Rome and the Maronites in the Renaissance and Reformation

Rome and the Maronites in the Renaissance and Reformation provides the first in-depth study of contacts between Rome and the Maronites during the fifteenth and sixteenth centuries. This book begins by showing how the church unions agreed at the Council of Ferrara-Florence (1438–1445) led Catholics to endow an immense amount of trust in the orthodoxy of Christians from the east. Taking the Maronites of Mount Lebanon as its focus, it then analyses how agents in the peripheries of the Catholic world struggled to preserve this trust into the early sixteenth century, when everything changed. On one hand, this study finds that suspicion of Christians in Europe generated by the Reformation soon led Catholics to doubt the past and present fidelity of the Maronites and other Christian peoples of the Middle East and Africa. On the other, it highlights how the expansion of the Ottoman Empire caused many Maronites to seek closer integration into Catholic religious and military goals in the eastern Mediterranean. By drawing on previously unstudied sources to explore both Maronite as well as Roman perspectives, this book integrates eastern Christianity into the history of the Reformation, while re-evaluating the history of contact between Rome and the Christian east in the early modern period. It is essential reading for scholars and students of early modern Europe, as well as those interested in the Reformation, religious history, and the history of Catholic Orientalism.

Sam Kennerley is Hannah Seeger Davis Postdoctoral Research Fellow at the Seeger Center for Hellenic Studies, Princeton University. He is co-editor of "The Reception of the Church Fathers and Early Church Historians in the Renaissance and Reformation, c.1470–1650", a special issue of the *International Journal of the Classical Tradition*.

Routledge Studies in Renaissance and Early Modern Worlds of Knowledge

Series Editors:
Harald E. Braun (University of Liverpool, UK) and Emily Michelson (University of St Andrews, UK)

SRS Board Members:
Erik DeBom (KU Leuven, Belgium), Mordechai Feingold (California Institute of Technology, USA), Andrew Hadfield (Sussex), Peter Mack (University of Warwick, UK), Jennifer Richards (University of Newcastle, UK), Stefania Tutino (UCLA, USA), Richard Wistreich (Royal College of Music, UK).

This series explores Renaissance and Early Modern Worlds of Knowledge (c.1400–c.1700) in Europe, the Americas, Asia and Africa. The volumes published in this series study the individuals, communities and networks involved in making and communicating knowledge during the first age of globalization. Authors investigate the perceptions, practices and modes of behaviour which shaped Renaissance and Early Modern intellectual endeavour and examine the ways in which they reverberated in the political, cultural, social and economic spheres.

The series is interdisciplinary, comparative and global in its outlook. We welcome submissions from new as well as existing fields of Renaissance Studies, including the history of literature (including neo-Latin, European and non-European languages), science and medicine, religion, architecture, environmental and economic history, the history of the book, art history, intellectual history and the history of music. We are particularly interested in proposals that straddle disciplines and are innovative in terms of approach and methodology.

The series includes monographs, shorter works and edited collections of essays. The Society for Renaissance Studies (http://www.rensoc.org.uk) provides an expert editorial board, mentoring, extensive editing and support for contributors to the series, ensuring high standards of peer-reviewed scholarship. We welcome proposals from early career researchers as well as more established colleagues.

21 Rome and the Maronites in the Renaissance and Reformation
The Formation of Religious Identity in the Early Modern Mediterranean
Sam Kennerley

22 Mathematics and the Craft of Thought in the Anglo-Dutch Renaissance
Eleanor Chan

For more information about this series, please visit: https://www.routledge.com/Routledge-Studies-in-Renaissance-and-Early-Modern-Worlds-of-Knowledge/book-series/ASHSER4043

Rome and the Maronites in the Renaissance and Reformation

The Formation of Religious Identity in the Early Modern Mediterranean

Sam Kennerley

LONDON AND NEW YORK

First published 2022
by Routledge
2 Park Square, Milton Park, Abingdon, Oxon OX14 4RN

and by Routledge
605 Third Avenue, New York, NY 10158

Routledge is an imprint of the Taylor & Francis Group, an informa business

© 2022 Sam Kennerley

The right of Sam Kennerley to be identified as author of this work has been asserted by him in accordance with sections 77 and 78 of the Copyright, Designs and Patents Act 1988.

All rights reserved. No part of this book may be reprinted or reproduced or utilised in any form or by any electronic, mechanical, or other means, now known or hereafter invented, including photocopying and recording, or in any information storage or retrieval system, without permission in writing from the publishers.

Trademark notice: Product or corporate names may be trademarks or registered trademarks, and are used only for identification and explanation without intent to infringe.

British Library Cataloguing-in-Publication Data
A catalogue record for this book is available from the British Library

Library of Congress Cataloging-in-Publication Data
Names: Kennerley, Sam, author.
Title: Rome and the Maronites in the Renaissance and Reformation : the formation of religious identity in the early modern Mediterranean / Sam Kennerley.
Description: Abingdon, Oxon ; New York : Routledge, 2022. | Includes bibliographical references and index.
Identifiers: LCCN 2021017021 (print) | LCCN 2021017022 (ebook) | ISBN 9780367760793 (hardback) | ISBN 9780367760809 (paperback) | ISBN 9781003165392 (ebook)
Subjects: LCSH: Catholic Church--Relations. | Maronites--Relations. | Church history--15th century. | Church history--16th century. | Mediterranean Region--Church history.
Classification: LCC BX4713.522 .K46 2022 (print) | LCC BX4713.522 (ebook) | DDC 281/.52--dc23
LC record available at https://lccn.loc.gov/2021017021
LC ebook record available at https://lccn.loc.gov/2021017022

ISBN: 978-0-367-76079-3 (hbk)
ISBN: 978-0-367-76080-9 (pbk)
ISBN: 978-1-003-16539-2 (ebk)

DOI: 10.4324/9781003165392

Typeset in Sabon
by SPi Technologies India Pvt Ltd (Straive)

Printed in the United Kingdom
by Henry Ling Limited

Für Lotte

Contents

Preface	*x*
List of Abbreviations	*xii*

Introduction 1

I Prelude   1
II Terminology and scope   2
III Summary of contents   3
Notes   6

**1   Franciscans, Jacobites, and the development of
Maronite historiography** 8

*I A summary history of the Maronites prior to the Council of
    Ferrara-Florence   8*
II The Maronites and the Council of Ferrara-Florence   9
*III Franciscans, Jacobites, and the development of Maronite
    historiography   12*
Notes   19

**2   Centre and periphery: Rome and Mount Lebanon in the
reign of Pope Leo X (1513–1521)** 24

I Introduction   24
II Rome is made to remember the Maronites   24
*III Francesco Suriano's reports on Maronite belief and
    practice: Tolerating religious difference on the eve of the
    Reformation   27*
*IV The Maronite delegation to the Fifth Lateran Council
    (1512–1517) and the development of Oriental studies in
    Renaissance Rome   29*
V Conclusion   32
Notes   32

viii   *Contents*

3   Negotiating a world in motion: Exchanges between
    Rome and the Maronites from Pope Clement VII (1523–1534)
    to Pope Marcellus II (1555)   36

I Historical and historiographical background   36
II Exchanges in the reign of Clement VII (1523–1534):
    Missing messengers and cardinal protectors   38
III Marcello Cervini and the pluri-confessional Rome of Paul III
    (1534–1549) and Julius III (1550–1555)   40
IV The exchanges between 1542 and 1544: The Maronite
    perspective   42
V The exchanges between 1542 and 1544: The response
    from Rome   46
VI Conclusion   49
Notes   52

4   Collaborations between Maronites, eastern Christians,
    and Catholic Orientalists in Rome during the cardinalate of
    Marcello Cervini (1539–1555)   57

I Introduction   57
II The Ethiopian community of early modern Rome,
    1404–1555: A very short history   58
III Polemical uses of the Ethiopian past. I: The Ethiopic Mass   59
IV Polemical uses of the Ethiopian past. II: The Ethiopic
    canons of the Council of Nicaea   62
V Two Syrian Jacobites in Counter-Reformation Rome: Peter
    of Damascus and Moses of Mardin   66
VI An Armenian catholicos and a Chaldean patriarch in Rome   72
VII Conclusion   76
Notes   79

5   The Maronites as anti-Ottoman agents: Their correspondence
    with Emperor Charles V (1519–1556)   86

I Introduction   86
II The letter of 1550: Characters and context   86
III The Maronites as anti-Ottoman agents   90
IV Conclusion   93
Notes   94

Contents ix

Conclusion 99

Note 102

Appendices 103

Bibliography 120

Index 135

Preface

The roots of this study can be traced back to early 2016, when I began work on editions and translations of the Greek Church Father John Chrysostom (c.350–407) produced by Catholic scholars during the Council of Trent. Besides trawling through bibliographies, this task involved a thorough reading of citations of Chrysostom in the acts of this council. One name kept appearing in both resources: Marcello Cervini. As I began to read more about him, it became clear that Cervini was interested not only in Greek patristics, but also in the past and present of a wide range of Churches in Africa and the Middle East. It also became clear that the best source for further research into Cervini would be the 75 volumes of his private archive stored at the Archivio di Stato in Florence, which remain one of the more puzzlingly underused resources for the history of the early sixteenth century.

Thanks to the generosity of the Istituto Sangalli, I was able to spend a month with these volumes in June 2018. The results exceeded my expectations. I was presented page after page of evidence about Cervini's interests in eastern Christianity from letters sent to him from throughout Christendom. But what jumped out at me most among this mass of documents were four letters written to Cervini by the Maronite patriarch of Antioch. I knew that Cervini was interested in eastern Christianity, but direct correspondence with a prelate from the Levant seemed highly unusual. Why would the patriarch of the Maronites have written to Cervini, as opposed to any other prelate or prince in the west?

Over time I decided that it was impossible to answer this question without contextualising these letters in a longer history of relations between the Maronites and the Catholic Church, beginning with the Council of Ferrara-Florence (1438–1445). This period has received less attention than the seventeenth and eighteenth centuries in recent research, but I found that it was populated by figures whose actions not only explained the events that I had encountered in Cervini's correspondence, but which were worth telling in their own right.

The following study therefore has two main aims. First, it will attempt to provide a new history of relations between Rome and Mount Lebanon

Preface xi

that aims to avoid the inaccuracies and partisanship of much historiography on this topic. Second, it will offer a new interpretation of Marcello Cervini, showing how and why this son of Montepulciano was appointed as cardinal protector of the Maronites, the decisions that he made as cardinal protector, and their effect. I also hope that readers will profit from the Appendices at the end of this study, in which I have edited sources that cannot be found in earlier collections of documents concerning the Maronites, most notably those of Tobias Anaissi.

My thanks go to Prof. Maurizio Sangalli and Michele Moromarco for making my time in Florence so pleasant and productive. Parts of this study have been presented at the seminars for Early Modern Intellectual History (Oxford) and Early Modern Scholarship and Religion (Cambridge). My thanks to the organisers and audiences of both seminars for their feedback, with a special mention to John-Paul Ghobrial, whose question about perpetual orthodoxy caused me to realise the significance of the fifteenth century for Maronite history and historiography. Dr Ghobrial also came to the rescue in the final stages of revision, placing me in contact with Rosemary Maxton and Lucy Parker, who translated Appendix IX. Richard Calis, Simon Ditchfield, Joseph Moukarzel, and Paolo Sachet all read this work and offered helpful advice. I have also been assisted in my research by conversations with Giuliano Tomei, and emails from Joan Greatrex, Tim Greenwood, Sundar Henny, Nelson Minnich, John O'Malley, Marianne Ritsema van Eck, whom I am pleased to acknowledge as a fellow Young Scholar of the Istituto Sangalli, and Michael Robson.

Sam Kennerley
Ely, 1 July 2021

Abbreviations

AAV	Vatican City: Archivio Apostolico Vaticano
BAV	Vatican City: Biblioteca Apostolica Vaticana
Bullarium Maronitarum	Tobias Anaissi, ed., *Bullarium Maronitarum*. Rome: Bretschneider, 1911
CC	Florence: Archivio di Stato, Carte Cerviniane
DBI	*Dizionario Biografico degli Italiani*

Introduction

I. Prelude

The profound changes that have taken place over the past decade within the discipline of early modern history can be summarised in the content of two lectures delivered at opposite ends of my academic career. In 2009, while an undergraduate at the University of St Andrews, I was first introduced to the Renaissance in a lecture by Chris Given-Wilson. The Renaissance I encountered was that of the rediscovery of antiquity and the development of humanism, an Italian story dominated by Florence, populated by philosophers like Marsilio Ficino, and studied by historians such as Paul-Oskar Kristeller.[1] Fast-forward ten years to another lecture on the Renaissance held at the University of Cambridge by Mary Laven. Students at this lecture were presented with a totally different Renaissance, one that extended from London to Istanbul via Augsburg and Vicenza, bound together by the movement of goods, ideas and people, and brought to life through the work of scholars like Lisa Jardine and Jerry Brotton.[2]

It is something of a platitude that each period re-writes the past in its own image. But like many platitudes, this one contains an element of truth. Major events and developments of the past decade – the Arab Spring, the ensuing wars in the Middle East and refugee crises in Europe, the corollary issue of discrimination faced by racial and religious minorities in the West, the rise of China, as well as the growing presence of the internet in our daily lives – have all focused attention on the history of connections between Europe and the wider world. It would be impossible to list all the articles and books that have appeared on this topic in the last year alone, even if we were to restrict our attention to the early modern period.[3] Indeed, the progress of research in this field is such that Richard Calis has reminded us that it is now no longer sufficient to simply present examples of connectivity in the early modern period, for that connectivity can now be taken for granted.[4]

The following study hopes to avoid this valid criticism by advancing a set of new conclusions about the history of ties between Rome and the Maronites. These conclusions will be outlined in the final part of this Introduction, but first it will be useful to provide a brief overview of the terminology and scope of this book.

DOI: 10.4324/9781003165392-1

2 Introduction

II. Terminology and scope

Basic facts about Rome are unlikely to require reiteration. However, the other partner of the dialogue studied here, the Maronites, may be less familiar to many readers of this book. The Maronites are one of the ancient Christian communities of the Levant. In the early modern period, they were mostly settled in Lebanon, with smaller communities in Cyprus, Jerusalem, and northern Syria. In language and liturgy, the Maronites have much in common with other local Churches, such as the Jacobites and the 'Nestorian' Church of the East. However, one key area in which the Maronites differ from other Christians of the Levant is their history of union with Rome, which they are widely agreed to have maintained since at least the thirteenth century.[5]

Union with Rome was and is one of the pillars of Maronite identity. As we will see in Chapter 1 in particular, most early modern sources and modern studies about the Maronites have therefore sought to document and dispute this union. Given the predominance of the theme in surviving sources and past historiography, the history of the union between the Maronites and Rome will be central to the analysis of the 'formation of religious identity' in this study. Indeed, as Chapters 3 and 4 will show, by studying the history of this union, we are provided with insights not only into the development of the religious identity of the Maronites, but also those of other eastern Churches, and even of Catholics in Rome.

At heart, the following study is therefore a history of the union between the Maronites and Rome. It surveys this history from the opening of the Council of Ferrara-Florence in 1438, to the death of Marcello Cervini in 1555. These years have been described under the rubric of 'Renaissance' and 'Reformation', controversial terms that have been chosen as they suggest the main themes of this investigation more effectively than alternatives such as 'early modern'. 'Renaissance' and 'Reformation' automatically conjure the history of scholarship and the history of religion in the fifteenth and sixteenth centuries, and these are indeed the historiographical traditions with which this book will engage.[6] A history of the Maronites that departs from scholarship and religion into less familiar realms such as social and economic history may well be possible, and would certainly be welcome, but such topics were not a preoccupation in the sources and debates that I encountered during my research. Indeed, such a study of the Maronites may be rendered more feasible once its author is freed from having to chase down the vast and scattered literature about their union with Rome, a freedom that present book hopes to provide.

Besides 'Renaissance' and 'Reformation', another contentious term used by this book is 'Mediterranean'. In the past two decades the Mediterranean has been the protagonist in a dizzying number of studies. It has been characterised as 'captive', 'converting', 'corrupting', 'great', and more besides.[7] The following book has no ambition to add to this nomenclature: it is a history in rather than of the Mediterranean.[8] However, in bringing to light developments in the neglected eastern coast of this sea, and following these developments as far as Saxony and Persia, I hope that this study might be useful to those with an interest in the history of the early modern Mediterranean.

One final note about terminology is in order. Recent histories of exchange, whether in the Mediterranean or in other theatres, have typically been written using metaphors of connection, crossing, or even entanglement.[9] By contrast, I have preferred to use the language of centre and periphery. These terms may remind some readers of the 'world systems' theory advanced by Immanuel Wallerstein, in which a thrusting, entrepreneurial western 'core' gradually absorbs its passive, eastern 'periphery'.[10]

As will be clear in what follows, I have indeed chosen 'centre' and 'periphery' because they are part of a language of contrast. However, unlike Wallerstein, I use this language to highlight situations in which the ostensible centre (Rome) was in fact dependent upon agents from the periphery (the Levant). In Chapters 1 and 2, for example, we will see how successive popes and cardinals in Rome were only able to communicate with Christians in the Levant thanks to the linguistic skill of Maronites such as Gabriel ibn al-Qilāʿī, and Franciscan friars like Francesco Suriano. Describing such situations in terms of centre and periphery forces us to confront our preconceptions about such events. In this case, the whole interest of the episode derives from the fact that we find it unexpected that the Maronites and Franciscans knew more about the languages and history of the Levant than did the popes and scholars of the golden age of Renaissance Rome. Once this prejudice has been confronted, it becomes possible to ask why such expectations have come into being in the first place. From there, we can query why figures such as al-Qilāʿī and Suriano have been omitted from the history of Catholic Orientalism. I believe that this and other episodes in the dialogue between Rome and the Maronites would have been less well-served by the language of interconnection, since its blander analogies close off avenues of thought that are sometimes best navigated through contrast.

Having outlined the terminology and scope of the present book, we can now turn to a chapter-by-chapter summary of its contents.

III. Summary of contents

The history of exchange between Rome and the Maronites has been the subject of some recent research. However, the majority of this research has concentrated on the final decades of sixteenth century or later.[11] The chronological focus of this historiography has been informed by the wealth and accessibility of sources for this period, produced in huge quantities by institutions of the Counter-Reformation like the Maronite College in Rome (founded 1584), and catalogued and stored at archives in Rome like that of the Propaganda Fide.[12] By contrast, the following study argues that the interaction between Rome and the Maronites during the

4   *Introduction*

Counter-Reformation can only be understood by reference to much earlier events. After an introduction to the early history of the Maronites, Chapter 1 begins in the mid-fifteenth century, when the growing presence of the Jacobite Church in Lebanon led sections of the Maronite community to doubt their historic union with Rome. These doubts were countered by the Franciscans of the Holy Land, above all by a Maronite Franciscan named Gabriel ibn al-Qilāʿī (c.1450–c.1516), whose letters and poems praised the union between Rome and the Maronites, and blamed figures of the past and present who had dared to challenge these ties. As this chapter demonstrates, Maronite historians of the Counter-Reformation such as Patriarch Stefanos al-Duwayhi (1670–1704) later reinterpreted al-Qilāʿī's works into a history of perpetual union between the Maronites and Rome. By exploring the genealogy of these ideas, this chapter shows that ongoing debates around perpetual union of the Maronites can ultimately be traced to a seventeenth-century re-interpretation of a fifteenth-century religious crisis. It therefore offers an alternative approach to the Maronite past than that of much modern historiography, which has often been a confessional response to the sources and interpretations that were presented by al-Duwayhi.[13]

Chapter 2 moves from the fifteenth century to the reign of Pope Leo X (1513–1521). Leo's reign is famous as a period in which the languages and history of the Middle East became a feature of scholarship in Rome. However, this chapter argues that even during Leo's reign the peripheries of the Catholic world possessed knowledge and resources that its metropole lacked. Indeed, it was only through actors in the peripheries that the Maronite embassy to the Fifth Lateran Council (1512–1517), which was ultimately responsible for stimulating the study of Arabic and Syriac in Rome, was able to depart from Lebanon in the first place. As well as demonstrating the impact of the peripheries of the Catholic world on its metropole, this chapter explores how Rome understood the faith of Christians in the Levant. We find that while Leo was aware that the Maronites did not follow all of Rome's doctrines and rites, in 1515 he nonetheless confirmed the Maronite patriarch Simon al-Hadathi in his office. In doing so, this chapter argues, Leo thereby accepted within the Catholic Church a people whose beliefs and customs he knew to differ from those of Rome – and all this just two years before the Reformation.

After surveying the tumultuous events of the Reformation and the Ottoman conquest of the Levant, Chapter 3 begins by considering the exchanges between the Maronites and Pope Clement VII (1523–1534). It argues that Maronite attempts to contact Rome were largely frustrated, and proposes that there was a gradual hardening of papal correspondence with Patriarch Musa al-Akkari at this time. A short introduction to the crucial source for this and the following chapters, the correspondence of Cardinal Marcello Cervini (1501–1555), is then followed by an evaluation of the letters exchanged between Cervini, Pope Paul III (1534–1549), and Patriarch Musa. The Maronite perspective on this correspondence is first examined, where it is argued that Patriarch Musa sought to establish diplomatic and educational exchanges in order to guarantee closer contact between the Maronites and Rome in the long term. This chapter then considers the Catholic response to the patriarch's letters, finding in them an intransigence that is traced back the Reformation. As such, this chapter argues that suspicions about the orthodoxy of other Christians generated by the Reformation changed Rome's approach to the Maronites, setting up the discussions of contact between Rome and other Christians from Africa and the Middle East that follow in Chapter 4.

Chapter 4 expands the argument of the previous chapter into a broader exploration of the presence of eastern Christians in Rome during the cardinalate of Marcello Cervini (1539–1555). This period merits particular attention, for it was during Cervini's cardinalate that scholars and prelates in Rome were exposed to eastern Christianity in a way unprecedented in recent history. In this period Catholics in Rome received embassies from the Armenian, Jacobite and 'Nestorian' Churches, and developed closer contact with the community of Ethiopians settled just behind the Vatican at Santo Stefano dei Mori. This chapter argues that Cervini played a vital role in developing these ties. Drawing on the cardinal's correspondence, it shows how Cervini created a network of Catholic Orientalists and eastern Christians in order to investigate the history and literature of the Armenian, Ethiopian, and Syrian Churches for new material in the fight against Protestantism. However, while some of these collaborations produced the results that Cervini had hoped for, this chapter will argue that they nonetheless had an unexpected consequence. The realisation that the eastern Churches were not as close to Rome as had been anticipated proved to be profoundly alienating for some of Cervini's Catholic collaborators, damaging the goodwill that had guided Catholic policy towards the eastern Churches since the Council of Ferrara-Florence.

The final chapter, Chapter 5, shifts its focus from Rome to Mount Lebanon in order to discover a previously overlooked Maronite perspective on exchange with Catholic Europe. It finds that, unlike other Churches, the Maronites not only sought ever-closer religious union with Rome during the Reformation, but that they even attempted to form military alliances with Catholic rulers like Charles V (1519–1556). This chapter concludes that the Maronites were much more interested in western powers than these rulers were in them, a policy of active engagement that set the stage for increased contact between the Maronites and Rome in the later sixteenth century.

Returning to Richard Calis' warning, it is hoped that this study has not just provided another example of early modern connectivity. My intention throughout has been to couple what and how I know the history of contact between Rome and the Maronites with why that history might matter. No doubt there will be oversights and mistakes. I am particularly conscious that my ignorance of Arabic has prevented me from engaging with sources written by al-Qilāʿī and al-Duwayhi quite as closely as I would have liked. Instead, the material studied here is primarily Latin and Italian. Assembling

6 *Introduction*

that material was no straightforward task. The sources studied here are scattered between Bkerké, Florence, Lisbon, and Rome. Many of them have never been studied in any language before, let alone in English. I therefore hope that this book will prove a useful point of departure for later histories of the Maronites, which should compare and contrast the western documents studied here with sources that were denied to me.

Notes

1 Paul Oskar Kristeller, *Renaissance Thought: The Classic, Scholastic and Humanist Strains* (New York: Harper & Row, 1961), esp. 3–23; Paul Oskar Kristeller, *Supplementum ficinianum* (Florence: Olschki, 1937).
2 Lisa Jardine and Jerry Brotton, *Global Interests: Renaissance Art between East and West* (London: Reaktion, 2000).
3 Much continental scholarship on this topic is cited in the special issue "Le lingue nella Roma della prima età moderna. Luoghi e risorse," *Rivista Storica Italiana* 132 (2020): 87–322. See also John-Paul Ghobrial, ed., *Global History and Microhistory* (Oxford: Oxford University Press, 2019), and Nicholas Hardy and Dmitri Levitin, eds, *Confessionalisation and Erudition in Early Modern Europe* (Oxford: Oxford University Press, 2020).
4 Richard Alexander Calis, "Martin Crusius (1526–1607) and the Discovery of Ottoman Greece" (PhD diss., Princeton University, 2020), 38.
5 Shafiq Abouzayd, "The Maronite Church," in *The Syriac World*, ed. Daniel King (London: Routledge, 2018), 731–50.
6 For a free-wheeling reflection on the period covered by these terms, see the special issue of the *Sixteenth Century Journal*, 50 (2019).
7 Daniel Hershenzon, *The Captive Sea: Slavery, Communication and Commerce in Early Modern Spain and the Mediterranean* (Philadelphia: University of Pennsylvania Press, 2018); Robert John Clines, "The converting sea: Religious change and cross-cultural interaction in the early modern Mediterranean," *History Compass* 17 (2019): 1–15; Peregrine Horden and Nicholas Purcell, *The Corrupting Sea: A Study of Mediterranean History* (Oxford: Basil Blackwell, 2000); David Abulafia, *The Great Sea: A Human History of the Mediterranean* (London: Allen Lane, 2011). For our period, Eric R. Dursteler, "On Bazaars and Battlefields: Recent Scholarship on Mediterranean Cultural Contacts," *Journal of Early Modern History* 15 (2011): 413–34 and Molly Greene, "The Early Modern Mediterranean," in *A Companion to Mediterranean History*, ed. Peregrine Horden and Sharon Kinoshita (Chichester: John Wiley & Sons, 2014), 91–106 are particularly perceptive.
8 Judith E. Tucker, "Introduction," in *The Making of the Modern Mediterranean*, ed. Judith E. Tucker (Oakland: University of California Press, 2019), 7.
9 Sanjay Subrahmanyam, *Empires between Islam and Christianity, 1500–1800* (Albany: State University of New York Press, 2019), 18–23; Brian A. Catlos, "Why the Mediterranean?" in *Can We Talk Mediterranean? Conversations in an Emerging Field in Medieval and Early Modern Studies*, ed. Brian A. Catlos and Sharon Kinoshita (Basingstoke: Palgrave Macmillan, 2017), 1–17.
10 Immanuel Wallerstein, *The Modern World-System*, 4 vols (New York: Academic Press, 1974–2011); see the comments in Sanjay Subrahmanyam, "Introduction," in *The Cambridge World History. Volume 6: The Construction of a Global World, 1400–1800 CE. Part I: Foundations*, ed. Jerry H. Bentley, Sanjay Subrahmanyam and Merry E. Wiesner-Hanks (Cambridge: Cambridge University Press, 2015), 10–11.

Introduction 7

11 See especially the following works by Robert Clines and Aurélien Girard: Robert John Clines, *A Jewish Jesuit in the Eastern Mediterranean: Early Modern Conversion, Mission, and the Construction of Identity* (Cambridge: Cambridge University Press, 2019), 90–136; Robert John Clines, "Between hermits and heretics: Maronite religious renewal and the Turk in Catholic travel accounts of Lebanon after the Council of Trent," in *Travel and Conflict in the Early Modern World*, ed. Gábor Golléri and Rachel Willie (London: Routledge, 2020), 108–26; Aurélien, Girard, "Was an Eastern Scholar Necessarily a Cultural Broker in Early Modern Europe? Faustus Naironus (1628–1711), the Christian East, and Oriental Studies," in *Confessionalisation and Erudition in Early Modern Europe* 240–63; Aurélien Girard, "Histoire connectée du monachisme oriental. De l'erudition catholique en Europe aux réformes monastiques au Mont Liban (XVIIe–XVIIIe siècles)," in *Scholarship between Europe and the Levant. Essays in Honour of Alastair Hamilton*, ed. Jan Loop and Jill Kraye (Leiden: Brill, 2020), 173–94; Aurélien Girard, "Le Collège maronite de Rome et les langues au tournant des XVIᵉ et XVIIᵉ siècles: éducation des chrétiens orientaux, science orientaliste et apologétique catholique," *Rivista Storica Italiana* 132 (2020): 272–99.

12 For the former institution, see Aurélien Girard and Giovanni Pizzorusso, "The Maronite College in early modern Rome: Between the Ottoman Empire and the Republic of Letters," in *College communities abroad: Education, migration and Catholicism in early modern Europe*, ed. Liam Chambers and Thomas O'Connor (Manchester: Manchester University Press, 2017), 174–97, and Girard, "Le Collège maronite de Rome"; for the latter, see Giovanni Pizzorusso, *Governare le missioni, conoscere il mondo nel XVII secolo. La Congregazione Pontificia de Propaganda Fide* (Viterbo: Sette città, 2018).

13 Contrast, for instance, the conclusions on this matter in Matti Moosa, *The Maronites in History* (Syracuse, NY: Syracuse University Press, 1986), which was written by a deacon of the Syrian Orthodox (Jacobite) Church, with those reached in Pierre Dib, *History of the Maronite Church*, trans. Seely Beggiani (Washington, DC: Maronite Apostolic Exarchate, 1971), which was written by a Maronite bishop.

1 Franciscans, Jacobites, and the development of Maronite historiography

I. A summary history of the Maronites prior to the Council of Ferrara-Florence

A lack of sources and several centuries of polemic have made it impossible to provide a comprehensive account of the early history of the Maronites. The very beginning of this history is especially obscure.[1] However, the Maronites often trace their origins to St Maron, a fourth-century monk whose existence is attested in the works of Theodoret of Cyrus and John Chrysostom.[2] Maron's followers are thought to have been based at the monastery of Beth Maron near Apamea, from which they evangelised the population of Lebanon and northern Syria.[3] The monks of Beth Maron enjoyed some contact with Rome at this time. An archimandrite named Alexander wrote to Pope Hormisdas in 517, to which this pope responded in 518.[4] Paul, the superior of Beth Maron, also attended the Council of Constantinople in 536.[5]

The first Maronite patriarch, John Maron, was probably elected towards the end of the seventh century.[6] But even before that time the Maronites were sufficiently integrated into the wider Christian world to have known and agreed with the Byzantine Emperor Heraclius's *Ecthesis* (638), a document that sought to solve contemporary Christological controversies by proposing that Christ had one will. This doctrine of 'Monothelitism' was condemned at the Sixth Ecumenical Council (680–681).[7] However, controversy has raged about whether the Maronites held Monothelitism to be orthodox even after this council.[8] The best that can be said is that some of those who considered themselves to be Maronites probably accepted Monothelitism long after its condemnation. Tūmā, the Maronite bishop of Kafartāb, for instance, is reported to have written a defence of Monothelitism in 1089.[9]

The history of the Maronites becomes somewhat clearer upon the irruption of Latin Crusaders into Lebanon in 1099. Chroniclers such as Raymond d'Aguilers and Jacques de Vitry record that groups plausibly identifiable as Maronites assisted the Crusaders on their way to Jerusalem during the First Crusade (1096–1099).[10] Attempts to renew or create a union between Rome and the Maronites eventually followed. The Maronites may have

DOI: 10.4324/9781003165392-2

The development of Maronite historiography   9

offered their submission to the papacy in 1139/40, and again in a famous episode recorded by William of Tyre that has been variously dated to 1180, 1181 or 1182.[11] That Rome had accepted the Maronites into communion around this time is suggested by the fact that the first papal privilege to the Maronites was issued in 1184.[12] Ties between Rome and the Maronites strengthened during the following century. In the course of a mission to the Levant, dated alternatively to 1203 and 1205, the papal legate Peter Capuano received another submission of loyalty from the Maronites.[13] A decade later, Pope Innocent III invited the Maronite Patriarch Jeremias El-Amsciti to attend the Fourth Lateran Council. Jeremias accepted this invitation, and on 3 January 1216 received from Innocent III a bull that confirmed the union between Rome and the Maronites.[14]

It is widely agreed that the union between Rome and the Maronites has held unbroken after 1216. But in a theme that will run throughout this and later chapters, it is important to stress that this union was not formed without resistance from some Maronites, nor maintained by the entire Maronite community.[15] In 1137, for example, some Maronites assisted local Muslims in capturing·the Crusader Count Pons of Tripoli.[16] The successor to Patriarch Jeremias El-Amsciti, Daniel of Shāmāt (1230–1239), encountered so much opposition to union with Rome among local Maronites that he was forced to move his residence to an area in which his flock was happier with their submission to the papacy.[17] Another patriarch, Lūqa al-Bnahrani, simply refused to accept messengers from the pope.[18]

Irrespective of their reception, exchanges between Rome and the Maronites were frequent as long as Latin Crusaders remained in Lebanon. However, the Mamluk expulsion of Crusaders from Lebanon in 1292 brought the Maronites into an Islamic empire once more. There is no sign of direct exchange between Rome and the Maronites for the next century, even though it would appear that the Mamluks were not always concerned by the threat of communication between Catholics and Christians in the Levant. For example, they permitted the Franciscans to re-establish themselves in Beirut in 1345.[19]

As we'll see, the Franciscans of Beirut were essential to the renewal of exchanges between Rome and the Maronites. These exchanges begin with the Council of Ferrara-Florence (1438–1445), the background to which we now turn.

II. The Maronites and the Council of Ferrara-Florence

After the disastrous loss at Manzikert in 1071, and the arrival of the First Crusade in Anatolia in 1096, the Byzantine Empire gradually disintegrated. Its territories were conquered and reconquered by a dizzying succession of Turks, Latins, Slavs, and even rival Byzantine rulers. Constantinople was governed by a Latin dynasty between 1204 and 1261, for example, while Athens served as the capital of a Catalan duchy between 1311 and 1388. However, by the first half of the fifteenth century, the principal threat to the

10 *The development of Maronite historiography*

Byzantine Empire were the Ottoman Turks. Their conquests in the Balkans and western Anatolia had surrounded Constantinople, which the Ottomans besieged for seven years in the 1390s, and again in 1422. Such an existential threat turned the Byzantine emperor John VIII Palaeologos (1425–1448) in favour of negotiations for union with Rome, which would have been a precondition to the dispatch of military aid from the Latin west.[20]

In retrospect, we know now that the assistance that John VIII acquired from the west made little difference. A Latin force led by Cardinal Giulio Cesarini was defeated at Varna on 10 November 1444. Just under a decade later, on 29 May 1453, the Ottomans took Constantinople.[21] However, these events were not inevitable in 1438, and decision-makers in Rome had good reason to be interested in the Byzantine emperor's overtures. The crusades are often thought of as a medieval phenomenon, alien to the world of the Renaissance. Yet the notion of a crusade against the Ottomans continued to animate the foreign policy of popes throughout the fifteenth century.[22] Besides a desire to keep the Ottomans out of Constantinople, there were also internal reasons for the popes to welcome steps towards a union of churches. The end of the Western Schism in 1417 was followed by the threat of conciliarism, as prelates at the Council of Basel (1431–1449) challenged the authority of Pope Eugenius IV (1431–1447) as head of the Catholic Church. A union between Constantinople and Rome arranged under Roman auspices would have provided a spectacular acknowledgement of papal supremacy, destroying the credibility of the opposition in Basel.[23]

The Council of Ferrara-Florence was therefore called with the intention of forging a new era in the history of Christian unity. After decades of wrangling in which cities as distant as Constantinople, Avignon, and Basel were proposed as sites for a council, Byzantine delegates arrived in Italy to conduct negotiations at Ferrara, and later Florence. Union between the Latin and Greek Churches was eventually declared in Florence on 6 July 1439.[24] These negotiations with the Greeks were followed by invitations to other Churches to unify themselves with Rome. Union with the Armenians was declared on 22 November 1439, with the Copts on 4 February 1442, and with the Jacobites of Syria on 30 September 1444.[25] Of all the eastern Christian groups who visited the Council, only the Ethiopians declined to unify with Rome. Their delegates protested, perhaps disingenuously, that they lacked the authority to make this decision on behalf of their emperor.[26]

The Maronites were equally entangled in this web of communication. In 1439, their patriarch Johannes al-Ghagi sent to Italy the superior of the Franciscan monastery in Beirut, Giovanni.[27] The mission of this Franciscan, however, differed from that commended to the envoys of other eastern Churches. Through his representative, Patriarch Johannes asked not for union to Rome, but rather proclaimed his fidelity to the Holy See, accepted the decisions of the Council of Ferrara-Florence in advance, and requested confirmation of his election as patriarch from the pope. From these promises and demands, we can deduce that Patriarch Johannes believed that his Church was already in union with Rome. As we've seen, such a belief was

The development of Maronite historiography 11

not without foundation. It was apparently common knowledge among the Maronites of the fifteenth century that Patriarch Jeremias El-Amsciti had already unified them to Rome in the reign of Pope Innocent III (1198–1216).[28]

The Franciscan envoy Giovanni returned to Tripoli in 1439 with gifts for Patriarch Johannes and confirmation of his election. However, Giovanni's return had the unintended consequence of arousing the suspicion of the Mamluk authorities, who it seems had begun to fear collaboration between local Christians and their co-religionists in the west. Subsequent attacks by the Mamluks forced Patriarch Johannes to retreat to the monastery of Qannubin in Mount Lebanon, which remained the home of later patriarchs throughout the early modern period.[29] The papacy certainly intended the Maronites to fulfil the role that the Mamluks had feared that they might play. In a letter of 16 December 1441 that responded to the events of Giovanni's return, Pope Eugenius IV cast the Maronites as a potential vanguard for the conversion of the Levant, reminding them that "you might preserve not only yourselves in the way of the Lord, but also guide and lead the peoples and nations of neighbouring regions to eternal life, to the benefit of your souls".[30] Such high hopes perhaps explain the papacy's interest in maintaining close ties with the Maronites. In the same letter that exhorted the Maronites to action, Eugenius sent to them the Franciscans Pietro da Ferrara and Antonio da Troia, in order to instruct the Maronites in the Catholic faith, and to correct any errors into which they may have fallen.[31] Their mission would appear to have been fruitful, as in 1444 Eugenius wrote again to Patriarch Johannes, noting that Antonio da Troia had informed him of Maronite acceptance of the decrees of the Council of Ferrara-Florence, and had brought to Rome a party of Maronites and Druze.[32] A year later, the Maronites of Cyprus joined their fellows on the mainland by declaring union with Rome.[33] The fact that the Maronites of Cyprus declared their union together with the Jacobites of the island, and after the Latin bishop of Rhodes had accused them of holding that Christ had one rather than two wills, has become a prime exhibit in the unresolved controversy about the prevalence of Monothelite beliefs among the Maronites in the fifteenth century that we will discuss in greater detail below.[34]

The dispatch of this Maronite delegation from Cyprus was apparently independent of the patriarch in Qannubin. Nor was this the only example of Maronite communities beyond Mount Lebanon conducting their own diplomacy with the Holy See. In 1439, the Maronites of Jerusalem sent a representative to the Council of Ferrara-Florence, receiving a letter from Pope Eugenius IV in return.[35] Jerusalem was in fact an important point of contact between Europe and the Middle East during the early modern period. This city was home to the Franciscans of the Holy Land, who also maintained smaller communities in other cities of the Levant.[36] The Franciscans of the Holy Land served as some of the most influential go-betweens for the Maronites of the fifteenth and sixteenth century, something especially true for the figure to whom we now turn.

12 *The development of Maronite historiography*

III. Franciscans, Jacobites, and the development of Maronite historiography

In late 1442 or early 1443, a Franciscan named Gryphon arrived in Jerusalem. Or that, at least, is the consensus of scholarship about him, which is dependent on a seminal article written over one hundred years ago by Henri Lammens.[37] Lammens's life of Gryphon is made difficult to verify by his erratic citation practice. But from his article and later studies, we can ascertain that Gryphon was Flemish, that he gained a doctorate in theology from the University of Paris, that he joined the Observant Franciscans in Italy, and that he travelled to the Holy Land, where he acquired a solid grasp of Arabic that he used in a lengthy stay among the Maronites of Mount Lebanon.[38] We can also be sure that Gryphon represented the Maronites before Pope Paul II (1464–1471), as his mission to Rome on their behalf is recorded in a papal bull that is of particular importance to the history and historiography of this community.

The bull in question, dated to 5 August 1468, begins and ends much like other documents issued from Rome to the Maronites. Paul II expressed his joy on receiving a letter from Patriarch Petrus bar Hassan (1468–1492), which, he said, had shown him that there were faithful Christians in even the most distant parts of the world. After exhorting Petrus to follow the good example of his predecessors, Paul confirmed his election as Maronite patriarch of Antioch. This bull, however, contains a core of patristic scholarship that stands out against earlier and later documents of this kind. Paul instructed Petrus to hold and teach the Catholic doctrine of Christ's two wills and natures. Citations from Athanasius and Cyril of Alexandria were adduced to prove this doctrine, which Paul wrote would be made even clearer through the decrees of the Sixth Ecumenical Council (680–681), a copy of which would accompany his letter to Mount Lebanon.[39]

Paul II's bull is significant, as it cautioned the Maronites against the doctrines of Monothelitism characteristic of other Churches in the region, such as the Syrian Jacobites. Although the Cypriot Maronites at the Council of Ferrara-Florence had abjured Monothelitism in 1445, Latin authors of the later fifteenth and early sixteenth century continued to argue that the Maronites were tainted by this heresy. In his *Trattato della Terra Santa* (1485), the Franciscan friar Francesco Suriano claimed that the first patriarch of the Maronites, John Maron, had been a follower of this doctrine.[40] Another contemporary Franciscan, Nicolas Glassberger, coupled this argument with the charge that the Maronites had lapsed into both Monothelitism and Monoenergism after the Fourth Lateran Council (1215), maintaining these heresies until Gryphon's arrival.[41] The fifteenth century indeed saw a notable increase in Jacobite influence in Mount Lebanon. From the beginning of this century, Jacobite Christians in Syria fled from Bedouin, Turcoman, and Kurdish raids to the refuge of Mount Lebanon, where they established a network of monasteries and bishoprics, and began to preach among the Maronites.[42] Based on such evidence, Matti Moosa

The development of Maronite historiography 13

proposed that until the late sixteenth century the Maronites held the same Monothelite beliefs as their Jacobite neighbours, differing from them only in acceptance of papal primacy.[43]

Moosa adduced the bull of Paul II as evidence for this argument. He argued that it showed Catholics were suspicious of Maronite beliefs, to the extent that they felt the need to instruct the Maronites about the Christology of the Catholic Church.[44] However, Paul II's bull was not the only document generated by Gryphon's visit to Rome in 1469. This friar also sent to Mount Lebanon his own account of the embassy, which presents a different take on the Maronite perception of the Christian world from that commonly encountered in secondary literature.[45]

In this account, Gryphon noted that there were many types of Christian in the world. The Maronites knew that they were not the same as other Christians, whether Greek, Nestorian, or Jacobite. Indeed, Gryphon continued, the Maronites considered all sects other than themselves to be heterodox. Yet it was clear that there had been many saints who were not Maronites, and saintly books that were written by authors who were not Maronite. The conclusion that the Maronites alone were orthodox was therefore impossible. That left the question of who the Maronites were, to which Gryphon provided an answer. Gryphon noted that the book of Clement showed that Rome was the foundation of faith, and that this same book observed that there were thousands of saints and doctors who lived among the Latins. In fact, he argued, the primary issue with Maronite self-identity as the only orthodox Church was that it omitted Latin writers and saints from the number of the orthodox. Having shown the orthodoxy of the Latins, Gryphon demonstrated that they and the Maronites shared certain similarities. Maronites and Latins alone followed the same manner of baptism, and from ancient times to the present, they had shared churches, worn the same vestments, and had celebrated the Mass in the same way. While knowledge of the book of Clement had inspired Patriarch Jeremias El-Amsciti to visit Innocent III in the thirteenth century, this patriarch was not the only Maronite to seek refuge in Rome. Instead, the Maronites had looked to the papacy from the distant past to the present, for the simple reason that they were united to Rome.[46]

Gryphon's account of his embassy allows a re-interpretation of Paul II's bull. In Moosa's analysis, this bull manifests papal suspicion of the Maronites. He therefore identified the pope as the primary actor in the drafting of the bull, but it is possible that Gryphon was the real influence in its composition. Gryphon's account shows that he was attempting to construct a Catholic identity for the Maronites by highlighting the similarities that existed between Catholics and Maronites and the ancient ties of trust that bound them together. Paul II's bull arguably achieved the same purpose. It provided an instrument through which Patriarch Petrus could enforce a Catholic, and therefore Maronite, answer to the Christological debates that were apparently of particular importance to his community. Later histories have generally attempted to show that all Maronites were

14 *The development of Maronite historiography*

always Catholic or always Jacobite. But Gryphon's many years in the Levant had perhaps taught him that the reality was more complex than that. From the documents generated by the 1469 embassy, it would appear that there were pro-Jacobite and pro-Catholic factions among the Maronites who were competing for the future religious direction of their people, and that Gryphon's mission to Rome was intended to ensure the triumph of the latter group.

We might argue that Gryphon's mission was successful. When visiting Mount Lebanon after Gryphon's death, Francesco Suriano noted that the Maronites considered Gryphon a saint, and that on the mention of his name, they would kiss their hands and place them on their heads as mark of reverence.[47] But this outcome was not inevitable by the time of Gryphon's mission to Rome in 1469. Just a year later, the governor (*muqaddam*) of Bsharri, Rizqāllah ibn Saifā, died. This was significant for the Maronites, as Bsharri was the district of Lebanon in which most Maronites lived, and where the patriarch had his seat. The role of *muqaddam* of Bsharri was hereditary. However, Rizqāllah's sons were too young to take up the post, causing it to pass to his nephew 'Abd al-Mun'im. And while Rizqāllah's family was traditionally Maronite, the new *muqaddam* 'Abd al-Mun'im favoured the Jacobites. His tenure as *muqaddam* appears to have involved a period of growth for the Jacobite community in Mount Lebanon, leading to sometimes violent clashes between Jacobites and Maronites.[48]

At around the time of 'Abd al-Mun'im's succession as *muqaddam*, Gryphon took further action to bolster the Catholic identity of the Maronites. He sent three young Maronites to Italy to receive their training there.[49] We know little of the life of one of these three, Francesco.[50] Another of the group, Johannes, returned to Mount Lebanon and was elected Maronite bishop of Aqura, but drowned in a shipwreck shortly afterwards.[51] By contrast, we know much more about the last of the three Maronites sent west by Gryphon, even if he is not quite as familiar to historians of the early modern period as he ought to be. This is Gabriel ibn al-Qilāʿī (c.1450–c.1516), whose life can be reconstructed from the immense number of translations, letters, tracts and poems that he produced, which are preserved in libraries throughout Europe and the Middle East.[52]

Al-Qilāʿī was born around the middle of the fifteenth century to a moderately prosperous Maronite family in the village of Lehfed. As a child, he had witnessed the deepening religious crisis in Mount Lebanon, recalling in later life how the villagers of 'Ayn Kfa had wanted to stone the Maronite patriarch Jacobus al-Hadathi (1445–1458) for his inaction against the Jacobites.[53] Having turned to the religious life – perhaps due to the cure of an eye illness that he attributed to the intercession of St Lucius – al-Qilāʿī likely spent his novitiate in Jerusalem, before being sent with his companions to Italy by Gryphon.[54]

Al-Qilāʿī is frustratingly vague about his education in Italy, stating that he gained a degree in theology, but without indicating where. The only place that he mentioned as regards his studies was the Franciscan convent of Ara Coeli in Rome, where he states that he completed his theological training. However, his seven-month stay at that monastery was unlikely to have been enough for a degree, suggesting that he studied elsewhere before finishing in Ara Coeli. Francesco Suriano, who knew him personally, claimed that al-Qilāʿī and his fellows became experts in canon law at Venice.[55] This would raise the possibility that al-Qilāʿī studied at Padua, since it was Venice's university town, and would be a good fit for other reasons. Padua had a Franciscan *studium*, and its university was frequented by Christians from the east.[56] But without any conclusive proof, the proposal that al-Qilāʿī studied at Padua must remain speculative.

Besides studying theology at Ara Coeli, al-Qilāʿī and his friend Johannes made use of their time in Rome by visiting local churches. They also faced the more unpleasant task of defending the Maronites from charges of heresy.[57] The question of the orthodoxy of the Christian east would indeed appear to have been on al-Qilāʿī's mind during his sojourn in Italy. His earliest known work is a translation of a papal letter of excommunication against the Greek Orthodox, which he translated into Arabic in Rome in 1483.[58]

It is possible that al-Qilāʿī returned to the Levant the same year as this translation. He was certainly back in the east by 1492, since a manuscript note in his hand informs us that in that year he was sent to check on the Maronites of the Cypriot town of Talo by his Franciscan superior in Jerusalem.[59] But as al-Qilāʿī's modern biographers have noted, the growing Jacobite presence in Mount Lebanon soon turned his attention to Maronite communities on the mainland.[60] On 12 December 1493, al-Qilāʿī wrote a letter to his home village of Lehfed from the Franciscan monastery in Beirut. In this letter, he admonished the people of Lehfed that the Christian duty to love one's neighbour did not extend to David, a native of the town who had left the Maronites to become a Jacobite bishop. Al-Qilāʿī warned the villagers that David's aim was to remove the Maronites from their ancestral obedience to Rome. Were that to happen, he cautioned, Lehfed's apostasy would result in conquest by the Turks, just as had been visited on towns and cities in the Balkans that had committed the same sin.[61]

The threat of heresy in his home village and the dire consequences that might follow added extra importance to al-Qilāʿī's next commission. Patriarch Simon al-Hadathi (1492–1524) wrote to the new Franciscan superior in Jerusalem, Francesco Suriano – whose *Trattato della Terra Santa* has been cited throughout this chapter – asking that he send al-Qilāʿī to spend the winter of 1494–1495 at the patriarchal seat in Qannubin. However, Patriarch Simon perhaps miscalculated by courting the attention of the Franciscans of the Holy Land, who were already nervous about the state of religion in Mount Lebanon. Although elected in 1492, Simon had yet to imitate his predecessors by sending an envoy to Rome for confirmation.[62] This omission meant that his visitors ultimately dictated the terms of their visit to him.

16 *The development of Maronite historiography*

Al-Qilāʿī was sent to Qannubin with a letter from Suriano that he had translated into Arabic.[63] In this letter, Suriano reminded Patriarch Simon of the act of faith that he and other representatives of the Maronites had signed in 1469 during Gryphon's mission to Mount Lebanon, and reproved him for not sending a similar document to Rome for his confirmation.[64] Al-Qilāʿī added to this pressure with a letter of his own. He wrote that Suriano had sent him to Qannubin in order to highlight traditions practiced by the Maronites that were not in accordance with those of Rome. He therefore outlined Catholic doctrine on the seven sacraments, and listed how the Maronites had broken them: the formula of baptism was wrong, confirmation was not practiced at all and extreme unction not enough, the manner of celebrating the Eucharist had been changed, communion was often taken without confession, married men and unsuitable candidates had been advanced to the priesthood, and the practice of marriage was errant. Patriarch Simon should prepare to announce these findings to the Maronite people on pain of excommunication, and ready himself for a visit from Suriano, who would report the events of his trip to the pope. To ensure that the Maronites had a lasting record of their Catholic history and beliefs, al-Qilāʿī would leave in Qannubin 14 papal bulls sent to the Maronites that he had translated into Arabic.[65]

However, when al-Qilāʿī arrived at this monastery in 1495, he had more than reform of Maronite traditions in his sights. In a letter from Qannubin dated to 5 August 1495, he complained that he had been at the monastery for five months without any Jacobite daring to engage him in disputation.[66] This was despite an extensive epistolary campaign, in which al-Qilāʿī claimed to have written well over four hundred letters.[67] Although he complained that he had received no response from his correspondents, the information that al-Qilāʿī provided about his contacts helps us to reconstruct the religious world of Mount Lebanon in the late fifteenth century. We find that he wrote to David of Lehfed, a Maronite who, as mentioned earlier, had become a Jacobite bishop, and to George ar-Rami, who called himself a Maronite despite his Monothelite beliefs.[68] Elsewhere al-Qilāʿī mentions other Maronites, such as his teacher Ibrahim ibn Dray, who held fast in union with Rome.[69] As such, it seems that the Christians of fifteenth-century Mount Lebanon could hold views that ranged from the total commitment to Rome shown by al-Qilāʿī and his friends, to the Jacobite leanings of George ar-Rami, while still calling themselves Maronites. Once again, we see that works that attempt to cast early modern Maronites as all Jacobites or all Catholics caricature the complexity of religious life in Mount Lebanon.

That is not to say that al-Qilāʿī's stay in Mount Lebanon in 1495 was entirely without controversy, however. In a poem called *Against those who sow tares among the Maronites*, al-Qilāʿī referred to how he had drawn up a book of doctrine after finding a Jacobite manuscript in the hands of the *muqaddam* Yusuf.[70] As has been noted by other authors, the description of this book closely matches the structure of al-Qilāʿī's *Exposition of the Faith*, a multi-part tract dated to 1495 in which al-Qilāʿī provides an ambitious

The development of Maronite historiography 17

defence of the fidelity of the Maronites to Rome.[71] In the first book of this tract, al-Qilāʿī adduced texts of the Greek and Latin Church Fathers (Severian of Gabala, Cyril of Alexandria, and Pope Leo I) that are essential to Roman Christology. These texts were complemented in the third book by discussions of Christology drawn from the works of the Franciscan theologian Duns Scotus (1266–1308), and a compendium of heresies assembled by the Dominican Nicholas Eymerich (d.1399).[72] Al-Qilāʿī augmented this discussion with a sacred history of the Maronites. He reminded his readers that their 'ancestors' had accepted the Council of Chalcedon, before providing a summary of relations between Rome and the Maronites until the embassy of Gryphon.[73] The second book of the *Exposition* expanded this history beyond Mount Lebanon. Al-Qilāʿī discussed the Incarnation and Ascension of Christ, and provided a list of popes from Peter to Alexander VI. An accompanying list of emperors and kings from Octavian to Louis IX of France was adduced to show that the Latins, rather than the Ethiopians, held the hopes of the Christians of the Holy Land.[74] This last point suggests disagreements among the Christians of Mount Lebanon about the identity of their real allies abroad. Besides Syrian Jacobites, al-Qilāʿī may have heard praise of the Ethiopian emperors from the small community of Ethiopian monks that is known to have existed in Mount Lebanon in the late fifteenth century.[75]

The *Exposition of the Faith* is perhaps the most impressive monument of al-Qilāʿī's scholarship. In this work he translated into Arabic texts and extracts from the whole history of western literature: classical authors like Plato, Seneca, and Cicero, patristic writers like Severian and Cyril, but above all scholastics such as Duns Scotus and, for the historical part of this work, Martin of Troppau (d. 1278).[76] From his version of the letter of excommunication against the Melkites in 1483 to his translation of Suriano's letter to Patriarch Simon in 1494, we have seen that al-Qilāʿī rendered difficult Latin texts into Arabic. Nor is this the full list of the works that he translated. To the works mentioned above, we can also add his Arabic versions of Ramon Lull's *Ars brevis* and *Liber de quinque sapientibus*, as well as his translations of Bernardino of Siena that he incorporated into his preaching.[77] The linguistic skill of western Orientalists of the fifteenth and early sixteenth centuries pales in comparison to the scale and complexity of al-Qilāʿī's translations. That al-Qilāʿī is less well-known than they are may be because he is not the kind of western intellectual, ideally with a connection to the printing press, who has tended to attract the attention of modern Orientalists in search of their intellectual ancestors.

While perhaps the text that best displays al-Qilāʿī's scholarship, the *Exposition of the Faith* was not his most influential work. As well as a translator, letter-writer, and controversialist, al-Qilāʿī was also a poet, in which capacity he set out the sacred history of the Maronites in greater detail than in his other texts. In his poem *On the Four Councils* (1507), for instance, al-Qilāʿī established a sacred history that showed how the Maronites had always been unified to Rome, informing his audience that

18 The development of Maronite historiography

John Maron had been consecrated patriarch by the pope with the commission to extirpate the Greeks, Jacobites, and Copts from Mount Lebanon.[78] Another poem, *On Mount Lebanon*, filled out this history to al-Qilāʿī's own day. Here he recounted how the Maronites had persisted in their ancestral faith to the time of Patriarch Lūqa al-Bnahrani, whose refusal to accept a Roman envoy, he claimed, had plunged the Maronites into a period of crisis that was matched in scale only by the contemporary growth of Jacobite influence.[79]

As is clear from *On the Four Councils* and *On Mount Lebanon*, al-Qilāʿī's poetry was another medium through which he aimed to make Maronites identify their ancestral faith with Rome. Poetry was perhaps especially suitable for this purpose, in that by being read aloud, it could reach an audience to whom al-Qilāʿī's histories were otherwise inaccessible.[80] There is evidence that his poems were recited, and the large number of manuscripts that contain his poetry suggests their success.[81]

Indeed, poems such as *On the Four Councils* and *On Mount Lebanon* were fundamental in crafting a Maronite identity not only through reading and recitation in the fifteenth century, but also through their impact on later histories of the Maronites. They were essential sources for later Maronite historians such as Patriarch Stefanos al-Duwayhi (1670–1704), who like al-Qilāʿī sought to demonstrate the historic union of the Maronites to Rome.[82] But despite their common goals, there were important differences between the ways in which these two Maronites conceived of their past. Al-Qilāʿī may have believed that at least some Maronites had always stayed true to the papacy from the time of John Maron, but he still criticised members of the church hierarchy and the wider Maronite community for their historic lapses from Rome. In this sense he may have been influenced by the Latin historiography of his time, which acknowledged that the Maronites had "returned and then fallen away" from Rome at various points in their history.[83] Indeed, in matters of doctrine and ritual, as well as in history, al-Qilāʿī consistently preferred Latin perspectives where they clashed with those of the Maronites.[84] But equally as important in forming this verdict may have been the undeniable defections from Rome that were caused by the rising influence of the Jacobites among the Maronite community in the fifteenth century. Al-Qilāʿī could not argue that Maronites had never abandoned their faith in Rome, as evidence to the contrary was all around him. Instead, he turned these defections into a polemical tool, arguing that whenever the Maronites had wavered from their union to Rome in the past, they had always been punished for it, creating a powerful incentive for his people to embrace what he thought to be the faith of their ancestors.[85]

As we will see in the following chapters, two centuries of missionary work cemented Maronite union with Rome and eliminated the Jacobite threat. This new religious context was matched by a new historiographical climate, in which the past fidelity of the eastern Churches to Rome became a battleground contested between Catholic and Protestant scholars. Fully embedded in this contest, al-Duwayhi therefore read al-Qilāʿī's history of

The development of Maronite historiography 19

the Maronites with different aims and expectations. While drawing heavily on his predecessor's work, he invariably contested al-Qilāʿī when the latter scholar accused the Maronites of lapsing from union with Rome. His refutation of al-Qilāʿī's criticisms of Patriarch Luqa is just one example of this.[86] For al-Duwayhi, the Catholicity of the Maronites left little space for lapsing or dissent, creating a history of unbroken union between Rome and Mount Lebanon that refined the earlier apologetics of Abraham Ecchellensis (d.1664) and Fausto Naironi (1628–1711).[87]

Much historiography on the Maronites still operates in the universalising shadow cast by these Counter-Reformation historians. Al-Duwayhi's claims are often repeated, while the sources on which he based his account remain largely unstudied. As a result, it has been forgotten that the idea of the perpetual union of the Maronites to Rome was born from a serious challenge to this union in the fifteenth century. Facing defections to the Jacobite Church in Mount Lebanon, Gryphon argued that the ancestral faith of the Maronites was that of the church of Rome. Through his letters, poetry, and pastoral work, al-Qilāʿī then injected this argument into the mainstream of Maronite identity and historiography. It was only later that al-Qilāʿī's sometimes critical portrayal of the Maronites was developed by historians of the Counter-Reformation, who rejected his criticisms of the past and overlooked the evidence of dissent that he recorded in his own time in order to create an image of perpetual union between the Maronites and Rome.[88]

One person who was apparently unmoved by al-Qilāʿī's threats and exhortations was the Maronite Patriarch Simon al-Hadathi. He declined to send to Rome for his confirmation until 1513, and even then his primary motivation may have been less devotion to the pope, than a desire to protect the growing Maronite community of Cyprus from the predations of Latin clerics on the island.[89] But whatever the patriarch's motivations, the exchanges between Rome and Mount Lebanon in the reign of Pope Leo X (1513–1521) that were sparked by this embassy proved decisive to the religious identity of the Maronites. It is to this topic that we now turn.

Notes

1 Paul Rouhana, "Identité ecclésiale maronite des origines à la veille du Synode libanais," *Parole de l'Orient* 15 (1988–1989): 215–21.
2 Elias El-Hāyek, "Struggle for Survival: The Maronites of the Middle Ages," in *Conversion and Continuity: Indigenous Christian Communities in Islamic Lands, Eighth to Eighteenth Centuries*, ed. Michael Gervers and Ramzi Jibran Bikhazi (Toronto: PIMS, 1990), 407–8.
3 Ibid., 411.
4 Ibid., 411.
5 Shafiq Abouzayd, "The Maronite Church," in *The Syriac World*, ed. Daniel King (London: Routledge, 2018), 731.
6 Ibid., 733; El-Hāyek, "Struggle for Survival," 413–14.
7 Abouzayd, "The Maronite Church," 733.
8 See below, Chapter 1:III.

20 The development of Maronite historiography

9 Kamal S. Salibi, *Maronite Historians of Medieval Lebanon* (Beirut: Catholic Press, 1959), 44.
10 Mariam de Ghantuz Cubbe, "Maroniti e Crociati dalla prima Crociata al 1215. Le fonti non maronite," *Studi e ricerche sull'Oriente cristiano* 6 (1983): 228–30; El-Hāyek, "Struggle for Survival," 418.
11 Kamal S. Salibi, "The Maronite Church in the Middle Ages and its Union with Rome," *Oriens Christianus* 42 (1958): 94–5 (c.1180); de Ghantuz Cubbe, "Maroniti e Crociati: Le fonti non maronite," 418 (1181); Wojciech Górecki, "The union between *Maronitae* and Rome (1182) as the context of relationships between the Franks and the Oriental Churches in the Crusader states in the 12th century," *Orientalia Christiana Cracoviensa* 2 (2010): 61–6 (1182).
12 Rudolf Hiestand, "Die Integration der Maroniten in die römische Kirche. Zum ältesten Zeugnis der pästlichen Kanzlei (12. Jahrh.)," *Orientalia Christiana Periodica* 54 (1988): 119–52.
13 Salibi, "The Maronite Church in the Middle Ages," 95 (1203); de Ghantuz Cubbe, "Maroniti e Crociati: Le fonti non maronite," 223 (c.1205).
14 Salibi, "The Maronite Church in the Middle Ages," 95–6; the bull is printed in *Bullarium Maronitarum*, 2–5.
15 Salibi, "The Maronite Church in the Middle Ages," 92.
16 Ibid., 92–3.
17 Ibid., 97.
18 On Patriarch Lūqa, see especially Mariam de Ghantuz Cubbe, "Le temps de Jérémie de Dmalsa, patriarche des Maronites (1283 environ): Problèmes ouverts et hypothèses," *Parole de l'Orient* 31 (2006): 451–504.
19 Salibi, "The Maronite Church in the Middle Ages," 100; Kamal S. Salibi, "The Maronite Experiment," in *Conversion and Continuity*, ed. Gervers and Bikhazi, 426. For the Mamluk period, see too Mariam de Ghantuz Cubbe, "Les trois expeditions des Mamelouks contre la montagne libanaise en 1292, 1300 et 1305, et les Maronites," *Orientalia Christiana Periodica* 81 (2015): 139–68.
20 Julian Chrysostomides, "The Byzantine Empire from the eleventh to the fifteenth century," in *The Cambridge History of Turkey. Volume I: Byzantium to Turkey*, ed. Kate Fleet (Cambridge: Cambridge University Press, 2010), 6–48.
21 Ibid., 48–9.
22 Norman Housley, *Crusading and the Ottoman Threat, 1453–1505* (Oxford: Oxford University Press, 2012).
23 Joseph Gill, *The Council of Florence* (Cambridge: Cambridge University Press, 1959), 21–95.
24 Ibid., 58–64 and 293.
25 Ibid., 307–35.
26 Salvatore Tedeschi, "Etiopi e Copti al Concilio di Firenze," *Annuarium Historiae Conciliorum* 21 (1989): 400.
27 Halim Noujaim, *I Francescani e i Maroniti (1233–1516)*, trans. Bartolomeo Pirone (Milan: Edizioni Terra Santa, 2012), 22–3.
28 Ibid., 64. The bull produced by this meeting is printed in *Bullarium Maronitarum*, 2–5.
29 Noujaim, *I Francescani e i Maroniti (1233–1516)*, 24–8; see however Salibi, "The Maronite Experiment," 427, which states that the patriarch's residence was attacked by a mob, which was suppressed by the Mamluks and local Maronite notables.
30 "Possistis non solum vos in via domini conservare, sed populos et nationes proximarum partium et regionum in animarum vestrarum lucrum dirigere, ac ad vitam ducere sempiternam." In Joseph Gill, ed., *Epistolae pontificiae ad Concilium Florentinum spectantes* (Rome: Pontificium Institutum Orientalium Studiorum, 1946), 3:43.
31 Ibid., 3:43.

The development of Maronite historiography   21

32 H. Lammens, "Frère Gryphon et le Liban au XVᵉ siècle," *Revue de l'Orient Chrétien* 4 (1899): 77–8; text printed in Gill, *Epistolae pontificiae*, 3:99–100.

33 Text in *Bullarium Maronitarum*, 14–16. The bull is dated there to VII nones Augusti, which is impossible as this date does not exist in the Julian calendar. The edition in Gill, *Epistolae pontificiae*, 3:105–8 gives a more plausible date of 7 August. For the Maronites of Cyprus, see Laurent Fenoy, "Refuge et réseaux: les chrétiens orientaux en Chypre entre 1192 et 1473," in *Espaces et réseaux en Méditerranée VIᵉ–XVIᵉ siècle. Volume 2: La formation des réseaux*, ed. Damien Coulon, Christophe Picard and Dominique Valérian (Saint-Denis: Bouchène, 2007), 187–206; Maria G. Skordi, *The Maronites of Cyprus. History and Iconography (16th–19th centuries)* (Nicosia: UNESCO, 2019).

34 Matti Moosa, *The Maronites in History* (Syracuse, NY: Syracuse University Press, 1986), 230–2. As noted earlier, Moosa had an axe to grind in this alternative history of the Maronites: he was a deacon of the Syrian Orthodox (Jacobite) Church.

35 Lammens, "Frére Gryphon," 72 (sending to Rome); Noujaim, *I Francescani e i Maroniti (1233–1516)*, 23 (receiving message from Rome, perhaps referring to letter to the Guardian of the Holy Land signalled in Gill, *Epistolae pontificiae*, 3:84).

36 For the Franciscans of the Holy Land, see most recently Marianne P. Ritsema van Eck, *The Holy Land in Observant Franciscan Texts (c.1480–1650)* (Leiden: Brill, 2019); Megan C. Armstrong, *The Holy Land and the Early Modern Reinvention of Catholicism* (Cambridge: Cambridge University Press, 2021).

37 Lammens, "Frére Gryphon" (see n.32 above).

38 Besides Lammens's article, see also Noujaim, *I Francescani e i Maroniti (1233–1516)*, 35–60; Moosa, *The Maronites in History*, 233–9; B. De Troeyer, "Gryphon, Griffoen van Vlaanderen, Griffo," in *Dictionnaire d'histoire et de géographie ecclésiastiques*, ed. R. Aubert (Paris: Letouzey et Ané, 1988), 22:453–5.

39 The text of Paul II's bull is printed in *Bullarium Maronitarum*, 22–5.

40 Girolamo Golubovich, ed., *Il Trattato di Terra Santa e dell'Oriente di Frate Francesco Suriano* (Milan: Tipografia editrice Artigianelli, 1900), 68.

41 *Analecta Franciscana, sive Chronica aliaque varia documenta ad historiam Fratrum Minorum spectantia* (Quaracchi: Ex Typographia Collegii S. Bonaventurae, 1887), 2:453.

42 Hector Douaihy, *Un Théologien Maronite: Gibra'il ibn al-Qalā'i, Evêque et Moine Franciscain* (Kaslik: Université Saint-Esprit, 1993), 167–73; Joseph Moukarzel, *Gabriel Ibn al-Qilāʿī († c. 1516). Approche biographique et étude du corpus* (Jounieh: PUSEK, 2007), 44–5.

43 Moosa, *The Maronites in History*, 231.

44 Ibid., 235–6.

45 Gryphon's account is printed in Noujaim, *I Francescani e i Maroniti (1233–1516)*, 63–5.

46 Ibid., 63–5.

47 Golubovich, *Il Trattato di Terra Santa di Francesco Suriano*, 70.

48 Kamal S. Salibi, "The *muqaddams* of Bsarri: Maronite Chieftains of the Northern Lebanon, 1382–1621," *Arabica* 15 (1968): 63–86; Douaihy, *Un Théologien Maronite*, 171–3; Moosa, *The Maronites in History*, 238–9. The broader history of Christianity in the Levant at this time is detailed in Thomas A. Carlson, *Christianity in Fifteenth-Century Iraq* (Cambridge: Cambridge University Press, 2018).

49 For the timing of al-Qilāʿī's vocation, see Moukarzel, *Gabriel Ibn al-Qilāʿī*, 49–50; for dispatch by Gryphon, see Golubovich, ed., *Il Trattato di Terra Santa di Francesco Suriano*, 70–1. It is possible that Gryphon sent other Maronites to learn in Italy. See for instance Geroldus Fussenegger, "De vita et scriptis

22 *The development of Maronite historiography*

Fr. Alexandri Ariosti," *Archivum Franciscanum Historicum* 49 (1956): 146, where we find mention of a Maronite, perhaps named Antonio, who acted as translator on Alessandro Ariosto's mission to the Levant.

50 Mentioned in Golubovich, *Il Trattato di Terra Santa di Francesco Suriano*, 71.

51 Ibid., 71; for his life and death, al-Qilāʿī's eulogy, described in Moukarzel, *Gabriel Ibn al-Qilāʿī*, 405–8.

52 See in general Moukarzel, *Gabriel Ibn al-Qilāʿī*.

53 Douaihy, *Un Théologien Maronite*, 171; Moukarzel, *Gabriel Ibn al-Qilāʿī*, 45.

54 Moukarzel, *Gabriel Ibn al-Qilāʿī*, 49.

55 Golubovich, *Il Trattato di Terra Santa di Francesco Suriano*, 70.

56 Paul F. Grendler, *The Universities of the Italian Renaissance* (Baltimore: Johns Hopkins University Press, 2002), 355–8.

57 Douaihy, *Un Théologien Maronite*, 180–1; Moukarzel, *Gabriel Ibn al-Qilāʿī*, 55; an extract from al-Qilāʿī's eulogy to Johannes mentioning this final episode is translated in Noujaim, *I Francescani e i Maroniti (1233–1516)*, 89.

58 See Moukarzel, *Gabriel Ibn al-Qilāʿī*, 239–40.

59 Ibid., 57–9.

60 Douaihy, *Un Théologien Maronite*, 183–7; Moukarzel, *Gabriel Ibn al-Qilāʿī*, 59.

61 Moukarzel, *Gabriel Ibn al-Qilāʿī*, 274–5 and 287–8.

62 Ibid., 277.

63 Al-Qilāʿī's Arabic translation of Suriano's letter survives in Bkerké: Bibliothèque de la Résidence patriarcale maronite, 113, 180–2, see Moukarzel, *Gabriel Ibn al-Qilāʿī*, 60 n.223. Large chunks of this letter are translated into Italian in Noujaim, *I Francescani e i Maroniti (1233–1516)*, 139–40.

64 Moukarzel, *Gabriel Ibn al-Qilāʿī*, 60–1.

65 Ibid., 250.

66 Ibid., 290.

67 Douaihy, *Un Théologien Maronite*, 187–96. I have not been able to consult Ray Jabre Mouawad, *Lettres au Mont-Liban d'ibn al-Qilai, XVe siècle* (Paris: Geuthner, 2001).

68 His letters to David and George are discussed in Moukarzel, *Gabriel Ibn al-Qilāʿī*, 287–90, and the letter to George is partially translated in Douaihy, *Un Théologien Maronite*, 187–8.

69 For Ibrahim ibn Dray and other pro-Roman Maronites, see Moukarzel, *Gabriel Ibn al-Qilāʿī*, 49 and 415.

70 Ibid., 412–13.

71 For the date of this tract, see ibid., 100.

72 Ibid., 96–9 and 104–7.

73 Ibid., 95–6.

74 Ibid., 99–104.

75 Ibid., 45; Fady Baroudi, "Jacobites, Ethiopians and Mount Lebanon," *Liban Souterrain* 5 (1998): 75–160; Ray Jabre Mouawad, "The Ethiopian Monks in Mount-Lebanon (XVth Century)," *Liban Souterrain* 5 (1998): 186–207.

76 Moukarzel, *Gabriel Ibn al-Qilāʿī*, 100–1.

77 Ibid., 223–32; Douaihy, *Un Théologien Maronite*, 197 and 227–37.

78 Moukarzel, *Gabriel Ibn al-Qilāʿī*, 401.

79 Ibid., 422–3; Salibi, *Maronite Historians*, 35–87.

80 Douaihy, *Un Théologien Maronite*, 197.

81 For evidence of recitation, see Moukarzel, *Gabriel Ibn al-Qilāʿī*, 398; al-Qilāʿī's poems and the manuscripts in which they can be found are described in ibid., 303–442.

82 Ibid., 418.

83 "Più volte [...] ritornati e poi prevaricati". Golubovich, *Trattato di Terra Santa di Francesco Suriano*, 68.

84 Douaihy, *Un Théologien Maronite*, 221–7.

The development of Maronite historiography   23

85 Salibi, *Maronite Historians*, 17.
86 Moukarzel, *Gabriel Ibn al-Qilāʿī*, 422 n.48; for other examples, see Salibi, *Maronite Historians*, 89–160.
87 For this broader context, see Aurélien Girard, "Quand les Maronites écrivaient en Latin: Fauste Nairon et la république des lettres (seconde moitié du XVIIe siècle)," in *Le latin des Maronites*, ed. Mireille Issa (Paris: Geuthner, 2017), 45–76; Aurélien Girard, "Was an Eastern Scholar Necessarily a Cultural Broker in Early Modern Europe? Faustus Naironus (1628–1711), the Christian East, and Oriental Studies," in *Confessionalisation and Erudition in Early Modern Europe: An Episode in the History of the Humanities*, ed. Nicholas Hardy and Dmitri Levitin (Oxford: Oxford University Press, 2019), 240–63.
88 When writing this analysis, I have been unable to consult Paul Rouhana, "La vision des origines religieuses des Maronites entre le XVe et le XVIIIe siècle: de l'évêque Gabriel Ibn-al-Qila'i († 1516) au patriarche Etienne Douaihy (1670–1704)" (PhD diss., Institut catholique de Paris, 1998).
89 Noujaim, *I Francescani e i Maroniti (1233–1516)*, 128; for the importance of Cyprus, see Moukarzel, *Gabriel Ibn al-Qilāʿī*, 64–5, and Skordi, *The Maronites of Cyprus*.

2 Centre and periphery
Rome and Mount Lebanon in the reign of Pope Leo X (1513–1521)

I. Introduction

The reign of Leo X (1513–1521) is iconic in the history of contacts between Rome and the Maronites. Maronite historians routinely quote with pride the pope's praise of their community as "roses among the thorns".[1] Similarly, Leo's pontificate is regarded as a significant period in the history of Catholic Orientalism, with pioneers such as Teseo Ambrogio and Johannes Potken beginning their studies of the languages of eastern Christianity.[2] As we will see, the Maronites were instrumental in this area too.

This chapter will retrace exchanges between Rome and the Maronites during Leo's pontificate. It will begin by reconstructing the correspondence between Leo and Patriarch Simon al-Hadathi between 1513 and 1515, showing how Rome was made to remember the existence of the Maronites due to the mediation of the Franciscans of the Holy Land. It will then analyse two previously unknown accounts of Maronite customs that were produced by one of these Franciscans, Francesco Suriano, arguing that his interventions were crucial to securing a positive outcome for the Maronite embassies to Leo X. Finally, this chapter will conclude by demonstrating the contributions of one Maronite ambassador to the development of Oriental scholarship in Rome.

Before proceeding, the reader should note that most of the events in this chapter occur between 1513 and 1516. Since there is no evidence of direct contact between the Maronites in Lebanon and the papacy from 1517 to 1522, only the final section about Oriental scholarship in Rome will consider the later years of Leo's pontificate. As such, this chapter will not discuss the Ottoman conquest of the Levant in 1516–1517 or the Reformation, since their impact on our topic was only felt after Leo's death. A reader who wishes to acquaint themselves with these developments can however find a summary of them at the beginning of the next chapter.

II. Rome is made to remember the Maronites

The influential exchanges between Rome and Mount Lebanon that took place the reign of Leo X had rather inauspicious beginnings. In 1513, Patriarch Simon al-Hadathi sent his emissary, a Maronite named Petrus, to Beirut

DOI: 10.4324/9781003165392-3

to check for ships sailing to the west. But once he had arrived, Petrus found that departures were planned much earlier than expected, leaving him no time to return to Qannubin in order to acquire the appropriate documents from his patriarch. Marco da Firenze, the superior of the Franciscan monastery in Beirut, therefore stepped in to assist this mission, sending Petrus to Italy with letters in which he reassured the pope of the Maronites' fidelity to Rome, and requested confirmation for Simon on the patriarch's behalf.[3]

Petrus's arrival in Rome appears to have been a cause for celebration. In two letters to Patriarch Simon and the Maronites dated to 25 and 27 May 1514, Pope Leo recalled that he threw his hands to the heavens in joy on receiving word from these "true sons of the holy Catholic faith, set among the infidel like lambs among the wolves".[4] However, Leo regretted that he could not fulfil the requests that Simon had made. The emissary Petrus was unwilling to carry out the ceremonies for union, and he had in any case arrived without letters from the patriarch. Leo was therefore returning Petrus to Mount Lebanon with his blessings and greetings to Patriarch Simon, whose wishes he promised not only to fulfil, but to exceed, should the patriarch complete the laudable path that he had embarked on. This would be done once Simon sent to Rome a request for confirmation in his own hand. Leo assured Simon that Rome, a city "flourishing in the study of every science", possessed learned men who could interpret the patriarch's Arabic letters for him.[5]

Leo's exhortations and promises to Simon indicate a desire to motivate the patriarch after what must have been the disappointing outcome of an embassy that had cost months of dangerous travel between Italy and the Levant. It is not impossible that Petrus's mission to Rome was doomed from the start by the lack of letters from Simon. But other factors may have been at play, too. By his own admission, Leo's joy on receiving word from the Maronites was accentuated by fact that he had never heard of them before.[6] It would appear therefore that Leo had not thoroughly read the short book about the future of the Church that Paolo Giustinian and Vincenzo Querini had submitted to him in July 1513, which lists the Maronites as one of the seven Christian peoples of Asia and Africa.[7] The sense that the Maronites had been forgotten in Rome is further borne out by the lack of any reference in Leo's letters to previous negotiations between Rome and the Maronites, such as had been commonplace in papal bulls of the fifteenth century. Patriarch Simon was as such paying the price for his and his predecessor's reluctance to engage with the papacy. There is no sign of any direct contact between the Maronites and the papacy in the period between 1478 and the start of Leo's reign. Any communication between Catholics and Maronites instead took place in the Levant, co-ordinated by the Franciscans of the Holy Land.

These friars at the periphery of the Catholic world were essential to Leo's plans, as is made clear in his letter of 25 May 1514 to Marco da Firenze, the superior of the Franciscan monastery in Beirut. Just as he had told the Maronites, Leo wrote to Marco that he could not confirm Patriarch

26 Centre and periphery

Simon in his office without documents in the patriarch's own hand. But he added a different reason for this, stating that he did not wish to confirm the patriarch in the present state of knowledge about the Maronites, "lest we approve as healthy what is actually harmful".[8] From this comment, we can gather that Leo perhaps had greater doubts about the Catholicity of the Maronites than he confessed in his letters to them. He therefore instructed Marco to make a thorough enquiry into Patriarch Simon. Marco was to discover how and by whom Simon was elected, where he had his seat, what vestments he wore, from whom the patriarchs customarily accepted holy orders and insignia, and how long he had been in office.[9] Moreover, he was to prepare a Latin translation of any letters that Simon sent to Rome in Arabic. This would imply that Leo wanted the translation to be prepared in the Levant, rather than in Rome. Despite the pope's boasts about the linguistic skill of Roman scholars in his letters to the Maronites, we see once more that the peripheries of the Catholic world had skills and knowledge that the metropole did not possess. There is indeed little doubt that the Franciscans of the Holy Land had a better grasp of Arabic than their Roman peers at this time, as in 1514 even pioneers of Oriental scholarship in Rome such as Teseo Ambrogio had yet to take up their study of Arabic or Syriac.[10]

Leo's exhortations bore fruit in 1515, when the Maronite emissary Petrus returned to Rome with a letter for the pope from Patriarch Simon.[11] After a lengthy confession of faith, Simon answered the questions that Leo had posed to Marco. The answers that he provided make this letter a precious source for Maronite worship in the early sixteenth century, not least in its thick description of the manner of composing the chrism, which we learn the Maronites made not only from oil and balsam, as in the Roman manner, but also from a range of spices and other ingredients.[12] Having answered Leo's questions, Simon repeated his request for confirmation, adding to this an appeal for vestments and other regalia for himself and his clergy, indulgences, a letter for the *muqaddam* Elias, and bulls that restored canonries to the Maronites of Cyprus and freed this community from certain taxes.[13] If that wasn't enough, he accompanied his letter with copies of bulls that earlier popes had sent to the Maronites.[14]

The failure of the earlier mission through lack of documentation perhaps inspired Patriarch Simon to take this maximalist approach. There was no lack of material for Leo to pour over, and the dispatch of these supporting texts appears to have had the desired effect. Leo confirmed Simon in his office as patriarch.[15] The pope claimed that this decision was motivated by his desire to follow in the footsteps of his predecessors, whose actions he had probably just learned about through the bulls that had been sent to him by Patriarch Simon. Indeed, from 1515 onwards, the letters of Leo and other popes routinely quote the bulls that had been sent by Simon.[16] We have just seen that the peripheries of Catholicism had knowledge and skills that the metropole lacked. From this example, we might add that provincial scholars and clerics had access to documentation unavailable in Rome, even documentation that had originally been written in the Eternal City.

Nonetheless, these bulls were not the only documents that influenced Leo's decision to confirm Simon as patriarch. The pope also mentioned that he had received letters from Francesco Suriano, which had reassured him that the Maronites were "good and true children" who differed from Rome in nothing that pertained to salvation.[17] Here, Leo may refer to two reports on Maronite belief and practice composed by Suriano, which are preserved today in the Archivio Apostolico Vaticano. To the best of my knowledge, neither has ever been mentioned in histories of the Maronites, despite their value as sources for the Christian traditions of sixteenth-century Lebanon.[18]

III. Francesco Suriano's reports on Maronite belief and practice: Tolerating religious difference on the eve of the Reformation

The first of Suriano's two reports responded to the questions about Patriarch Simon that Leo had asked Marco da Firenze to investigate. Marco must therefore have transmitted Leo's letter to Suriano, and it appears that Suriano travelled from Jerusalem to Mount Lebanon in order to answer the pope's questions. In his letter to Leo, Patriarch Simon mentioned that the Franciscan custodian of the Holy Land had visited them. In this way, Simon referred honorifically to Suriano through the office that this Franciscan had filled until just a few months earlier.[19]

Suriano's first report about the Maronites shows that he found most of Leo's queries easy to answer. He noted that papal bulls recorded Antioch as the patriarch's seat, described the vestments that the patriarch wore and how he accepted holy orders, and confirmed that Simon had been in office for about 30 years. The manner in which Maronite patriarchs were elected, however, demanded a longer answer. In his letter to Leo, Patriarch Simon had claimed that elections were carried out by 12 priests of good character, who were isolated from one another in different cells, and required to write a name on a piece of paper until they all suggested the same candidate. In Simon's account, this candidate would then be unproblematically accepted by the rest of the Maronite clergy and people.[20] Suriano's report contrasts with this description. He wrote that only two archbishops and four bishops gathered for the election, and that they selected one of their number as a candidate. This candidate would then be proposed to the Maronite clergy and people, who had the power to reject him and force the suggestion of another name. Once a candidate had been acclaimed by the clergy and people, 60 ducats would be sent to the Muslim governor of Tripoli in order to obtain their consent for the choice of the new patriarch.[21]

That the patriarch of the Maronites owed his election to popular acclaim and payment to local Muslim authorities paints a somewhat less exemplary picture than the one that Simon had presented to Leo. Suriano discussed further errant practices in his second report, titled "the customs of the Maronite people and clergy".[22] He noted that the Maronites followed the Greeks by keeping a stock of pre-consecrated hosts to administer to the

28 Centre and periphery

dying. Their priests were married, and they used some vestments differently from the Latins. He also recorded a complex code around acceptance of the Eucharist, such as the belief that it was a sin to spit on the same day as taking Communion, to wash one's mouth with water in Communion, if a beard hair entered the mouth, or to take Communion on the same day that one suffered an effusion of blood from the nostrils or teeth. He found similar codes of conduct around baptism, where women were said to delay the baptism of their child until after the fourth day, in the belief that to do otherwise would make their milk sinful. As regards marriage, Suriano concluded that "no-one was more ignorant about grades of relation and spiritual knowledge" than the Maronites.[23] But what scandalised him most was that there were only three or four priests who heard confession in Mount Lebanon. He therefore recommended that the pope provide a dispensation for parish priests to confess their parishioners.[24] Suriano had first-hand knowledge of this dearth of confessors in Mount Lebanon, reporting in his *Trattato della Terra Santa* that he had received confession from Maronites in Arabic while in the Levant, and adding that the Maronites frequently had recourse to Franciscans for this purpose.[25]

Despite what he had observed in Mount Lebanon, in his *Trattato* Suriano stated that he had confidence in the Catholicity of the Maronites, believing them to have gone astray due to the lack of instruction, rather than any natural depravity.[26] We learn from Leo's letters to Patriarch Simon that Suriano took the same favourable stance when representing the Maronites before the pope, with whom he probably discussed these matters in Rome in 1515.[27] In this manner, Suriano joined a longer tradition of Franciscan emissaries who represented the Maronites as Catholics despite their knowledge of discrepancies between Rome and Mount Lebanon. Before Suriano, Gryphon had apparently interceded with the pope in order to allow the Maronites to keep certain customs typical of the oriental Churches.[28]

Perhaps we need not be too surprised by Gryphon and Suriano's favourable interventions on behalf of the Maronites. Missionaries are often willing to accommodate the customs of their target audience within the faith that they are promoting. One need only think of the Chinese rites controversy a century after these events, which was caused by the considerable latitude for Confucian practices that the Jesuits gave to Chinese Catholics.[29] Instead, what is more striking is the papacy's approach to these 'errant' customs. In two bulls of 1 and 20 August 1515, Leo replied to Simon that he was sending Franciscans to correct the Maronites, probably to enforce the specific changes mentioned there, such as using only oil and balsam in the chrism, and to ensure that the faithful confessed at least once a year. He also highlighted some serious doctrinal omissions from Simon's confession of faith, such as the lack of any mention of the *filioque*.[30] Leo must then have known that the Maronites were not in full agreement with Roman doctrine and practices when these bulls were written. In replying to Simon, he was therefore faced with two options. He could insist on full conformity to Rome before granting the patriarch's requests, which ran the risk of losing the Maronites' interest in maintaining ties with the papacy. On the other hand, he could issue a benevolent reply, which might secure the Maronites' trust, but would confirm Simon based purely on promises of change that Leo might have known his missionaries would not insist upon too harshly, and would leave other matters mentioned in Suriano's report, such as the fact that the Maronite clergy could marry, entirely unresolved. Leo chose the second course of action. Just two years before the outbreak of the Reformation, the papacy had therefore shown that it could tolerate within Catholicism a people whose customs and beliefs it knew to differ from those of Rome.

It is possible that international politics partly explain Leo's benevolent reply to Patriarch Simon. The French had just invaded northern Italy, in a campaign that would soon culminate at the battle of Marignano (13–14 September 1515).[31] Any recognition of Rome's authority was therefore especially precious, and Leo indeed used the Maronite embassy to bolster his standing on the European stage. He had the bulls to Patriarch Simon printed together with documents relating to his other great triumph of this time, the abrogation of the Pragmatic Sanction of Bourges.[32] Moreover, crusading was as much an ambition of Leo's papacy as it was of other popes in the fifteenth and sixteenth centuries. But as previous studies have shown, there is no indication that Leo saw the Maronites as potential allies in a crusade against the Mamluks or the Ottomans in the Levant.[33] Doctrine and ecclesiology instead provide the most rewarding perspectives through which to assess the bilateral relationship between Rome and the Maronites. As we will see in Chapter 5, military matters were instead a major factor of Maronite contacts with Catholic secular powers, especially with Habsburg Spain.

IV. The Maronite delegation to the Fifth Lateran Council (1512–1517) and the development of Oriental studies in Renaissance Rome

After he had presented his reports about the Maronites to Leo, Francesco Suriano was dispatched to Qannubin with the new superior of the Franciscan monastery in Beirut, Giovanni Francesco da Potenza, to communicate the pope's responses to Simon.[34] Leo was true to his original promise to not only fulfil, but also to exceed the patriarch's requests. Besides Simon's confirmation, Leo sent Suriano east with indulgences and letters that freed the Maronites of Cyprus from certain taxes, as well as restoring them to the church of St John in Nicosia.[35] The Catholic hierarchy may also have come to value the influence of secular figures among the Maronites, since Leo sent a letter to the *muqaddam* Elias, as Simon had requested.[36] These bulls, letters, and indulgences were accompanied by an enormous list of gifts, which were enumerated by Simon in a letter to Leo of 14 February 1516.[37] There we find a wealth of clerical vestments and church decorations, such as chasubles, copes, an altar-cloth, maniples, a mitre, and a

30 *Centre and periphery*

pallium, the last two of which are especially significant. The use of the pallium was only granted by the pope to Catholic prelates, and Suriano had observed that the Maronites alone among the eastern Churches used the mitre, as Catholics did.[38] It therefore appears that the intention of these gifts was to display the union between Rome and the Maronites by dressing Simon as a Catholic prelate. The force of this display was enhanced by the ornamentation of these vestments and decorations. The altar-cloth sent to Simon, for instance, featured an image of St Thomas inspecting Christ's wounds.[39] This picture of faith confirmed against doubt and adversity was perhaps suitable for a people whom Rome believed to have returned to the fold while surrounded by heretics and non-believers. Leo therefore provided Simon not only with doctrines and vestments, but also with an iconography of faith and obedience that was tailored to the unique situation of the Maronites. We might speculate that this iconography was intended to support other media like poetry and sermons in proclaiming the union between Rome and Mount Lebanon to those who lacked the ability to read the texts in which this union had been secured. However, the written word was not neglected in this embassy. Simon also mentioned that he had received a "liber pontificalis" from Leo, which may be the book of this name to which Leo pointed Simon for guidance on the Catholic mode of preparing the chrism.[40]

The letter in which Simon listed the gifts that he had received from Leo was likely translated in the Levant by Suriano, since he is recorded as the 'interpreter' of the embassy that transported these gifts east.[41] It was then carried back to Rome by Suriano's travel companion, Giovanni Francesco da Potenza, who was accompanied by three Maronites sent by Simon and the *muqaddam* Elias.[42] These emissaries arrived in Rome in time for the eleventh session of the Fifth Lateran Council (1512–1517) in December 1516, where they proclaimed Simon's obedience to Rome, and read out a letter in which the patriarch promised to follow the Catholic Church in the doctrines and customs where Leo and Suriano had found that the Maronites were wanting.[43]

Suriano's apparent absence from the party that returned to Rome is a small detail that perhaps led to major developments in the history of Oriental scholarship in Europe. In 1516, Cardinal Bernardino Carvajal asked Teseo Ambrogio to verify whether or not the Maronite Mass was in accordance with that of the Catholic Church. Ambrogio had been given this job despite the fact that he had no prior experience of Syriac or Arabic, so we can assume that there was no scholar in Rome who was known to be better qualified for the task. To complete this mission Ambrogio relied on a Jew named Joseph, who worked with one of the Maronite emissaries, the sub-deacon Elias ibn Ibrahim, to translate the Maronite Mass from Syriac into Arabic, and then into Latin.[44]

This episode highlights the extent to which Catholic scholars in the early years of the sixteenth century depended on the Jewish community of Rome as translators of texts in Oriental languages, a point also clear from Johannes

Potken's initial recourse to the Jews of the city in his attempts to understand Ge'ez, the language of the Ethiopian Orthodox Church.[45] However, this dependence appears to have diminished during and after the Fifth Lateran Council, when Catholics increasingly approached eastern Christians in Rome for the same purposes. Potken eventually learned Ge'ez from the Ethiopians resident at the church of Santo Stefano dei Mori, for instance.[46] The arrival of the Maronite delegation offered similar prospects for grappling with the languages of the Levant. The Maronite subdeacon Elias ibn Ibrahim stayed in Rome until 1521, where he taught Syriac and Arabic to western scholars, and copied manuscripts in these tongues.[47] Many of these manuscripts were copied at the monastery of Santa Maria della Pace, which may have served as Elias's base during his western sojourn.[48] His pupils and clients read like a who's-who of early Oriental scholarship in Rome. He taught Arabic and Syriac to Teseo Ambrogio, who is widely regarded as the first western scholar of the early modern period to learn the latter language.[49] He also offered copies of the Maronite Psalter to Bernardino Carvajal and Giles of Viterbo, an important Hebraist of the time.[50] Finally, he worked on copies of the Gospels in Syriac and Arabic for Alberto Pio da Carpi.[51] The manuscript of the Arabic Gospels that Elias worked on for Alberto Pio gains added interest from the fact that it was completed with Leo Africanus, the North African convert to Christianity famously studied by Natalie Zemon Davis.[52]

Here as elsewhere, Leo's role as a patron of Oriental scholarship has probably been exaggerated.[53] Simply because this early efflorescence of Catholic Orientalism occurred in Rome during his papacy does not mean that he should be afforded credit for it. Elias copied his manuscripts for Carvajal in order to thank the cardinal for his hospitality, for example, while Alberto Pio likely patronised the copying of biblical texts in Arabic and Syriac as part of his plans for a polyglot Bible.[54] Instead of giving all the credit to Leo, the contribution of eastern Christians to the early history of western Orientalism requires greater acknowledgment. In his seminal work on the first Oriental manuscripts to enter the Vatican Library, Giorgio Levi della Vida rightly hailed Elias's role in establishing the study of Oriental languages in Rome. Elias's pupils would in fact go on to teach or inspire the next generation of western Orientalists, thereby securing for this discipline a lasting place in European scholarship.[55]

Elias's work as a scribe and teacher ended abruptly in 1521. In that year he left Rome, perhaps as a result of the death of Leo X. However, he still had an important role to play in fostering connections between Rome and Mount Lebanon. In May 1522, Elias returned to Rome with a Maronite priest named Musa al-Akkari, in order to submit the obedience of Patriarch Simon to the new pope, Adrian VI (1522–1523). But within a year both Pope Adrian and Patriarch Simon were dead. Clement VII (1523–1534) was elected in Rome, while in Mount Lebanon the priest Musa was elected as the new patriarch of the Maronites, beginning a lengthy patriarchate that would last until 1567.[56]

32 Centre and periphery

V. Conclusion

The reign of Leo X marks the end of a distinctive period in the history of contact between Rome and Mount Lebanon, which extends from the Council of Ferrara-Florence to the Fifth Lateran Council. At the start of this period, the rise of Jacobite influence led to the creation of pro-Jacobite and pro-Roman parties among the Maronites. Franciscans such as Gryphon, al-Qilāʿī and Suriano therefore strove to build a Catholic identity for the Maronites, with lasting effects on the history and historiography of this people. At the same time, these Franciscans kept alive communication between the popes and the Maronite patriarchs, even through periods in which these prelates seemed uninterested in or forgetful of their counterpart across the sea. The labour of these friars was crowned by the intense exchange of embassies in the reign of Leo X, which shaped the future of Rome and Mount Lebanon in different ways. Rome was changed by Elias's copying of manuscripts and his teaching of Arabic and Syriac, which cemented Oriental scholarship in the city and then in Europe more widely. The impact of these exchanges on the Maronites was arguably even more profound. Despite the best efforts of the Franciscans of the Holy Land, Patriarch Simon was reluctant to communicate with Rome throughout most of his long reign. This all changed between 1514 and 1516, when Leo X vested huge intellectual and material resources in winning over the allegiance of Simon and his people. Leo's reign therefore marks the end of a period of introspection among the Maronites, and the beginning of a new era in which their patriarchs sought closer contact with Rome and the wider Catholic world.

As we will see, this goal defined the long patriarchate of Musa al-Akkari. Musa and his flock were however looking out onto a dramatically changed world. In 1517, the Ottoman Sultan Selim I completed the conquest of Lebanon, Syria, Egypt, and the holy places of Arabia. In distant Wittenberg, Martin Luther's protest set the Reformation into motion. The impact of these events upon papal contacts with the Maronites was only felt by Leo's successors, whose exchanges with Patriarch Musa will be the subject of the following chapter.

Notes

1 "[V]eluti rosas inter medias spinas". *Bullarium Maronitarum*, 47.
2 Giorgio Levi della Vida, *Ricerche sulla formazione del più antico fondo dei manoscritti orientali della Biblioteca Vaticana* (Vatican City: Biblioteca Apostolica Vaticana, 1939), 99–141; Robert J. Wilkinson, *Orientalism, Aramaic and Kabbalah in the Catholic Reformation: The First Printing of the Syriac New Testament* (Leiden: Brill, 2007), 1–62.
3 Halim Noujaim, *I Francescani e i Maroniti (1233–1516)*, trans. Bartolomeo Pirone (Milan: Edizioni Terra Santa, 2012), 128.
4 "[T]amquam agnos in medio luporum sic veros S. Catholicae fidei filios, in medio infidelium constitutos". *Bullarium Maronitarum*, 29. The letters are printed in ibid., 27–30.

Centre and periphery 33

5 "[I]n hac nostra Urbe orbis principe et omnium doctrinarum studiis florentissima, multorum habebimus arabicarum notarum peritos et interpretes". Ibid., 28.

6 "[S]ublatis manibus in altum gratias Deo Omnipotenti immensas egimus, qui tot animas fideles et sibi debitas, de quibus antea notitiam non habebamus, nobis notas esse voluisset". Ibid., 29.

7 "Maronitae enim illi sunt, qui Libanum montem et circa eum adjacentia loca occupant. Gabrielem [al-Qilāʿī] namque virum ex eodem S. Francisci Ordine, linguarum peritia insignem in Episcopum receperunt, qui eos Ecclesiae Romanae obedientia custodit, conservavitque". Paolo Giustinian and Vincenzo Querini, "Libellus ad Leonem X," in *Annales Camaldulenses*, ed. Giovanni-Benedetto Mittarelli and Anselmo Costadoni (Venice: Pasquali, 1773), 9:660. That Leo indeed did not read the *Libellus* is affirmed in Carlo Falconi, *Leone X, Giovanni de' Medici* (Milan: Rusconi, 1987), 311–12.

8 "[S]uper omnia diligentissime animadvertens, ne in eis articulis, quae ad salutem animarum necessaria sunt, aliquo modo a veritate et S.R.E. ritu discrepent, ne aliquid pestiferum, ut sanum approbemus". Ibid., 26.

9 Ibid., 26.

10 For his studies, see Giorgio Levi della Vida, "Teseo Ambrogio degli Albonesi," *DBI* 2 (1960); the improbability of Leo X's boast was noted by the same author in Giorgio Levi della Vida, *Ricerche*, 110 n.1.

11 Printed in Tobias Anaissi, ed., *Collectio documentorum Maronitarum* (Livorno: Fabbreschi, 1921), 33–42. Anaissi dates this letter to 1514, following the colophon "anno Christi 1514, octava die mensis Martii". However, this letter clearly responds to Leo's bulls of May 1514, and is in turn referred to in Leo's responses to Simon of August 1515, so should be dated to March 1515. It is translated into French and analysed in Miriam de Ghantuz Cubbe, "La lettre du Patriarche Maronite Šamūn Butros de Hadet au Léon X (1515)," *Orientalia Christiana Periodica* 76 (2010): 389–432.

12 Anaissi, *Collectio documentorum*, 36.

13 Ibid., 40–1.

14 This can be inferred from Leo's letter to Simon of 1 August 1515, where these bulls are mentioned: "Nuper autem idem Nuncius tuus ad nos rediens literas tuas, arabico vulgari syriace scriptas, ac originales literas fel. Rec. Innocentii Tertii, et Alexandri Quarti, in quibus etiam Innocentii Tertii literae commemorantur, nec non Eugenii Quarti, Nicolai Quinti, Calixti Tertii, et Pauli Secundi Romanorum Pontificum, et praedecessorum nostrorum". *Bullarium Maronitarum*, 45.

15 Ibid., 49.

16 See, for instance, letters of later popes throughout the sixteenth century in ibid., 53, 57, 67–8, 71.

17 "Ac demum ex literis dilecti filii Francisci Suriani [...] intelleximus, te ac Maronitas omnes se ortodoxae fidei nostrae veros esse cultores, et observatores, et Sanctam Romanam Ecclesiam, tanquam bonos et dilectos filios, plurimum venerari, ac in his, quae ad animarum salute requiruntur, et necessaria sunt, ab eadem minime discrepare". Ibid., 46.

18 These reports are extant in two later copies: AAV: Misc. Arm. VI, 39, 16r, 23r–24v (incomplete copy) and 17r–19v (complete copy). They are transcribed below in Appendix I.

19 "[G]uardianus Hierosolymitanus, qui nobiscum fuit". Anaissi, *Collectio documentorum Maronitarum*, 41.

20 Ibid., 37.

21 AAV: Misc. Arm. VI, 39, 18v–19r.

22 "Mores cleri ac populi Maronitarum quos ego inueni". Ibid., 19v.

23 "Nemo fuit multum ignoranter circa gradus affinitatis et spiritualis cognationis in Matrimoniis contrahendis". Ibid., 19v. For Maronite marriage around this

34   *Centre and periphery*

time, see Michel Aoun, "Le mariage dans l'église Maronite d'après un rituel manuscrit du XVI siècle (Vat. Syr. 52)," *Parole de l'Orient* 23 (1998): 111–65; Fouad El-Hage, *Kitâb al-Nâmûs d'ibn al-Qilâ'î dans l'histoire juridique du marriage chez les Maronites* (Kaslik: Université Saint-Espirit, 2001).

24 AAV: Misc. Arm. VI, 39, 19v.

25 Girolamo Golubovich, ed., *Il Trattato di Terra Santa e dell'Oriente di Frate Francesco Suriano* (Milan: Tipografia editrice Artigianelli, 1900), 14 and 70.

26 "Per mancamento più presto de non haver homini docti et predicatori, che per inata malitia". Ibid., 69.

27 *Bullarium Maronitarum*, 46.

28 Ibid., 46. Due to this distinction between practice and theory, I disagree with image of Catholic intransigence proposed in the useful study by Petro B.T. Bilaniuk, *The Fifth Lateran Council (1512–1517) and the Eastern Churches* (Toronto: Central Committee for the Defence of Rite, Tradition and Language of the Ukrainian Catholic Church in USA and Canada, 1975), 155–88.

29 On this topic, see Pierre-Antoine Fabre and Ines Županov, eds, *The Rites Controversies in the Early Modern World* (Leiden: Brill, 2018).

30 *Bullarium Maronitarum*, 33–4 and 46–9.

31 Kenneth M. Setton, *The Papacy and the Levant (1204–1571)*, vol. 3, *The Sixteenth Century to the Reign of Julius III* (Philadelphia: The American Philosophical Society, 1984), 159–61; Maurizio Gattoni, *Leone X e la geopolitica dello Stato Pontificio (1513–1521)* (Vatican City: Archivio Segreto Vaticano, 2000).

32 Bilaniuk, *The Fifth Lateran Council (1512–1517) and the Eastern Churches*, 170.

33 Besides there being no trace of the Maronites in the exhaustive study by Setton, *The Papacy and the Levant*, 3:142–97 or Nelson H. Minnich, "Lateran V and the Call for a Crusade," in *Begegnung der Kirche in Ost und West im Spiegel der synodalen Strukturen*, ed. Johannes Grohe et al (Sankt Ottilien: EOS, 2017), 207–36, see too the reservations in Mariam de Ghantuz Cubbe, "I rapporti fra Leone X e i Maroniti," *Studi e ricerche sull'Oriente Cristiano* 9 (1986): 149–73.

34 *Bullarium Maronitarum*, 33–4. For identification of Giovanni Francesco da Potenza as the Franciscan superior in Beirut, see Noujaim, *I Francescani e i Maroniti (1233–1516)*, 142.

35 The indulgence of 20 August 1515 can be found in AAV: Misc. Arm. VI, 39, 15r–16r. For the text, see below Appendix II. For documents relating to Cyprus, see *Bullarium Maronitarum*, 30–1 and 37–9.

36 *Bullarium Maronitarum*, 36–7.

37 *Sacrorum Conciliorum nova et amplissima collectio*, ed. Giovanni Dominico Mansi et al (Paris: Welter, 1901), 32:1011–12.

38 Golubovich, *Trattato di Terra Santa di Francesco Suriano*, 68.

39 "Pallium altaris brochati in velluto rubeo imaginem B. Thomae continens digitum in latus Salvatoris mittentis [sic]". Mansi, *Sacrorum Conciliorum nova et amplissima collectio*, 32:1011.

40 Ibid., 32:1012 (receipt of *liber pontificalis*); *Bullarium Maronitarum*, 48 (for guidance from this book about chrism).

41 The emissaries of sent to Simon are named as Giovanni Francesco da Potenza and "Francesco Reatino interprete'" by the patriarch in a letter to Leo of 14 February 1516, see Anaissi, *Collectio documentorum Maronitarum*, 42 and Mansi, *Sacrorum Conciliorum nova et amplissima collectio*, 32:1012. This has created an imaginary Franciscan called 'Francesco Reatino', but it is clear that this figure is Suriano, since he mentions that he was sent with Giovanni Francesco da Potenza to take presents to the Maronites in the reign of Leo X. See Golubovich, *Trattato di Terra Santa di Francesco Suriano*, 71. The same conclusion is reached in the short life of Suriano by Francesco Surdich, "Suriano,

Francesco," *DBI* 94 (2019).

42 Anaissi, *Collectio documentorum Maronitarum*, 42 and Mansi, *Sacrorum Conciliorum nova et amplissima collectio*, 32:945. Cf. Mansi, *Sacrorum Conciliorum nova et amplissima collectio*, 32:1013 and 1014, which records Joseph and one Elias only. For the identities of the three Maronite emissaries, see Nelson H. Minnich, "The Participants at the Fifth Lateran Council," *Archivium Historiae Pontificiae* 12 (1974): 166–7.

43 Mansi, *Sacrorum Conciliorum nova et amplissima collectio*, 32:942–5. Onorato Bucci, "La Chiesa Maronita al Concilio Lateranese V," in *Alla ricerca di soluzioni: Nuova luce sul Concilio Lateranese V*, ed. Nelson H. Minnich (Vatican City: Libreria Editrice Vaticana, 2019), 335–45, commits too many errors of fact to be of much use; by contrast, Bilaniuk, *The Fifth Lateran Council (1512–1517) and the Eastern Churches*, 170–4 offers a thorough reconstruction of events.

44 Levi della Vida, "Teseo Ambrogio degli Albonesi"; for Elias's rank and full name, see Minnich, "The Participants," 166–7 n.38.

45 "Querens itaque interpretem per quem cum eis loqui plenius possem, nec illum in Urbe gentium olim domina, etiam neque inter Hebreos quidem reperiens idoneum". Quoted in Renato Lefevre, "Giovanni Potken e la sua edizione romana del Salterio in etiopico," *La Bibliofilia* 68 (1966): 307.

46 Ibid., 289–308.

47 Elias is known to have copied the following manuscripts: Innsbruck: University Library, 401; Modena: Biblioteca Estense, J.6.3.104 and α.U.2.6; Paris: Bibliothèque nationale de France, Syr. 44; St Petersburg: National Library of Russia, Syr. 2; BAV, Vat.sir.9, 15, 265; Munich: BSB, Syr. 3. See Levi della Vida, *Ricerche*, 99–108 and 133–9; supplemented by Jean Gribomont, "Gilles de Viterbe, le moine Élie, et l'influence de la littérature maronite sur la Rome érudite de 1515," *Oriens Christianus* 18 (1970): 125–9; Michael Breydy, *Geschichte der Syro-Arabischen Literatur der Maroniten vom VII. bis XVI. Jahrhundert* (Opladen: Westdeutscher Verlag, 1985), 213; Robert J. Wilkinson, *Orientalism, Aramaic and Kabbalah*, 18; Margherita Farina, "La circulation de manuscrits syriaques en Orient et entre Orient et Occident entre la fin du XVᵉ et le XVIᵉ siècle," in *Les chrétiens de tradition syriaque à l'époque ottoman*, ed. Bernard Heyberger (Paris: Geunther, 2020), 97 n.11.

48 See for instance the colophons to Vat.sir.9 and Vat.sir.15 in Stefano Evodio Assemani and Giuseppe Simone Assemani, *Bibliothecae Apostolicae Vaticanae codicum manuscriptorum catalogus* (Rome: Typographia linguarum orientalium, 1758), I/2:22–3 and 57–8.

49 Wilkinson *Orientalism, Aramaic and Kabbalah*, 3 and 11.

50 Vat.sir.265 and Innsbruck: University Library, 401 respectively.

51 Levi della Vida, *Ricerche*, 103–8.

52 This is Modena: Biblioteca Estense, J.6.3.104. See Levi della Vida, *Ricerche*, 103–8; Natalie Zemon Davis, *Trickster Travels: A Sixteenth-Century Muslim Between Worlds* (London: Faber and Faber, 2007).

53 Falconi, *Leone X*, 477–507.

54 Wilkinson, *Orientalism, Aramaic and Kabbalah*, 18; Levi della Vida, *Ricerche*, 103–8.

55 Levi della Vida, *Ricerche*, 134 n.1.

56 Breydy, *Geschichte der Syro-Arabischen Literatur der Maroniten*, 213–14.

3 Negotiating a world in motion

Exchanges between Rome and the
Maronites from Pope Clement VII
(1523–1534) to Pope Marcellus II (1555)

I. Historical and historiographical background

1517 was marked by two events that changed the political and religious
geography of the early modern Mediterranean. In the south-east corner of
that sea, the last Mamluk Sultan, Tumanbay (1516–1517), was executed
by the Ottomans in Cairo after defeat at the battle of al-Ridaniyya. His
death was the culmination of a year of losses to the Ottoman Sultan Selim I
(1512–1520), which had seen Lebanon, Syria, Egypt, and the holy cities of
Medina and Mecca pass from Mamluk to Ottoman control. The Maronites
now found themselves subjects of a different empire, while Rome and the
Catholic powers of Europe were confronted by a single, often-hostile state
that dominated the eastern Mediterranean.[1]

Later that year, on 10 November 1517, an Augustinian friar named Martin
Luther fixed his *95 Theses* to the door of the Schlosskirche in Wittenberg.
Luther's original hope was for a scholastic debate, but his protest eventually
spiralled into what we now know as the Reformation. Latin Christendom
was split between Catholics, who acknowledged the supremacy of the pope,
and various Protestant Churches, who did not. During the sixteenth century,
Protestantism became the religion of many formerly Catholic states, from
polities in the Holy Roman Empire, to certain Swiss cantons, the Tudor
realms (1534, and again in 1558), Denmark (1537), and Sweden-Finland
(1593).[2] It also made inroads into France, Italy, and, to a lesser extent, Iberia. Those who remained Catholic found their religious lives re-organised
by the Council of Trent (1545–1563), with dissent suppressed by the Spanish and Roman inquisitions.[3] Yet despite its obvious impact on Italy, France,
and Iberia, the Reformation has not been considered an important moment
for the religious history of the Mediterranean. Scholars such as Renate Dürr
and Richard Calis have, however, sought to challenge this view.[4] Whether
it was Greek prelates hauled before the Roman inquisition for 'heretical'
beliefs, or Ethiopian monks engaging Luther in theological debate, it is
becoming increasingly clear that eastern Christians were important actors
in the history of the Reformation.[5]

Nonetheless, 'great events' such as the Ottoman victory at al-Ridaniyya
and Luther's posting of the *95 Theses* only become 'great' if they set into

DOI: 10.4324/9781003165392-4

Negotiating a world in motion   37

motion thoughts and actions that subsequently confirm their significance. It took almost three years for Leo X to declare Luther a heretic, for example, while Ottoman control over new provinces like Lebanon was challenged by a series of rebellions throughout the 1520s. The gradual process of historical change perhaps explains why there is no sign of the Reformation or the Ottoman conquests in the exchanges between Rome and the Maronites during the reign of Leo X that we studied in the previous chapter. But while it doubtless took some time for these interactions to be impacted by such developments, it may not have taken quite as long as has been implied in modern scholarship. As we saw in the Introduction, recent research has shown that the Maronites were eventually integrated into the confessional struggles of the Reformation, as well as the anti-Ottoman plans of Catholic powers. Yet these developments have only been traced from the 1560s, in the first case as a result of the Council of Trent, and in the second as a consequence of the battle of Lepanto (1571).[6]

The omission of the Maronites from the religious and political history of the period between 1517 and 1571 is partly the result of a lack of reference material on this subject. Pierre Dib's oft-cited *History of the Maronite Church* devotes just two pages to these years, and, as we will see, commits serious factual errors along the way.[7] Another standard guide, Matti Moosa's *The Maronites in History*, entirely overlooks the period from the reign of Leo X (1513–1521) to the patriarchate of Michael ar-Russi (1567–1581).[8] The absence of any accessible survey means that the history of exchanges between the Maronites during this sixty-year period can only be recovered from specialist literature, as well as the analysis of primary texts.

In light of this background, the present chapter has two primary aims. First, it will use previously unstudied archival sources to reconstruct the history of exchanges between Rome and the Maronites from the reign of Pope Clement VII (1523–1534) to that of Pope Marcellus II (1555). At one level, this account is intended as a work of reference that will compensate for the omission of this period from earlier studies. Such a goal will necessitate the close scrutiny of sources to resolve the factual problems they present, the sort of analysis that studies of better-known periods can avoid by reference to earlier literature.

Second, this chapter has a historiographical as well as a narrative aim. On one hand, it will draw attention to the Maronite perspective on exchanges with Rome, arguing that Patriarch Musa al-Akkari sought to integrate the Maronites into the world of European Catholicism more closely than his predecessors had attempted. On the other, it will propose that the Reformation influenced Rome's response to this patriarch, thereby showing that the Reformation was a factor in Catholic approaches to non-Latin Christians even before the Council of Trent. This argument will be expanded in the following chapter, which explores collaborations between Catholics, Maronites, and eastern Christians in Rome from 1540 and 1555. The final chapter of this book will then consider the possible limitations of the Reformation as an explanatory key, highlighting the political, anti-Ottoman

38 *Negotiating a world in motion*

concerns that drove the Maronites to correspond with the Habsburg Emperor Charles V (1519–1556).

II. Exchanges in the reign of Clement VII (1523–1534): Missing messengers and cardinal protectors

The history of exchanges between Rome and the Maronites in this forgotten period begins in January 1526, when Pope Clement VII appointed a Franciscan named Bernardino Cortone da Udine as nuncio to the Maronites, as well as to the patriarch and the king of the Armenians.[9] This embassy again stresses the limitations of Roman knowledge about the wider Christian world in the early sixteenth century, for there was no king of Armenia reigning at that time. But before Bernardino could depart to this imagined prince, news that Musa al-Akkari had been elected patriarch of the Maronites reached Rome, forcing the reconceptualisation of his embassy. In July 1526, Clement supplied Bernardino with a letter for Musa.[10] Just as his cousin Leo X had done, Clement also equipped Bernardino with letters to the patriarch's chief allies in the Levant, namely the *muqaddam* 'Abd al-Mun'im III, as well as the Franciscan Guardian of the Holy Places in Jerusalem.[11] What little we know of Bernardino and his aims similarly conformed to the example of recent missions. Clement referred to Bernardino as a doctor of theology, continuing the tradition of learned ambassadors to the Maronites that had been the norm since Gryphon.[12] The purpose of Bernardino's mission was to comfort the Maronites, and to provide Musa with confirmation of his election as patriarch.[13]

Despite the extensive preparations for his departure, there is no evidence that Bernardino made it to Mount Lebanon. Travel in the early modern world could be perilous, especially when, like Bernardino, travellers were forced to pass through regions destabilised by war. A later Catholic emissary, Giovanni Battista Vecchietti (1552–1619), was for example enslaved twice in a single attempt to cross the Mediterranean from the Levant to Italy.[14] The Maronites appear to have taken matters into their own hands in the absence of any word from Rome. In late 1526 or early 1527, a Maronite archbishop named Antonius was dispatched to Rome with a monk called Elias. Yet disaster struck once more. Antonius died in a shipwreck, but Elias, who made it to Rome, was sent back to Mount Lebanon with another confirmation for Musa.[15] As we will see, it however appears that this Maronite was also unable to complete the return journey to Mount Lebanon.

After the tragedy of Antonius and Elias's mission, Musa transmitted his letters for Clement through Latin messengers, who were perhaps present in the Levant as merchants or pilgrims. A Roman citizen named Celso Jubileo carried a letter from Musa to Clement in 1530. Nonetheless, it was only in 1531 that the pope replied to Musa, prompted by another letter from the patriarch.[16] Musa's letters of 1530 and 1531 do not survive, but their contents can be inferred from Clement's reply. First, Musa seems to have asked the pope for vestments and church ornaments. Clement rejected

Negotiating a world in motion 39

this demand, ordering Musa to submit the request for confirmation that he wrongly asserted the patriarch's predecessor had promised but failed to deliver to Leo X. The pope's command would imply that neither Bernardino nor Elias had reached Mount Lebanon with his earlier letters of confirmation, leading Musa to seek this authorisation once more. In turn, the fact that Musa asked for confirmation appears to have misled bureaucrats in Rome into concluding that Clement had never confirmed Musa in the first place. Such miscommunication has caused some historians to assert that Musa was not confirmed as patriarch until the reign of Pius V (1559–1565).[17] Instead, we can assert that he was confirmed by Pope Clement VII, but that accidents of travel and record-keeping meant that this confirmation took much longer to reach him.

Musa's first aim in contacting Rome – to obtain confirmation of his election as patriarch – is the same as that which had spurred his predecessor Simon al-Hadathi to send envoys to Leo X. However, Musa made another petition to Clement VII that was new in exchanges between Rome and Mount Lebanon. He asked Clement for a cardinal protector for his people. In making this request, Musa showed his knowledge of recent developments in the Roman curia. The office of cardinal protector was then relatively new, with most European nations only gaining a protector by 1520. There is still much to know about the role of the cardinal protector, but it appears that their duty was to monitor the spiritual welfare and doctrinal purity of the people to whom they had been entrusted.[18]

Clement looked favourably upon this request, appointing the 'cardinal of Santa Croce' as protector of the Maronites.[19] The absence of any identifier in Clement's reply except for the title of 'cardinal of Santa Croce' has led to confusion about the person whom he appointed to this office. A standard guide to Maronite history, Pierre Dib's *History of the Maronite Church*, claims that the cardinal mentioned there was Marcello Cervini.[20] Cervini was indeed referred to by contemporaries as 'Santa Croce' after his titular church, but this identification is impossible, for the simple reason that Cervini did not enter the cardinalate until 1539.[21] In 1531, the cardinal of Santa Croce was instead Francisco Quiñones, a former general of the Franciscans who is now best-known for supervising an extremely controversial reform to the Roman breviary.[22]

While it is nowhere mentioned in Clement's reply, Quiñones was not the first cardinal protector of the Maronites. He was preceded in this role by an even earlier cardinal of Santa Croce, Bernardino Carvajal. The events that led to Carvajal's election are obscure, but that he held this office is recorded in a lectionary that the Maronite emissaries Elias and Musa gifted to him when they visited Rome in 1522.[23] This lectionary is the unique piece of evidence for Carvajal's protectorate of which I am aware, and Quiñones's tenure is just as poorly documented. The only evidence that I have found of relations between Rome and Mount Lebanon during the latter's time as cardinal protector (1531–1540) is a request in 1535 for the confirmation of a new Maronite bishop of Tripoli. This dearth of documentation suggests

40 *Negotiating a world in motion*

that Quiñones was not too interested in his Maronite charges, a contention further supported by the fact that it was Marino Grimani, rather than Quiñones, who raised the confirmation of this bishop to the consistory.[24]

Yet if Dib was wrong to assert that Cervini was appointed cardinal protector of the Maronites in 1531, he was correct to state that Cervini served in this capacity at some stage. It is simply that Cervini's appointment occurred later than has been thought. A document appointing Rodolfo Pio da Carpi and Gianbernardino Scotti as cardinal protectors of the Maronites in 1556 mentions that this office had been vacated through Cervini's death the previous year. This indicates that Cervini was the third cardinal protector of the Maronites, taking on this role after Quiñones's death in 1540.[25]

In contrast to his predecessors, ample documentation survives for Cervini's career as cardinal protector of the Maronites. Indeed, this documentation provides an essential resource upon which to construct a history of exchanges between Rome and the Maronites from Cervini's appointment as cardinal protector in 1540 to his death in 1555. But before proceeding to an account of these exchanges, it is first necessary to outline the context in which they are best understood. Such a task requires a short introduction to Cervini's life, as well as to the eastern Christian presence in Rome during the reigns of Paul III (1534–1549) and Julius III (1550–1555).

III. Marcello Cervini and the pluri-confessional Rome of Paul III (1534–1549) and Julius III (1550–1555)

Marcello Cervini was born on 6 May 1501 in Montefano, a small town in the Marche region of central Italy. After an education at his family home and in Siena, Cervini travelled to Rome in 1524, where he impressed Clement VII by disproving prophecies about an impending flood of the city. While at Clement's court, Cervini got to know Cardinal Alessandro Farnese, a connection that served him well when this cardinal was elected as Pope Paul III in 1534. For the next two decades Cervini distinguished himself as a politician and administrator, whether in his service as ambassador to France and the Holy Roman Empire (1538–1539), as papal legate to the Council of Trent (1545–1548), or in the revived Roman inquisition. Such service was rewarded by a rapid ascent through the curial hierarchy. Cervini was created cardinal in the consistory of 19 December 1539, receiving the title of Santa Croce almost a year later on 5 November 1540.[26] His career was capped by election as Pope Marcellus II on 9 April 1555. However, Cervini died just three weeks later, making his reign as pope the shortest in recorded history.[27]

Research about Cervini has typically restricted his concerns to western Europe. However, recent work by Giacomo Cardinali and Paolo Sachet has elucidated his interests in the wider world.[28] Such interests are manifest in one Cervini's first acts after his appointment as cardinal, a commission of a world map that was completed and framed by 24 September 1544.[29] This map of the world was later complemented with specialised maps of

Negotiating a world in motion   41

other areas, including the Red Sea.[30] At the same time, Cervini furnished his household with eastern goods, acquiring Ottoman carpets from Venice through his agent Antonio Lorenzini.[31] In addition to these furnishings, Cervini's bookshelves were lined with manuscripts in eastern languages, and printed texts about the orient.[32] Food from the east even graced his table, such as a gift of dried roe (*bottarga*) sent to him by the bishop of Corfu, Giacomo Cauco.[33]

However, Cervini was not the only prelate in Rome who was interested in the eastern Mediterranean. Such interests could be easily stimulated in a resident of the papal city. As we will see in greater detail in the next chapter, the Rome of Paul III and Julius III was a pluri-confessional city, in which Catholics, Protestants, eastern Christians, Muslims, and Jews rubbed shoulders – albeit with varying degrees of friction.[34] Besides Cervini, cardinals such as Reginald Pole, Alessandro Farnese, Bernardino Maffei, and Rodolfo Pio da Carpi all consumed goods from the east, financed scholarly and political projects, and hosted eastern Christians and Catholic Orientalists in their palaces.[35] Institutions such as the Vatican Library, with its growing collection of Oriental manuscripts, as well as the church and hostel of Santo Stefano dei Mori, which were put aside for the use of pilgrims from Africa and the Middle East, also offered space for collaboration and conflict.[36] An example of the connections across empires and confessions that were possible in Rome at this time is offered in the surprising life of the chaplain of Gian Pietro Carafa. Carafa was the arch-inquisitor of this period, who would later rule as the notoriously intransigent Pope Paul IV (1555–1559).[37] Yet his chaplain had anything but an orthodox upbringing. He was an Ethiopian named Yohannes who was born in Cyprus to refugees from Egypt, who had been originally ordained on that island by a Jacobite bishop, and who would later die there as the first black nuncio in the early modern history of the Catholic Church.[38]

Cervini's first-hand acquaintance with people and goods from the eastern Mediterranean was not therefore unusual in the Rome of Paul III and Julius III. Instead, what is exceptional is the quantity and quality of documentation that testifies to his connections with the Maronites and other Christians from Africa and the Middle East. From his residence in Rome, and others in Trent, Bologna, and Gubbio, Cervini maintained a vast network of correspondence, much of which is now preserved in the Archivio di Stato in Florence.[39] Cervini's letters indicate how much a highly-placed and well-connected prelate could know about the world that they lived in, as well as the motivations that spurred them to seek this knowledge. They show that he received news about the Reformation in northern Europe from correspondents across the Alps, such as Johannes Cochlaeus and Friedrich Nausea, as well as from exiled northern prelates resident in Italy, for example the bishop of Uppsala, Olaus Magnus. Contacts in the Venetian domains provided him with a steady stream of information about eastern affairs, while his frequent absences from Rome, caused first by his duties as papal legate to the Council of Trent, and later by lengthy stays at

42 *Negotiating a world in motion*

his bishopric in Gubbio, led Roman correspondents to update him about events in the city.

Cervini's itinerant life and long career at the highest levels of curial diplomacy therefore make his correspondence an indispensable source for any history of contacts between Rome and the wider world in the mid-sixteenth century. The broader range of these contacts will be explored in the next chapter. But for present purposes, what is of most interest are four letters sent to Cervini by the Maronite Patriarch Musa al-Akkari.[40] Only one of these letters has been published and analysed before, and even there some problems remain.[41] The remainder of this chapter will therefore combine these letters with other sources to provide a history of exchanges between Rome and Mount Lebanon during Cervini's tenure as cardinal protector of the Maronites.

IV. The exchanges between 1542 and 1544: The Maronite perspective

There is no trace of direct communication between Patriarch Musa and the papacy in the decade after 1531. This period of silence was broken in February 1542, when Musa sent a letter to Pope Paul III. In this letter, Musa complained that the subjection of his people to the 'pagan' Turks had impelled him to dispatch to Rome Felice da Venezia, the commissioner and procurator for the Guardian of the Holy Places in Jerusalem. Musa tasked this Franciscan with doing reverence to Paul III, and alerting him to the problems faced by the Maronites. Chief among these was that his people had not received a visitor from Rome since the reign of Leo X, a claim that again suggests that the emissaries sent by Clement VII had failed to reach their destination.[42] Musa therefore requested such a visitor, asking that they carry to the Levant papal letters commanding the Maronite clergy and people to obedience to Rome, and excommunicating any transgressors. Finally, Musa begged Paul III to have the Franciscan custodian of the Holy Places send six of his confreres to Mount Lebanon in order to teach the Maronites how to read and write Latin. Musa was confident that the faith of his people, proven in the time of Leo X, would ensure a positive outcome for his requests.[43]

It was therefore Musa, rather than Paul III, who re-established contact between Rome and Mount Lebanon after a decade-long hiatus. It is worth dwelling on the reasons that Musa provided for this step. Here, we can begin with the patriarch's statement that he had written to Rome due to oppression by the Ottomans. Although Musa's letter discusses Ottoman oppression in the vaguest terms, the conquests of 1516–1517 were indeed followed by the persecution of some religious groups in Lebanon. There were massacres of the Druze in 1523 and 1524, for example.[44] Similarly, a 1548 *fatwa* by the Ottoman jurist Ebu's-Suud Efendi created a legal framework for the persecution of Shiites, and an important Shiite scholar from Lebanon, Zayn al-Din ibn ʿAli, was executed in 1558.[45] But in contrast to the experiences of

Negotiating a world in motion 43

the Druze and Shiites, it is difficult to find a concrete example of Ottoman oppression against the Maronites. This may be because we know very little about the day-to-day life of the Maronites under Ottoman rule, which might bring to light less specular instances of persecution. Later Jesuit missionaries to Lebanon indeed referred to the arbitrary detention of Maronite priests by Ottoman authorities.[46] However, a recent study has suggested that the Maronites were protected by the real force in Lebanese politics at this time, the Turcoman warlord Mansur Assaf, who ruled as the de-facto Ottoman governor of Lebanon from 1528 to 1579.[47]

Rather than difficulties with Muslim authorities, Musa's letter suggests that his problems were caused by one of the rival churches established in the Ottoman Empire. For all his protestations about the proven Catholicity of the Maronites, the patriarch implied that his flock was divided about their faith. Had his people been unanimously in favour of Rome, there would have been no reason to request a commissioner to carry bulls to Mount Lebanon that commanded obedience to the pope, and excommunicated those who refused. The patriarch was vague about the causes of this request, but we can locate them in the wider religious history of Lebanon. Musa's letter was sent during the reign of the Melkite Patriarch of Antioch Dorotheus III (1541–1543), who began his period of office by attempting to unify his Church with the Maronites.[48] Dorotheus's success in this regard is unknown, but his plans may well have led to the development of pro- and anti-Rome factions in the Maronite community similar to those that formed due to Jacobite influence in the fifteenth century.[49] If this reconstruction of events is correct, Musa probably appealed to Paul III in 1542 in order to bolster his authority among his flock. A bull from the papacy would have provided the patriarch with support of a powerful external ally, whose provisions the six Franciscans that Musa requested from Jerusalem would no doubt have been expected to enforce.

Once more, Musa's letters show that events and initiatives in the peripheries, rather than any action from the metropolis, were the main driver of contact between the Maronites and Rome in the sixteenth century. Rome is often compared to a magnet, but a more appropriate metaphor might be an oasis, since groups of all kinds travelled to the city of their own volition in order to draw on the resources that were uniquely on offer there.[50] As Musa's letter shows, one of the resources in Rome most prized by eastern Christians was the pope's power of arbitration in disputes within or between Churches.[51] We will see in the next chapter that eastern Christian embassies commonly went to Rome for this purpose, whether that was to secure the pope's confirmation of a contested election, or to obtain his support against a rival Church's claims to the same see.

In aiming to use the pope as an arbiter in a local dispute, Musa therefore acted in a way similar to other prelates from the Levant. However, his letter to Paul III also suggests that he also had another goal in mind. Besides requesting documents from Rome, Musa asked the pope to send six Franciscans to Lebanon in order to teach the Maronites Latin. The linguistic

44 *Negotiating a world in motion*

skill of these friars was in fact as essential to communication between Rome and Mount Lebanon in 1542 as it had been in the reign of Leo X. Knowledge of Arabic and Syriac was still limited in Rome, and Musa's request for Latin teachers suggests that there was restricted knowledge of western tongues among the Maronites. Indeed, it is likely that Musa's letter to Paul III was translated by the Franciscan emissary Felice da Venezia. This letter is only known from an Italian translation, which contains peculiar spellings from the Venetian dialect that are comparable to those used by Felice in his life of Ginepro of Catania.[52]

In requesting these Franciscans from Jerusalem, Musa's letter to Paul III shows a desire to expand the knowledge of Latin among his flock in Lebanon. However, a previously unpublished letter from the patriarch to Marcello Cervini indicates that he also sent Maronites to study in capital of Catholicism.

Despite dispatching Felice to Paul III in February 1542, Musa had yet to receive word from him over a year later. He therefore decided to write to Cervini for news about this mission. The patriarch's letter, dated to 5 April 1543, is one of the more striking documents in Cervini's correspondence. It immediately draws the eye due to its language and script, a style of Arabic written in Syriac characters that is commonly called 'karshuni'.[53] In this letter, Musa informed Cervini that was sending to Rome another emissary, a Maronite deacon named Sarkis, in order to check on Felice and this Franciscan's fellow ambassador, a Maronite named Peter. He implored Cervini to take care of Sarkis, and requested that he help this deacon to "learn speech and reading and writing".[54]

Musa declined to mention which languages he hoped that Sarkis would master. But since he had sent this deacon to Rome, we can speculate that he intended Sarkis to learn Latin and Italian. It appears that Sarkis already had some grasp of this second tongue. In another letter to Cervini of 5 April 1543, Musa wrote that he had commanded Sarkis to pen a letter in Italian, through which Cervini might understand the content of the karshuni brief. The letter that Sarkis wrote is possibly this second letter of 5 April 1543, since it is written in Italian, and serves mostly to summarise the content of the karshuni letter. This letter is labelled as a 'Translation' in Cervini's archive, but the fact that it includes much more content than the karshuni brief suggests that is instead an original composition.[55]

Cervini's correspondence and sources in the Vatican do not provide any further evidence about Sarkis's career in Rome, through which we might confirm whether or not he stayed there to learn Latin and Italian. However, Musa's letter of introduction for this deacon highlights another, perhaps more successful attempt by the patriarch to develop a clergy that had been trained in Italy. Besides complaining about Felice, in this letter Musa mentioned to Cervini that he had received no word from a Maronite bishop of Beirut named Simeon, whom he had sent to Rome "to learn the rites and customs of the Roman Catholic Church, in order to then canonically instruct our people here".[56]

Negotiating a world in motion 45

Other evidence suggests that Musa may have sent Simeon to Rome long before 1542. However, this letter is the earliest unambiguous record of his stay in that city.[57] As it implies, Musa had dispatched Simeon to Italy to learn languages and Catholic doctrine, with the expectation that he would then return to Mount Lebanon, and educate the Maronites in these matters. But Simeon only completed half of this arrangement. He found it more attractive to remain in the west as a scribe and translator, occupying the same roles as other 'keepers' of eastern learning recently described by John-Paul Ghobrial.[58] Indeed, while disappointing his patriarch's expectations, we will see in the next chapter that Simeon's decision to stay in Italy caused him to become an indispensable intermediary between Rome, the Maronites, and other Christians from the Levant in the later 1540s.

The letters that Musa sent to Paul III and Cervini between 1542 and 1543 allow some insight into the Maronite perspective on their exchange with Rome. As noted above, Musa's motivations and aims are often familiar from previous contacts between Rome and Mount Lebanon. Like him, earlier patriarchs had offered obedience to Rome as a means of securing papal intervention in local disputes. His desire to train Maronites in Rome also has a precedent in Gryphon's dispatch of al-Qilāʿī and his companions to Italy, while his requests for a cardinal protector continued a tradition that had been established under his predecessor Simon al-Hadathi. However, the connections between Rome and Lebanon that Musa had inherited were extremely fragile. His urgent requests for assistance show that, despite a century of work by the Franciscans of the Holy Land and some earlier patriarchs, not every member of his flock was convinced about obedience to Rome. It was also difficult for Musa to secure the external intervention that he desired. It seems that he wrote to Rome six times between 1526 and 1542 before he received a reply. Such a period of silence may well have deterred a patriarch whose commitment to Rome was less genuine.

But instead of cutting ties from an unresponsive Rome, Musa sought to make contact with the papacy in a much more proactive way than earlier patriarchs. Indeed, his letters to Rome suggest that he had a particular goal in mind. They show that Musa pursued diplomatic and educational policies that would strengthen ties between Rome and the Maronites in the long term. His initiative secured a second cardinal protector for the Maronites in 1531, turning what could have been an exceptional appointment into a recognised office in the curia. In this way, Musa established a stable point of contact in Rome to which the Maronites could turn when they required assistance from the pope. While we do not know much about Quiñones's tenure as cardinal protector, correspondence between Maronite patriarchs and later holders of this office indicate that the latter took an active role in representing Maronite interests in the curia.[59] Musa's ambitions to improve knowledge of Italian and Latin among his flock pursued the same end. By training Maronites in these languages both in Lebanon and in Rome, Musa would have enabled his people to better communicate with the past and present of the wider Catholic Church. His repeated attempts to train

46 *Negotiating a world in motion*

Maronites in Rome might even be seen to presage the foundation of the Maronite College there in 1584, since this college was established with the same aim of educating young Maronite men in Latin language and theology, who were then meant to return to Lebanon to teach the wider Maronite community.[60]

Musa's letters therefore show that he sought to integrate the Maronites into Latin Catholicism much closer than his predecessors had done. This integration may well have been unprecedented, but the patriarch appears to have believed that it would be painless. However, the reply that he received from Rome turned out to be quite different to that which he had anticipated.

V. The exchanges between 1542 and 1544: The response from Rome

As we saw earlier, Musa was prompted to check on his emissaries, Felice and Peter, after receiving no word from them for over a year after their departure. However, the patriarch's concerns about these ambassadors were unwarranted. They had clearly communicated his letter to Paul III in 1542, since the pope responded to Musa with a bull dated to 21 September of that year. In this bull, Paul looked favourably upon the requests that Musa had made. He appointed as visitor to the Maronites the Guardian of the Holy Places, Dionisio Saorgano, and instructed this Guardian to send Franciscans of the Holy Land to Mount Lebanon.[61] The remainder of Paul's reply exhorted Musa and his flock to obedience to the Catholic Church, the terms of which Paul wrote that Dionisio and his Franciscans would further explain to Musa.[62] As Musa had requested, Paul also wrote a letter urging the Maronite clergy and people to obedience to Rome.[63]

These documents were exactly what Musa had hoped to obtain from Rome. Yet the number and intricacy of the terms that they contained may have surprised him, given the confidence that he had expressed in his and his people's Catholicity. Paul reiterated elements from earlier papal bulls to the Maronites, insisting on adherence to the *filioque* and observance of Chalcedon and other councils approved by Rome. However, these familiar stipulations were joined by a range of new demands that related not to doctrine, but to customs and discipline among the Maronites. Paul reminded Musa of the need to follow Rome as regards the observation of the articles of faith, the seven sacraments, and the times of fasting and celebration of the Mass. He further cautioned the patriarch not to permit unqualified priests, laymen, or heretics to administer the sacraments, to control drunkenness among his clergy, and to avoid the overuse of excommunication.[64]

None of these additional points had been raised in Musa's letter to Paul. Instead, it is likely that they had been brought to the pope's attention by the Franciscan Felice da Venezia. We have seen that another Franciscan, Francesco Suriano, also reported what he saw as errant customs of the Maronites to Leo X.[65] Later Franciscans would do the same, and they were in any case the only Catholic group at this time that had sufficient acquaintance with the Maronites to provide such detailed reports.[66] But while Felice was continuing practices established in earlier exchanges with the Maronites, there was an important distinction between the way in which Paul III responded to his embassy, and how Franciscans of the past had been received by earlier popes. For example, Suriano's report on the errant customs of the Maronites was omitted from Leo's correspondence with Patriarch Simon despite the gravity of the problems that he had observed, such as the existence of married clergy. By contrast, Paul III's bull included a wide range of alterations to Maronite customs that had been brought to his attention, thereby making these changes a necessary part of Catholic observance. Aurélien Girard has shown that Catholics after the Council of Trent sought to bring Maronite customs into line with those of Rome, until a backlash from the Maronites caused them to take a more cautious approach to the rites of the eastern Churches. From Paul III's bull, we can see that the interventionist attitude that characterises the early phase of this supposedly post-Tridentine story existed even before the first session of this council had been held.[67]

Besides reforming Maronite customs, Felice was entrusted with another mission in Mount Lebanon. Like Suriano, he was sent back to the Levant with a checklist of points to investigate among the Maronites. But whereas Suriano was asked to find basic information about Patriarch Simon's life and election, Felice was commissioned to make a thorough enquiry into the intellectual heritage of the Maronites. With the assistance of Musa and other members of the Maronite hierarchy, Felice was instructed to make an index of books in Maronite possession, and to enquire about the existence of Greek texts in Antioch and other nearby cities. He was to pay particular attention to histories of the church, copies of the Constitutions and Canons of the Apostles, and of the acts and canons of church councils, especially whether Maronite manuscripts contained more than 20 canons of the first Council of Nicaea. Moreover, he was to check whether the Maronites had the same number of books of the Bible as were found in Latin and Greek manuscripts, and to obtain copies of Scripture in Syriac, as well as in Syriac written in Hebrew characters. Finally, Felice was required to ask Musa and the Maronites whether they thought that Syriac was the same as the 'ancient Chaldean' language that was spoken by Jesus, and whether they thought that their copies of Matthew were written in the same language as that in which this Gospel was originally composed. Medallions and inscriptions were also to be acquired or illustrated.[68]

This set of instructions is anonymous, but its concerns and assumptions suggest an author immersed in a specific scholarly context. This author had a strong interest in antiquities and the textual heritage of non-Latin Churches, especially in manuscripts of the church councils and Scripture. It was for such reasons that Giacomo Cardinali recently detected the hand of Cervini behind this document.[69] Interests in medals, coins, inscriptions, Scripture, and conciliar texts can indeed be found throughout Cervini's correspondence.[70] Nonetheless, a word of caution is needed before entirely attributing this text to Cervini. The document is anonymous, so it is impossible to know

48 *Negotiating a world in motion*

whether Cervini was its sole author. The least that can be said is that he was almost certainly one voice in its composition, where the strongest proof is probably the simplest. Cervini was the cardinal protector of the Maronites when this document was drafted in 1542, and can as such be expected to have been involved in the planning of Felice's return to Mount Lebanon. Indeed, a letter sent to Cervini by Musa al-Akkari in 1550 indicates that he had personally replied to the patriarch, promising in the name of the pope to send Franciscans to the Maronites.[71] Cervini therefore knew the documents that Felice had communicated to Rome in 1542, and probably supplied the Franciscan with his own response to Musa when he returned to Lebanon in 1543.[72] This in turn suggests that Cervini may have also helped to draft other documents, such as the instructions discussed above, that Felice carried back to the Levant.

Once more, we see that Cervini was involved in Rome's exchanges with the Maronites to a greater extent than his predecessors had been. The terms of this document indicate why that may have been the case. As we will see in the next chapter, during the 1540s Cervini created a network of eastern Christians and western Orientalists dedicated to the study of the past of non-Latin Churches, whose overriding purpose was to use such material in controversy against the Protestant Churches. The document that Felice carried back to Lebanon in 1542 manifests exactly the same set of concerns, down to its interest in the canons of the Council of Nicaea that we will see Cervini and his collaborators later explored in Ge'ez and Arabic.[73] What this document presents is therefore a coherent attempt to involve the Maronites and their history in Rome's struggles against Protestantism. It is as such the earliest witness to the attempts of Cervini and his network to enlist the churches of the Middle East and Africa in this direction, suggesting that his encounters with the Maronites may have conditioned how the cardinal and his collaborators later interacted with representatives of the Armenian, Ethiopian, and Syriac Churches.[74]

Further documentation from Cervini's correspondence allows us to trace the next steps of Felice's mission. He appears to have returned to Mount Lebanon with the bull entrusted to him by Paul III, as on 19 September 1543 Musa wrote another letter to Cervini that acknowledged its reception. However, in this same letter Musa claimed to have been puzzled by the fact that Felice returned from Rome without other items that he had expected to find. He wrote that Felice had come to Lebanon without a mitre, chalice, or bishop's staff, all of which Musa stated he lacked in his monastery of Qannubin. This letter of 19 September 1543 served to introduce to Cervini another emissary, a Maronite deacon named George, whom Musa had sent to do obedience to Paul III and his cardinals, and to beg Cervini to ask the pope to send these vestments to him. As Musa reminded Cervini, such duties fell to him as protector of the patriarch and his people.[75]

Musa's anxiety to acquire these vestments can be explained by their symbolic significance. We saw in Chapters 1 and 2 that earlier popes

Negotiating a world in motion 49

typically gifted vestments once they had accepted the Maronite patriarch's submission of obedience to Rome, making them an outward display of the patriarch's status as a Catholic prelate. Indeed, Felicita Tramontana has stressed the importance of vestments and church furnishings to displays of Catholic identity in confessionally-mixed territories such as the Levant.[76] However, Paul III's letters to Musa between 1542 and 1543 contain no reference to such items. George's embassy further disappointed Musa's expectations. On 18 September 1544, almost a year after this Maronite had been sent to Rome, Paul III appointed the Franciscan Guardian of the Holy Places, a Bosnian named George, as commissioner to the Maronites. This George was provided with instructions to teach the Maronites about Catholic observance, and to correct or reform them in the manner outlined in Paul's 1542 bull. But there was no mention of the vestments that Musa desired.[77]

It is doubtful that George visited the Maronites to enforce the provisions of this new bull. He travelled to the Holy Land in 1544, but died there the following year. Felice da Venezia was then appointed president of the Franciscans of the Holy Land, presiding over a difficult period in which these friars were forced to cede their church under the Cenacle to the Ottoman authorities in Jerusalem.[78] The problems faced by the Franciscans of the Holy Land may explain why, after these intensive exchanges between 1542 and 1544, there is no sign of further contact between Rome and the Maronites until 1550. That year Musa wrote another letter to Cervini, but it is more informative about Maronite connections to Emperor Charles V than it is about their ties to Rome. As such, it will be analysed in the discussion dedicated to this topic in Chapter 5. This letter of 1550 was then followed by another five years of silence until 19 September 1555, when Patriarch Musa requested a new protector to replace the deceased Pope Marcellus II.[79]

VI. Conclusion

It is possible that future research will discover more sources about the exchanges between Rome and the Maronites from the reign of Clement VII to that of Marcellus II. But in the absence of additional documentation in the archives and reference works consulted for this study, we can move from an account of events to a broader consideration of how and why Rome's approach to the Maronites changed within this period.

Earlier we saw that Patriarch Musa pursued diplomatic and educational policies with the aim of tying the Maronites more closely into the wider Catholic world. The emissaries who conveyed these goals to Rome were initially received with the same liberality that marked their reception under Leo X, as seen for example in Clement VII's willingness in 1526 and 1527 to confirm Musa without any real knowledge of who he was. However, this enthusiasm began to wane in the later years of Clement's reign. Although granting the Maronites a cardinal protector, in 1531 Clement refused to

50 *Negotiating a world in motion*

provide the traditional gift of vestments until the patriarch had submitted another request for confirmation. This tough line hardened still further under Clement's successor Paul III, who weighed down the conditions of the Maronites' closer integration to the wider Catholic world with unprecedented demands for changes to their customs.

Within thirty years, the goodwill and openness that had characterised Leo's exchanges with the Maronites had therefore turned into suspicion and intransigence. In this way, the history of contacts between Rome and Mount Lebanon can be mapped onto a broader theme in early modern history. Fraud and its detection have been a perennial concern of human history, theorised and practiced from the ancient world to the present. However, historians such as Perez Zagorin and Miriam Eliav-Feldon have adduced good evidence to show that the denizens of the early modern Mediterranean were particularly exercised by the discernment of fact from fiction.[80] Theirs was a world inhabited by spectacular impostors such as David Reuveni, who arrived in Italy in 1524 claiming to be the ambassador of a huge Jewish kingdom that sought an alliance against the Ottomans, and Ṣagā Krestos, who a century later presented himself to various European courts as the rightful emperor of Ethiopia.[81] However spectacular, the impostures practiced by Reuveni and Ṣagā Krestos were by no means exceptional in the early modern period. They were instead just two of the more extreme products of an age in which dissimulation was an accepted or even encouraged part of everyday life. There were many factors behind this widespread practice of deceit. Surprisingly high mobility allowed for the invention of new identities, particularly when that mobility occurred between places that had been rarely, if ever connected before 1500. Apocalyptic expectations assured that the more dramatic of these identities were often well-received. In other cases, individuals caught in the path of expanding empires or religions might dissemble out of necessity. As a result, Reuveni and Ṣagā Krestos were joined by ranks of false prophets, fake saints, and Nicodemites who turned to imposture or dissimulation out of conviction, personal gain, or survival. Such deception both shaped and was shaped by the documentation that sought its discovery, such as inquisitorial manuals, passports, and even wanted posters. Not without reason has dissimulation been considered an important part of the state and confession-building initiatives of the early modern period.[82]

There were therefore a host of reasons that could have led Clement VII and Paul III to adopt a more suspicious approach towards the Maronites. However, forms of deception, the suspicions that they inspired, and the means of their detection all varied in time and place. In the Iberian peninsula, for example, suspicion was largely directed towards recent Muslim and Jewish converts to Catholicism, who were the chief concern of the Spanish inquisition after its foundation in 1478.[83] By contrast, Protestants in the England of Elizabeth I (1558–1603) suspected 'popish' plots by local Catholics, which the government monitored through spies and double-agents.[84] In the Ottoman Empire, some Muslims who resented the rapid social ascent

Negotiating a world in motion 51

of more recent converts to Islam sought to undermine their careers by doubting their command of their new faith.[85]

In aiming to understand why Rome's approach to the Maronites shifted in the reigns of Clement VII and Paul III, it is therefore essential to concentrate on the local religious context of sixteenth-century Italy. Here there can be little doubt that the Reformation was the principal factor in Rome's new attitude of suspicion. Rather than Jews or Muslims, the Catholic Church in Italy was primarily concerned with Protestant threats to orthodoxy. As Jane Wickersham has reminded us, the bull *Licet ab initio*, which re-established the Roman inquisition in 1542, did so with Protestantism as its primary target.[86] This bull quickly flushed out some high-profile crypto-Protestants, perhaps most notably the vicar-general of the Capuchins, Bernardino Ochino.[87] Statistical studies have also shown that Protestantism preoccupied inquisitors in Italy. Protestantism dominated the caseload of the inquisition in Venice, for example, which tried 717 cases of Lutheranism, compared to 34 for Judaising, and just 10 for Islam, in the years between 1547 and 1585.[88]

Of all possible factors, it is therefore most likely that the Reformation had trained Catholics in Italy to doubt the faith of other Christians to a greater extent than had been true in the reign of Leo X. The changed tone of papal bulls suggests that this suspicion was then applied to the Maronites, with a bridge between these phenomena provided by the personnel in Rome who managed the papacy's response to the Maronites. Besides serving as cardinal protector of the Maronites, for example, Cervini took an active role in the prosecution of Protestantism even before his formal appointment as an inquisitor in 1546.[89] That the Reformation was a major influence in his contacts with the Maronites is clear from the documents that Felice da Venezia carried east in 1542/3, which, as we have seen, sought both to bring Maronite customs into conformity with Rome, and to channel Maronite texts into Catholic refutations of Protestant Church history. It is possible that these instructions from Rome were acted upon by Patriarch Musa. Al-Duwayhi records that Musa held a 'synod' in 1557, an event that might be connected to the copying of a manuscript of canon law by this patriarch in 1559.[90]

The confessionalisation of correspondence between Rome and the Maronites from the reign of Clement VII to that of Marcellus II therefore implies that the Reformation was a factor in how Rome interacted with Christians from the Ottoman Empire even before the Council of Trent.[91] Whereas earlier popes had been happy to accept the Maronites as Catholics in spite of the problems reported to them, bitter experience of the Reformation led later Catholic prelates to reject compromise, and to insist more than ever on orthodoxy in doctrine and custom. However, it was not just Rome's contacts to the Maronites that changed at this time. The next chapter will explore how the Reformation also redefined interactions between Rome and Christians from Africa and the Levant from 1540 to 1555, interactions in which the Maronites served as privileged interlocutors.

52 *Negotiating a world in motion*

Notes

1 Ebru Boyar, "Ottoman Expansion in the East," in *The Cambridge History of Turkey. Volume III: The Ottoman Empire as a World Power, 1453–1603*, ed. Suraiya N. Faroqhi and Kate Fleet (Cambridge: Cambridge University Press, 2013), 96–114; Abdul-Rahim Abu-Husayn, *The View from Istanbul. Lebanon and the Druze Emirate in the Ottoman Chancery Documents, 1546–1711* (London: I.B. Tauris, 2004), 11.

2 See the useful chronology in Ulinka Rublack, *Reformation Europe*, 2nd ed. (Cambridge: Cambridge University Press, 2017), xiii–xvi.

3 John O'Malley, *Trent: What Happened at the Council* (Cambridge MA: Harvard University Press, 2013); Virgilio Pinto Crespo, *Inquisición y control ideológico en la España del siglo XVI* (Madrid: Taurus, 1983); Andrea Del Col, *L'Inquisizione in Italia. Dal XII al XXI secolo* (Milan: Mondadori, 2006).

4 Renate Dürr, "The World in the German Hinterlands: Early Modern German History Entangled," *Sixteenth Century Journal* 50 (2019): 148–55; Richard Alexander Calis, "Martin Crusius (1526–1607) and the Discovery of Ottoman Greece" (PhD diss., Princeton University, 2020).

5 Sam Kennerley, "Identity, inquisition and censorship in the *editio princeps* of Theodoret of Cyrus's anti-heretical works (1545–1547)," forthcoming in the journal *Erudition and the Republic of Letters*; Stanislau Paulau, *Das andere Christentum. Zur transkonfessionellen Verflechtungsgeschichte von äthiopischer Orthodoxie und europäischem Protestantismus* (Göttingen: Vandenhoeck & Ruprecht, 2020), 21–72.

6 For the post-Trent period, see the works by Robert Clines and Aurélien Girard cited in the Bibliography; for Lepanto, see Maria Antonietta Visceglia, "Roma, il papato e le emergenze del Mediterraneo tra Cinque e Seicento," in *La Roma dei papi. La corte e la politica internazionale (secoli XV–XVII)*, ed. Elena Valeri and Paola Volpini (Rome: Viella, 2018), 323–66.

7 Pierre Dib, *History of the Maronite Church*, trans. Seely Beggiani (Washington DC: Maronite Apostolic Exarchate, 1971), 98–100.

8 See the skip in Matti Moosa, *The Maronites in History* (Syracuse NY: Syracuse University Press, 1986), 241–5.

9 AAV: Arm. XL, 11, 72r–73v. Another copy of this letter, Lisbon: National Library of Portugal, 303, 343v–344v, is dated to 20 July 1526, the same date that Bernardino's mission was discussed in the consistory.

10 See Appendix III. Campeggi's intervention in the consistory of 20 July 1526 suggests that Bernardino's mission had been prompted by a letter of obedience sent by Musa: "R.^{mus} Dominus Cardinalis Campegius proposuit fratrem Franciscum de Vtica Sancti Francisci de obseruantia mittendum fore ad Maronitas et quod petunt auctoritate apostolica confirmationem Patriarchae Maronitarum electi, et negocium fuit remissum eidem R.mo Domino Cardinali Campegio". AAV: Arch. Concist., Acta Vicecanc. 3, 119r.

11 "Addidmus Breuia aliquot in commendationem tuae fraternitatis et populorum eorundem ad dominos temporales praecipueque Macchademum vestrum". AAV: Arm. XL, 12, 7r. For the letter to the Guardian, See Appendix IV.

12 "[S]acrae Theologiae professorem". AAV: Arm. XL, 12, 7r.

13 "Itaque delegimus dilectum filium Bernardinum de Vtino ordinis minorum et sacre Theologie professorem nostrum et huius Sancte Sedis Nuntium, per quem confirmationem ipsam ad te mitteremus". Ibid., 7r.

14 Mario Casari, "Vecchietti, Giovanni Battista," *DBI* 98 (2020).

15 See Appendix V.

16 *Bullarium Maronitarum*, 55. The draft of this letter in AAV: Arm. XL, 41, 39r–39v shows that Anaissi made some mistakes, for instance "Alexandrum de la Balle Romaniensem" should be 'Bononiensem'. Musa later used another member of della Balle family, Galeazzo, as a messenger to Rome: see Appendix XII.

Negotiating a world in motion 53

17 Dib, *History of the Maronite Church*, 98–100.
18 Josef Wodka, *Zur Geschichte der nationalen Protektorate der Kardinäle an der römischen Kurie* (Innsbruck: Felizian Rauch, 1938), 2–32. Matteo Sanfilippo and Péter Tusor, eds, *Gli "angeli custodi" delle monarchie: I cardinali protettori delle nazioni* (Viterbo: Sette città, 2018) is exclusively concerned with the seventeenth and eighteenth centuries.
19 *Bullarium Maronitarum*, 56.
20 Dib, *History of the Maronite Church*, 98–100.
21 AAV: Arch. Concist., Acta Vicecanc. 5, 120v and 136r.
22 For Quiñones, see Ignacio Tellechea Idígoras and Víctor Sánchez Gil, "Testamento del Cardenal Quiñones Protector de la Orden Franciscana (OFM) y Gobernador de Veroli († 1540)," *Archivum Franciscanum Historicum* 96 (2003): 129–59. His breviary is the subject of Sam Kennerley, "The Reception of John Chrysostom and the Study of ancient Christianity in early modern Europe, c.1440–1600" (PhD diss., University of Cambridge, 2017), 223–57.
23 The note in the lectionary is Salamanca: Biblioteca Universitaria, 2647, 298r. As so often in this study, my thanks go to Dr Joseph Moukarzel for reference to this source.
24 "Romae, die Lunae: paenultima Augusti. MDXXXV. Fuit Consistorium in aedibus S.^ti Marci. Referente R.^mo Car.^le de Grimani. Ecclesiae Tripolensis in Syria vacanti per obitum Simonis Monachi ordinis Maronitarum, qui habitant Montem Libanum, fuit prouisum de persona Iosephi Monachi eiusdem ordinis, suadente hoc per litteras Patriarcha Antiocheno: Qui dictum Iosephum Monachum ad Pont. Miserat: Cum facultate exercendi Pontificalia in Ciuitate Antiocensis tamen de consensu Patriarchae praedicti". AAV: Arch. Concist., Acta Vicecanc. 5, 26r.
25 *Bullarium Maronitarum*, 65.
26 AAV: Arch. Concist., Acta Vicecanc. 5, 120v and 136r.
27 Giampiero Brunelli, "Marcello II, papa," *DBI* 69 (2007); Chiara Quaranta, *Marcello II Cervini (1501–1555). Riforma della Chiesa, concilio, Inquisizione* (Bologna: Il Mulino, 2010); Massimo Firpo, *La presa di potere dell'Inquisizione romana* (Rome-Bari: Laterza, 2014), 206–27.
28 Giacomo Cardinali, "Ritratto di Marcello Cervini en *orientaliste* (con precisazioni alle vicende di Petrus Damascenus, Mose di Mardin ed Heliodorus Niger)," *Bibliothèque d'Humanisme et Renaissance* 80 (2018): 77–98 and 325–43; Paolo Sachet, *Publishing for the Popes: The Roman Curia and the Use of Printing (1527–1555)* (Leiden: Brill, 2020), 173–84.
29 CC 20, 32r, 34v, 46r, and 51r; CC 23, 9v.
30 CC 44, 94v.
31 CC 41, 53r.
32 Giorgio Levi della Vida, *Ricerche sulla formazione del più antico fondo dei manoscritti orientali della Biblioteca Vaticana* (Vatican City: Biblioteca Apostolica Vaticana, 1939), 192–3; for printed texts about eastern affairs, see Paola Piacentini, *La biblioteca di Marcello II Cervini* (Vatican City: Biblioteca Apostolica Vaticana, 2001), 11, 69, 71, 100–1 and 147.
33 CC 42, 13r.
34 See Irene Fosi, "The Plural City: Urban Spaces and Foreign Communities," in *A Companion to Early Modern Rome, 1492–1692*, ed. Pamela M. James, Barbara Wisch, and Simon Ditchfield (Leiden: Brill, 2019), 169–83; and for a later period, eadem, *Convertire lo straniero. Forestieri e Inquisizione a Roma in età moderna* (Rome: Viella, 2011). This topic is also the theme of Emily Michelson and Matthew Coneys, eds, *A Companion to Religious Minorities in Early Modern Rome* (Leiden: Brill, 2020). The notes to Matteo Sanfilippo, "Il controllo politico e religioso sulle comunità straniere a Roma e nella penisola," in *Ad ultimos usque terrarum terminos in fide propaganda: Roma fra promozione e difesa della fede in età moderna*, ed. Massimiliano Ghilardi, Gaetano Sabatini, Matteo

54 *Negotiating a world in motion*

Sanfilippo and Donatella Strangio (Viterbo: Sette città, 2014), 85–110 are rich with less-commonly cited works.

35 The reader is referred to the *Dizionario Biografico degli Italiani* for the lives of these cardinals.

36 Levi della Vida, *Ricerche*, 109–98; Mauro Da Leonessa, *Santo Stefano Maggiore degli Abissini e le relazioni romano-etiopiche* (Vatican City: Tipografia Poliglotta Vaticana, 1929); Ilaria Delsere and Osvaldo Raineri, *Chiesa di S. Stefano dei Mori: Vicende edilizie e personaggi* (Vatican City: Edizioni Capitolo Vaticano, 2015), 112–72.

37 Firpo, *La presa di potere dell'Inquisizione romana.*

38 Matteo Salvadaore, "African Cosmopolitanism in the early modern Mediterranean: the diasporic life of Yohannes, the Ethiopian pilgrim who became a Counter-Reformation bishop," *Journal of African History* 58 (2017): 61–83.

39 Florence: Archivio di Stato, Carte Cerviniane [CC].

40 CC 41, 99r–99v, 101r–101v, 102r–102v; CC 45, 3r.

41 Giacomo Cardinali, "Ritratto di Marcello Cervini en *orientaliste*," 325–43; two of these letters are cited in Sachet, *Publishing for the Popes*, 174 n.94.

42 See above, Chapter 3:II.

43 The letter is printed in Tobias Anaissi, ed., *Collectio documentorum Maronitarum* (Livorno: Fabbreschi, 1921), 44–7; that instruction in Latin is intended is clear from Paul's response, printed in ibid., 57–8.

44 Abu-Husayn, *The View from Istanbul*, 14–15; William Harris, *Lebanon: A History, 600–2011* (Oxford: University Press, 2012), 93.

45 Stefan Winter, *The Shiites of Lebanon under Ottoman Rule, 1516–1788* (Cambridge: Cambridge University Press, 2010), 15 and 20–6.

46 Robert John Clines, "Wayward Leadership and the Breakdown of Reform on the Failed Jesuit Mission to the Maronites, 1577–1579," *Journal of Early Modern History* 22 (2018): 230.

47 Harris, *Lebanon: A History, 600–2011*, 85–90.

48 Constantin A. Panchenko, *Arab Orthodox Christians under the Ottomans, 1516–1831*, trans. Brittany Pheiffer Noble and Samuel Noble (Jordanville NY: Holy Trinity Seminary Press, 2016), 253–4.

49 See above, Chapter 1.

50 The broader history of the impact of the 'periphery' of the Catholic world on its European centre is explored in Simon Ditchfield, "The 'Making' of Roman Catholicism as a 'World Religion'," in *Multiple Reformations? The Many Faces and Legacies of the Reformation*, ed. Jan Stievermann and Randall C. Zachman (Tübingen: Mohr Siebeck, 2018), 189–203.

51 Robert John Clines, "Pope as Arbiter. The Place of Early Modern Rome in the Pan-Mediterranean Ecumenical Visions of Eastern Rite Christians," in *A Companion to Religious Minorities in Early Modern Rome*, 55–88.

52 Printed in Cesare Cenci, "Il martirio di fra Ginepro da Catania secondo il codice Canoniciano italiano 203," *Archivum Franciscanum Historicum* 55 (1962): 378–81.

53 On karshuni, see Joseph Moukarzel, "Maronite Garshuni Texts: On their Evolution, Characteristics, and Function," *Hugoye* 17 (2014): 237–62.

54 See Appendix IX.

55 See Appendix X.

56 "[N]e manco habbiamo hauuto notitia del R.^{do} vescouo di Baruti nominato Simeon Marunita, qual habbiamo mandato agli Piedi di sua santità in loco nostro, accioche impari gli Rite et santte costumi della chiesia catholica di Roma, per poter poi canonicamente instruir questi Populi nostri di qua Autoritate accepta a Pontefice". CC 41, 101r. For the full text of this letter, see Appendix X.

57 The Bavarian Orientalist Johann Albrecht Widmanstetter referred to Simeon as his teacher in Syriac, which teaching probably took place at some point during Widmanstetter's stay in Rome between 1527 and 1539. Although falling within that range, Stefano Assemani's claim that Simeon arrived in 1535 to seek a dispensation from residence in his diocese of Tripoli is incorrect. Assemani's source, al-Duwayhi, misunderstood a letter of that date that appointed a Maronite named Joseph as bishop of Tripoli, following the death of another Maronite named Simon. The different names and sees of these bishops mean that they cannot be the same person. For Widmanstetter and Simeon, see his note of "Symeon Episcopus Libani, praeceptor meus" in Munich: Bayerische Staatsbibliothek, Rar. 155, [sig]a***3.v; for Assemani, see Stefano Evodio Assemani, *Bibliothecae Mediceae Laurentianae et Palatinae codicum manuscriptorum orientalium catalogus* (Florence: ex Typographio Albiziniano 1742), 91–2; the letter to Joseph can be found in Appendix VII of the present book.

58 John-Paul Ghobrial, "The Archive of Orientalism and its Keepers: Re-Imagining the Histories of Arabic Manuscripts in Early Modern Europe," *Past & Present* 230 (2016): 90–111.

59 For example, Antonio Carafa's role in organising the Jesuit Eliano's mission to Lebanon, for which see Robert John Clines, *A Jewish Jesuit in the Eastern Mediterranean: Early Modern Conversion, Mission, and the Construction of Identity* (Cambridge: Cambridge University Press, 2019), 90–149.

60 Aurélien Girard, "Le Collège maronite de Rome et les langues au tournant des XVIe et XVIIe siècles: éducation des chrétiens orientaux, science orientaliste et apologétique catholique," *Rivista Storica Italiana* 132 (2020): 272–99.

61 For him, see Girolamo Golubovich, ed., *Biblioteca bio-bibliografica della Terra Santa e dell'Oriente francescano* (Florence: Quaracchi, 1929), 6:151 n.1.

62 *Bullarium Maronitarum*, 58.

63 See below, Appendix VIII. My thanks to Dr Joseph Moukarzel for the images of this letter.

64 *Bullarium Maronitarum*, 58.

65 See above, Chapter 2:II–III.

66 For a later Franciscan report, see Appendix XIII.

67 Aurélien Girard, "*Nihil esse innovandum*? Maintien des rites orientaux et négociation de l'union des églises orientales avec Rome (fin XVIe mi–XVIIIe s.)," in *Réduire le schisme? Ecclésiologies et politiques de l'Union entre Orient et Occident (XIIIe–XVIIIe siècle)*, ed. Marie-Hélène Blanchet et Frédéric Gabriel (Leuven: Peeters, 2013), 337–52.

68 The instructions are printed in Cardinali, "Ritratto di Marcello Cervini *en orientaliste*," 343.

69 Ibid., 328–35.

70 For Cervini's interests in Scripture and conciliar texts, see Chapter 4:III–IV. His interest in antiquities is a recurring theme in his correspondence with Bernardino Maffei, for instance CC 20, 14r, 84v, 78v; CC 19, 20r–20v, 16r–16v.

71 "Et perche V.S.R.^{ma} già mi promise per nome della s.^{ta} di nostro signore di mandare alcuni padri a uiuere con noi in monte libano, affine d'instituirci secondo il rito et consuetudine della Sta madre chiesa Romana, le ricordo riuerentemente questo nostro desiderio essere maggiore che fusse mai". CC 45, 3r; printed in Cardinale, "Ritratto di Marcello Cervini en orientaliste," 342. I owe this realisation to Giuliano Tomei.

72 This letter awaits discovery. Dr Joseph Moukarzel has informed me that Cervini's letters to Musa cannot be found in the patriarchal library in Bkerké. Private correspondence, 29 January 2020.

73 Chapter 4:IV.

56 *Negotiating a world in motion*

74 I build here on Sam Kennerley, "The Reception of John Chrysostom," 204–13; this theme is also noted in Cardinali, "Ritratto di Marcello Cervini en orientaliste," 329.

75 "[T]u frater protector noster es in omnibus nostris necesitatibus". CC 41, 102v. See Appendix IX.

76 Beat Kümin and Felicita Tramontana, "Catholicism Decentralized: Local Religion in the Early Modern Periphery," *Church History* 89 (2020): 281–3.

77 Ibid., 62–3. George is called 'Bononiensi' there, but for his Bosnian identity, see Golubovich, *Biblioteca bio-bibliografica della Terra Santa e dell'Oriente francescano*, 8:8.

78 Ibid., 8:150 n.2, and 8:152–3; also ibid., 9:69, which recounts a mission to Malta by Felice in 1542.

79 See below, Appendix XII.

80 Perez Zagorin, *Ways of Lying. Dissimulation, Persecution, and Conformity in Early Modern Europe* (Cambridge MA: Harvard University Press, 1990); Miriam Eliav-Feldon, *Renaissance Impostors and Proofs of Identity* (London: Palgrave, 2012).

81 Eliav-Feldon, *Renaissance Impostors*, 68–80 (for Reuveni); Matteo Salvadore, "'I Was Not Born to Obey, but Rather to Give Orders': The Self-Fashioning of Şäga Krestos, an Ethiopian Traveler in 17th-century Europe," *Journal of Early Modern History* 25 (2021): 1–33.

82 Valentin Groebner, *Who Are You? Identification, Deception, and Surveillance in Early Modern Europe* (New York: Zone Books, 2007).

83 Eliav-Feldon, *Renaissance Impostors*, 17–32.

84 Zagorin, *Ways of Lying*, 132–52; John Bossy, *Under the Molehill: An Elizabethan Spy Story* (New Haven: Yale University Press, 2001).

85 Tijana Krstić, *Contested Conversions to Islam: Narratives of Religious Change in the Early Modern Ottoman Empire* (Stanford: Stanford University Press, 2011), 1–2.

86 Jane K. Wickersham, *Rituals of Prosecution. The Roman Inquisition and the Prosecution of Philo-Protestants in Sixteenth-Century Italy* (Toronto: University of Toronto Press, 2012), 9–10.

87 Del Col, *L'Inquisizione in Italia*, 305–8.

88 John Tedeschi, with William Monter, "Toward a Statistical Profile of the Italian Inquisitions, Sixteenth to Eighteenth Centuries," in John Tedeschi, *The Prosecution of Heresy: Collected Studies on the Early Modern Inquisition* (Binghamton NY: MRTS, 1991), 105.

89 Quaranta, *Marcello II Cervini*, 123–4.

90 Michael Breydy, *Geschichte der Syro-Arabischen Literatur der Maroniten vom VII. bis XVI. Jahrhundert* (Opladen: Westdeutscher Verlag, 1985). The manuscript is Oxford: Bodleian Library, Syr. 170 (Hatton Or. 25).

91 For a similar argument about the Reformation as a motor for religious intolerance beyond the Latin west, but dated for the Catholic world only after Trent, see Carina L. Johnson, "Idolatrous Cultures and the Practice of Religion," *Journal of the History of Ideas* 67 (2006): 597–621.

4 Collaborations between Maronites, eastern Christians, and Catholic Orientalists in Rome during the cardinalate of Marcello Cervini (1539–1555)

I. Introduction

As well as proving pivotal to exchanges between Rome and the Maronites, Cervini's cardinalate between 1539 and 1555 was an exceptional period in Rome's contact with Christians from Africa and the Levant. During this period emissaries came to Rome from Armenia, the Jacobite Church in Syria, and the 'Nestorian' Church of the East for the first time since the Council of Ferrara-Florence. These emissaries were often hosted by the community of Ethiopian pilgrims resident at Santo Stefano dei Mori, which grew to its greatest extent at this time.

Giorgio Levi della Vida and Robert J. Wilkinson have provided indispensable outlines of the eastern Christian presence in mid-sixteenth-century Rome, as well as of the collaborations between eastern Christians and western Orientalists that took place in the city.[1] However, further detail can now be added to their accounts. A significant amount of research into eastern Christians in Rome has been published since these authors wrote their surveys.[2] Yet this research has commonly focused on the relations between Rome and a particular eastern Church, leaving the broader picture unclear. Moreover, neither Levi della Vida, Wilkinson, nor their successors made use of Cervini's unpublished letters in Florence, which are as essential to understanding Rome's relations to these Churches as they are to reconstructing Catholic exchanges with the Maronites.

In light of this background, the following chapter has two primary aims. Taking Cervini and his correspondence as its centre, its first aim is to provide a panoramic overview of the eastern Christian presence in Rome between 1539 and 1555. This overview will begin with collaborations between Catholic scholars and the Ethiopian community of Rome, before analysing the reception of embassies sent by the Syrian Jacobites, Armenians, and the 'Nestorian' Church of the East. Through these examples we will see that Maronites, as well as Ethiopians, served as privileged intermediaries between Rome and the eastern Churches in the mid-sixteenth century.

The second aim of this chapter is to consider the motivations that brought eastern Christians to Rome, and to assess how they were received by Catholics in that city. It will again be shown that eastern Christians took

DOI: 10.4324/9781003165392-5

58   *Eastern Christianity, Catholic Orientalism*

the initiative in these exchanges, travelling to Rome for reasons that ranged from military intervention to the use of the printing press. By contrast, we will see that the Council of Trent was never a cause of attraction. For the Catholic side of these exchanges, further evidence will be adduced to show that the Reformation coloured Rome's perception of other Christians from Africa and the Levant. Finally, this chapter will end with a summary of how Catholic relations with other Churches changed between the Council of Ferrara-Florence and Cervini's death in 1555.

II. The Ethiopian community of early modern Rome, 1404–1555: A very short history

As noted in the previous chapter, it is becoming increasingly clear that Rome was a pluri-confessional city throughout the early modern period.[3] Yet even once that fact is acknowledged, it is still striking that Rome's largest eastern Christian community was not from the nearby Levant, but rather from distant Ethiopia. Explaining this phenomenon requires a brief excursus into the longer history of contact between Ethiopia and Rome.

Just like their Roman counterparts, the rulers of Ethiopia adopted Christianity in the fourth century. Its national Church, however, took a different path when it rejected the Council of Chalcedon (451 AD), becoming a 'Monophysite' Church headed by the Jacobite Patriarch of Alexandria. Long associated in medieval Europe with the mythical kingdom of 'Prester John', authentic ambassadors from Ethiopia arrived in Rome for the first time in 1404. Later embassies followed throughout the fifteenth and early sixteenth centuries, mainly visiting Rome to draw western works of art and craftsmen to Ethiopia, as well as to obtain military support against neighbouring states.[4] Some of these ambassadors also claimed to have travelled to Rome to discuss church union, but such assertions should be treated with caution. Of all the eastern delegations present at the Council of Ferrara-Florence, for example, only the Ethiopians declined to sign a union with Rome when the opportunity was presented to them.[5] Despite this refusal, Catholics seem not to have doubted the orthodoxy of Ethiopian Christianity until the middle of the sixteenth century, for reasons that will be discussed in greater detail below.[6]

This trickle of embassies was engulfed by a stream of Ethiopian pilgrims that poured into Rome throughout the early modern period. As the site of the tombs of the Apostles Peter and Paul, Rome was an important stop on a pilgrimage route that led from Ethiopia to Jerusalem, Italy, and finally Santiago de Compostela.[7] This peculiarly Ethiopian pilgrimage route ensured that Ethiopians were much more frequent visitors to Rome than other eastern Christians. Almost fifty Ethiopian pilgrims were attested in Rome in the fifteenth century, and many more probably visited the city without leaving a trace of their existence.[8] Indeed, by the end of the fifteenth century, the number of Ethiopian pilgrims in Rome had grown to such an extent that they occupied the church and hostel of Santo Stefano, a complex of

Eastern Christianity, Catholic Orientalism   59

buildings that was (and still partly is) located just behind the modern Vatican basilica. This occupation was initially informal, but the continuous arrival of further pilgrims perpetuated the arrangement to such an extent that the church became known as Santo Stefano dei Mori (St Stephen's 'of the Moors').[9] In 1548, Pope Paul III (1534–1549) formally conceded Santo Stefano to the use of Ethiopian pilgrims and other eastern Christian visitors to Rome, and under Julius III (1550–1555) this community seems to have expanded to its greatest extent. A total of 41 Ethiopian pilgrims were attested in Santo Stefano in 1551, almost equal to the entire number that are known to have visited Rome in the previous century.[10] During Cervini's cardinalate the leading figure of this community was an Ethiopian named Tasfā Ṣeyon, an important intermediary between Catholics and the eastern Churches whom we will often encounter in the following pages.[11]

The concentrated presence of these Ethiopian pilgrims made Santo Stefano a privileged site for collaboration between western Orientalists and eastern Christians. A German priest named Johannes Potken had, for example, worked with them between 1511 and 1513 to print the Psalter and the Song of Songs in the liturgical language of the Ethiopian Church, Ge'ez.[12] Santo Stefano retained this status during Cervini's cardinalate. It was a central node in the network of eastern Christians and western Orientalists that he created with the aim of discovering of further resources in the fight against Protestantism. As regards the Ethiopians of Rome, Cervini's correspondence preserves evidence of two projects in this direction, as well as their contrasting outcomes. First there was an attempt to use the Ethiopic Mass to defend the apostolic origin of its Roman counterpart, which largely followed the plans that Cervini had devised for it. Second was an enquiry into the Ge'ez tradition of the canons of the Council of Nicaea (325 AD), which had the unintended result of causing some of Cervini's Catholic collaborators to lose faith in the orthodoxy of the Ethiopian Church. The following analysis will discuss these initiatives in turn, considering what they might tell us about us about the aims and expectations of both Ethiopians and Catholic Orientalists in early modern Rome.

III. Polemical uses of the Ethiopian past. I: The Ethiopic Mass

Marcello Cervini's contacts with the Ethiopians of Rome are first attested on 14 March 1546, when he wrote a letter to the papal secretary Bernardino Maffei. In this letter, Cervini recounted a conversation that he had had with Tasfā Ṣeyon, in which Tasfā had informed him that the Ethiopic Mass contained practices such as prayers for the dead and the invocation of saints that Catholics also followed, but which Protestants did not. Since the Ethiopian Church had been evangelised by an Apostle, Cervini concluded, these similarities showed that prayers for the dead and the invocation of saints were apostolic in origin. The continued observation of these practices by Catholics therefore proved that they, rather than Protestants, were the true heirs to the faith of the Apostles in the present.[13]

60 *Eastern Christianity, Catholic Orientalism*

Cervini's aim to use Ethiopian evidence against Protestantism shows that the confessional goals we have seen drove his contacts with the Maronites similarly shaped his communication with other eastern Christians. Indeed, Cervini's letter to Maffei indicates that he sought to enlist the Maronites in this campaign to prove the apostolicity of the Mass through the traditions of the eastern Churches. Cervini noted that a "Maronite archbishop or bishop" had informed him that the Maronite Mass contained the same customs as those used in Rome.[14] This anonymous prelate was undoubtedly Simeon, the Maronite bishop of Beirut who had been resident in Rome since at least 1542.[15] As we will see later, Simeon acted as an interlocutor between Cervini and non-Latin Churches on several other occasions between 1539 and 1555. But for reasons that remain obscure, no further use seems to have been made of the information that he furnished Cervini about the Maronite Mass.[16]

By contrast, Cervini's letters indicate that he acted upon the conversation that he had had with Tasfā Ṣeyon about the Ethiopian Mass. Between June and July 1547, Tasfā and a Catholic scholar named Pier Paolo Gualtieri translated the Ethiopian Mass into Latin for Cervini.[17] Their translation was then printed in Rome between 1548 and 1549, featuring a preface to Paul III and concluding annotations that were written in Tasfā's voice.[18] These paratexts explicitly recognised papal supremacy, and stressed the commonalities between Rome and the Ethiopian as well as the Greek and Egyptian Churches.[19]

Cervini had therefore achieved his goal of weaponising the Ethiopian Mass against Protestantism. But for his part, Tasfā may have had other aims in mind for this text. Lucy Parker has recently argued that encounters between Catholics and eastern Christians look different when viewed from an eastern Christian rather than a Roman perspective. She found that some eastern Christians who regarded themselves as unified with Rome included in their religious identity not just 'Catholic' doctrines such as papal supremacy, but also reverence for figures who had been anathematised by the popes. Whereas earlier historians have typically attributed such syncretism to ignorance of Catholic doctrine, Parker argued it was instead the result of an alternative approach to orthodoxy.[20]

These insights can be applied to the edition of the Ethiopian Mass. The paratexts to this edition blend acknowledgement of papal supremacy with prayers for the Jacobite Patriarch of Alexandria, whom Tasfā's Latin contemporaries would have regarded as schismatic.[21] These elements appear contradictory when assessed from a Roman perspective, and one interpretation would be to criticise Tasfā for 'failing' to realise this conflict. However, another, more fruitful approach might be to use these apparent contradictions to highlight how Tasfā understood his Church's relations to Rome. Unlike some of his Ethiopian contemporaries, Tasfā never had himself re-ordained as a Catholic priest.[22] But this may have been because he understood his Church as already in union with Rome. Tasfā's prefaces proclaimed to Paul III that the Ethiopians "are and want to be Catholics", and begged the pope to protect them from European slander to the contrary.[23]

Tasfā's desire to prove his nation's orthodoxy to Latin Catholics in this edition can only be understood when placed in the wider context of Ethiopian history. He had arrived in Rome around 1536 in the midst of a war between Ethiopia and the sultanate of 'Adal, where Ethiopia was on the losing side until the death of the 'Adali sultan Gragn in 1543. Tasfā spent the rest of his life in Rome attempting to enlist Catholic support in the reconstruction of his homeland. He was, for instance, instrumental in persuading the Jesuits to embark on their mission to Ethiopia in 1555, having pressed home the importance of this project during a personal meeting with their founder Ignatius Loyola.[24] Guided by the advice of trusted informants like Tasfā, the Jesuits expected to find a warm reception in Ethiopia. The reality proved rather different, and the Jesuits and their flock were eventually ejected from Ethiopia in 1632.[25]

Once more, the edition of the Ethiopic Mass shows that the eastern Christian perception on contacts with Rome can only be understood by reference to developments beyond Europe. Such conclusions are in keeping with recent emphasis on the agency of eastern Christians during their contacts with Rome. But at the same time, it is equally important to avoid caricaturing Catholic perspectives on such connections, something that can only be achieved by accurate contextualisation within European history. In this case, Cervini's interest in the Ethiopic Mass between 1546 and 1549 coincided with his service as papal legate to the Council of Trent. It is broadly accepted that eastern Christians played no part in this council during Cervini's time at Trent. Invitations for eastern Christians to attend the council were only sent during its final bout of meetings between 1562 and 1563, for example.[26] Nonetheless, the exclusion of living eastern Christians from this instrument of the Counter-Reformation does not mean that Cervini and his Catholic contemporaries disregarded eastern Christians in the confessional conflicts of the sixteenth century. In his letter to Maffei, Cervini explicitly noted that his interest in the Ethiopian Mass was to prove the apostolic origins of Catholic traditions, an interest that we see reflected in his use of this translation at the Council of Trent. When Cervini commissioned the Jesuit Alfonso Salmeron to defend the Mass at this council, for instance, Salmeron drew on the Ethiopic Mass to prove the orthodoxy of its Roman counterpart.[27]

The translation of the Ethiopic Mass therefore demonstrates that some Catholics in Rome understood eastern Christian evidence to be a valid instrument in the defence of Catholic doctrine against Protestantism. Cervini's correspondence implies that he was the driving force behind this understanding. True, the translation of the Ethiopic Mass would have been impossible without the linguistic skill of Tasfā Ṣeyon and Pier Paolo Gualtieri. But it is unlikely that their collaboration would have existed without Cervini's desire to obtain a Latin translation of the Mass, and presumably his willingness to cover the costs associated with the project.

Cervini's investigations into the Maronite and Ethiopian Mass have been largely forgotten, due to the fact that his interest in them can only be

62 Eastern Christianity, Catholic Orientalism

recovered from his unpublished correspondence. Nonetheless, this was not the only time that Cervini led a collaboration between Catholics and the Ethiopians of Rome. His engagement with this community is preserved in much greater detail in letters about another translation from Ethiopic that he coordinated in the summer of 1547.

IV. Polemical uses of the Ethiopian past. II: The Ethiopic canons of the Council of Nicaea

On 4 June 1547, Cervini received a letter about Tasfā Ṣeyon from a client named Guglielmo Sirleto. Sirleto was a Calabrian scholar, who in later life became one of the leading figures in the development of Rome's policies towards other Churches. However, at this time he was a relatively recent arrival in Rome, and just beginning his career in Cervini's household.[28]

In this letter, Sirleto reported to Cervini a conversation about Tasfā that he had had with a Spanish scholar named Francisco Torres.[29] Torres had told Sirleto that Tasfā owned a Ge'ez copy of the canons of the Council of Nicaea (325 AD), which apparently contained over 80 canons from this council. Sirleto naturally felt the need to write to Cervini about this discovery. At a stroke, Tasfā's manuscript quadrupled the number of canons of this key early council that were known to Catholics from Greek and Latin evidence. Torres appears to have shared Sirleto's enthusiasm. Sirleto reported that this Spanish scholar was planning to have Tasfā explain the canons to him, and even to have them translated.[30]

It would appear that Cervini stepped in at this point. He wrote to Sirleto on 27 June 1547 and 1 July 1547, noting that he had exchanged letters with Tasfā about the Ge'ez manuscript of the canons. In these letters Tasfā had indicated his willingness to display the Ge'ez manuscript of the canons of Nicaea to Sirleto, and to assist him in their translation. Cervini therefore equipped Sirleto with a letter that he felt would encourage Tasfā to show him the manuscript.[31]

With this letter in hand, Sirleto visited Tasfā together with Pier Paolo Gualtieri, the Catholic scholar whom we met in the analysis of the Ethiopic Mass above. As Cervini had hoped, Tasfā showed his manuscript of the canons of Nicaea to these Latin visitors and explained its contents to them. However, problems began to occur once this Ethiopian source was subjected to scrutiny. Tasfā claimed that there were 318 canons in his manuscript. By contrast, Sirleto protested that that was a misunderstanding, since he knew that 318 bishops had attended the council. His suspicions deepened as Tasfā continued to work through the manuscript. Once they reached the twentieth canon, there was a break in the manuscript, at exactly the same point where the Latin and Greek traditions also stopped. Sirleto and Gualtieri therefore wanted to compare the Ethiopic canons to their Latin and Greek equivalents, but Tasfā argued that such a comparison would be futile. He stated that the canons of Nicaea had been originally written in Ge'ez, making the Latin and Greek manuscripts that were

Eastern Christianity, Catholic Orientalism   63

familiar to western scholars derivative of an earlier Ethiopian tradition. Sirleto was incredulous at this claim. He protested that the council had been held in Greek-speaking territory, and that early historians such as Eusebius suggested that the canons had been written in Greek, since they never mentioned that they had drawn on them in translation. Sirleto's dismay was compounded when Tasfā argued that the first canon of Nicaea justified circumcision, a common practice among Ethiopian Christians, but not among Roman Catholics. Sirleto concluded to Cervini that, in future, it would be essential to get hold of someone who understood Ethiopic and who knew how to express themselves, in order to ensure that Ethiopic material was faithfully translated.[32]

The detail of this letter brings to life the methods and expectations that Catholics and eastern Christians brought to their collaborations in early modern Rome. We can almost see Sirleto and Gualtieri listening intently as Tasfā explained to them the content of his manuscript. This explanation would most likely have been in Latin or Italian, since these were the tongues that all three men knew. Gualtieri was an Italian classicist who had learned Ge'ez, while Tasfā had taken Latin lessons, and had probably picked up Italian during his lengthy stay in Rome. Sirleto's case is more complex. Early biographers claimed that Sirleto knew various Oriental tongues, for which his offer in these letters to help with translations from Ge'ez would seem to provide confirmation.[33] However, a scholar might assist on a translation without having any real knowledge of the language that they were translating. William Morris's early translations of the Icelandic sagas, for instance, saw him work into more poetic English a literal translation that had been prepared by a native speaker of Icelandic, with whom he would then check his emended version against the original.[34] A similar process of collaboration may have taken place in early modern Rome. We can see from this letter that Tasfā orally summarised the content of the canons for his Catholic audience. Sirleto's role as a 'translator' in this and other cases may then have been limited to finding the right Latin or Italian words to express terms explained to him by his eastern interlocutors, something that he could do without acquiring an independent knowledge of Oriental languages like Ge'ez.

Sirleto therefore relied upon collaboration to access material in Oriental languages. This may have created an environment in which Tasfā felt able to express certain interpretations of his manuscript, through which we can perhaps catch glimpses of an Ethiopian understanding of church history. Tasfā's claims that the canons of Nicaea supported the Ethiopian practice of circumcision, and most remarkably that these canons had been originally written in Ge'ez, adduced ancient Christian sources to support the orthodoxy and pre-eminence of the Ethiopian Church. In this matter Tasfā was no different to his Latin collaborations, who objected to his comments when they differed from a distinctly Roman Catholic interpretation of orthodox belief and practice. Sirleto compensated for his linguistic deficiencies by evaluating what he was told through textual criticism and his vast

64   *Eastern Christianity, Catholic Orientalism*

erudition. His knowledge of church history allowed him to counter Tasfā's claims about the number of canons and their original language, while his observation that the twentieth canon was followed by a pause in the manuscript caused him to suspect that any canon thereafter was a later addition. This collaboration, therefore, seems to have achieved the opposite effect to that intended, making eastern and western scholars more aware of the differences, rather than the similarities, that existed between the Ethiopian and Roman Churches. As we saw with the Maronites in earlier chapters, such acknowledgement of difference could lead to negotiations that strengthened the ties between Rome and Christian communities in the Middle East and Africa. But in this case, the discovery of difference led to a growth in suspicion. After this episode Sirleto came to suspect Tasfā's competence and honesty. He would later forward to Cervini an alternative translation of a crucial part of the Ethiopic Mass that had been completed by another Ethiopian resident at Santo Stefano, thereby challenging on confessional grounds Tasfā's status as a 'keeper' of learning about eastern Christianity.[35]

In contrast to Sirleto, Cervini appears to have retained both his confidence in Tasfā, and his interest in the Ge'ez manuscript of the canons of Nicaea. From Bologna, he continued to write to Sirleto about the progress of study on these canons, and his patience was rewarded when Gualtieri found among the additional canons of the Ethiopian tradition one that offered a clear acknowledgement of papal supremacy.[36] Gualtieri's Latin translation of this canon survives today in BAV: Vat.et.2, accompanied by Latin summaries of the remaining canons, and the Ge'ez text of those found in the Ethiopic tradition. This manuscript was owned by Cervini,[37] whose considerable interest in the eastern tradition of the Council of Nicaea is shown by the fact that he also owned an Arabic manuscript of these additional canons. Cervini's manuscript later served as an exemplar for the Latin translation of these Arabic canons, completed by Francisco Torres and a Turkish convert to Catholicism who took the baptismal name of Paolo Orsini.[38]

Unlike Tasfā and Gualtieri's translation of the Ethiopic Mass, the Latin version of the canon in favour of papal supremacy prepared for Cervini never reached print. It only exists in Cervini's manuscript copy. We need not look too far for why this text suffered such limited dissemination. The Ethiopic canons of Nicaea had failed to yield a usable defence of Catholic practices, such as Cervini and his Catholic collaborators had found in the Ethiopian Mass. Even if one canon defended papal supremacy, it was extracted from a text whose authenticity Sirleto had shown that a hostile scholar could easily challenge. The diverse fortunes of these translations highlight an important qualification in our assessment of the interest of Catholics in eastern Christianity during the early Reformation. We saw earlier that the Ethiopic Mass provides clear evidence that Catholic scholars valued eastern Christian sources in the defence of Catholic doctrine against Protestantism. Yet the translation of the Ge'ez canons of Nicaea shows that this was as far as some Catholics wished to engage with eastern

Christianity. It appears that Sirleto at least was interested in Ethiopic texts and traditions only in so far as they defended the apostolicity and orthodoxy of the Roman Church.

As noted earlier, much recent scholarship has rightly sought to restore the agency of eastern Christians in their contacts with Rome. However, this new focus should not lead us to assume that we already know everything that there is to know about European perspectives on these exchanges. In Rome as in the Levant, there was a variety of possible approaches to eastern Christianity. Not every Roman scholar shared Sirleto's doubts about Tasfā, for example. In contrast to this Calabrian scholar, Pier Paolo Gualtieri seems to have been curious about Ethiopia even when detached from the utility of Geʿez sources in religious polemic. Tasfā named Gualtieri as a spiritual son of the Ethiopian monk Tekla Haymanot, indicating a deeper affection for Ethiopia that was valued by members of the Ethiopian community in Rome.[39] Religion also proved no impediment in Gualtieri's interactions with the Armenian Catholicos Stefanos V during the latter's visit to Rome between 1548 and 1550. While conscious of the doctrinal differences that divided them, Gualtieri fondly recalled the conversations about eastern affairs that he had held with this prelate and his entourage, suggesting that at least some members of Cervini's network formed friendships with eastern Christians that crossed confessional lines.[40]

The recognition that there was a variety of Catholic approaches to eastern Christianity as well as eastern Christian interactions with Catholicism makes it essential to understand the specific motivations that drove key figures such as Cervini to cultivate connections to the eastern Churches. There were many reasons that may have led him into contact with Ethiopian Christians, ranging from simple curiosity, to a concern with their possible strategic role as allies against the Ottomans. However, like the contacts with the Maronites that we studied in the previous chapter, Cervini's letters about the Ethiopian Mass and the Geʿez canons of Nicaea kept show that his primary interest was the applicability of Ethiopian Christianity to polemics against Protestantism. In both cases, Cervini's interactions with Ethiopian Christianity were guided by the search for new ways of proving doctrines that had been rendered controversial by the Reformation, above all papal supremacy. This confessional focus was also at the heart of two other explorations of Ethiopian culture in which Cervini is known to have been involved. Cervini was the dedicatee of the *Chaldeae seu Aethiopicae linguae institutiones* (1552), a grammar of Geʿez composed by Mariano Vittorio with assistance from Pier Paolo Gualtieri and the Ethiopians of Rome. Vittorio's preface to this edition pointed to how the study of eastern tongues might show the apostolicity of Catholicism against Protestant detractors, and attributed to Cervini the realisation that Geʿez preserved ancient Christian writings lost in other languages. Vittorio also credited Cervini for having the New Testament printed in Geʿez.[41] The claim that Cervini was responsible for this famous edition is exaggerated, as the planning and printing of the Geʿez New Testament in Rome between 1546 and

66   *Eastern Christianity, Catholic Orientalism*

1549 was achieved by collaboration between the Ethiopians of Santo Stefano and a wide variety of Catholic scholars and prelates.[42] That he was a part of this collaboration is however suggested by the fact that he received a personalised copy of the Ge'ez New Testament, one of a number of such copies that appear to have been distributed to patrons of this ambitious project.[43]

In sum, Cervini's letters about the Ethiopian community of Rome reinforce the conclusions of the previous chapter. There, we saw that Cervini sent Franciscans to Mount Lebanon to investigate the value of Maronite texts in confessional polemic against Protestantism. Here, we have seen that these same concerns also drove the collaborations that he arranged between Maronites, Ethiopians, and Catholic Orientalists. Moreover, in recording Sirleto's doubts about the orthodoxy of Tasfā Ṣeyon, Cervini's letters further highlight the growing suspicion with which eastern Christians were received by Catholics in Rome. Cervini's ability to bring Catholics and eastern Christians together, as well as the friction that might arise from the meeting of these different worlds, is further manifest in his encounters with another eastern Christian group: the Syrian Jacobites.

V. Two Syrian Jacobites in Counter-Reformation Rome: Peter of Damascus and Moses of Mardin

The Jacobite (or Syrian Orthodox) Church derives its name from Jacob Baradeus, a bishop of Edessa who led resistance to the Council of Chalcedon (451) in the Levant during the sixth century. The Jacobites had made contact with Rome during the twelfth century, and, as we saw in Chapter 1, signed what was probably a fleeting union with Rome at the Council of Ferrara-Florence in 1444. But like other eastern Churches, connections between the Jacobites and Rome only intensified from the mid-sixteenth century. Cervini's correspondence again provides indispensable material for this history.[44]

On 18 November 1544, Johann Albrecht von Widmanstetter wrote a despairing letter to Cervini from the Bavarian capital of Landshut. Widmanstetter recounted how a Jacobite deacon named Peter of Damascus had flown into a rage with one of his servants, purchased a two-handed sword, and marched about Landshut threatening to kill some of the town's inhabitants. The affair was so serious that even Duke Ludwig X of Bavaria became involved. Widmanstetter and the duke managed to calm Peter down and find out what he wanted. Peter demanded the pay that he was due from Widmanstetter, a horse, and spending money for himself and a companion to Rome, all of which were granted. This arrangement would bring to an end Peter's thoroughly miserable stay in Landshut, which had seen him accuse Widmanstetter of plots against his life, while failing to teach this Orientalist any Arabic. This was despite an agreement to offer such teaching that he had made in Rome with Widmanstetter – and with Cervini.[45]

Eastern Christianity, Catholic Orientalism 67

Peter of Damascus was not the first eastern Christian to instruct Widmanstetter in the languages of the Levant. This Bavarian Orientalist is regarded as one of the first Europeans to obtain a scholarly knowledge of Syriac and Arabic, much of which he gained during a lengthy stay in Italy between 1527 and 1539.[46] Particularly important in this regard was Simeon, the Maronite bishop of Beirut, whom Widmanstetter acknowledged as his 'teacher'.[47] We saw in Chapter 2 that the Maronite subdeacon Elias taught Arabic and Syriac to a generation of Catholic Orientalists in the Rome of Leo X. Simeon's teaching of Widmanstetter, a central figure in the next generation of Catholic Orientalists, further highlights the important role of the Maronites in the early modern history of Orientalist scholarship in the Latin west.

Widmanstetter returned to Rome in October 1543.[48] His original intention was to pursue a legal case in the curia, but it was probably on this trip that he met Peter of Damascus. The agreement that Widmanstetter made with Peter in Rome is outlined in his letter to Cervini, where we see that he had agreed to pay Peter 24 *scudi* a year in exchange for instruction in Arabic. It appears that Cervini was the guarantor of this agreement, as both parties had recourse to his protection once they fell out in 1544. Peter threatened that he would complain to Cervini about the treatment he had received, while the purpose of Widmanstetter's letter was to obtain cash from Cervini in order to defray the costs of a tutor whom he seems to have considered the cardinal's responsibility. Widmanstetter indeed credited Cervini with dispatching Peter from Rome to Landshut.[49] Based on this evidence, we can speculate that Cervini, knowing of Widmanstetter's earlier studies of Arabic, and his desire to deepen his knowledge of the language, brought him into contact with Peter in Rome, who as a native speaker would have seemed an appropriate candidate as a tutor for this Bavarian Orientalist.

Such an agreement could only have been made if Cervini already knew Peter before Widmanstetter's return to Rome in October 1543. This knowledge would however appear to have been limited, as Cervini miscalculated Peter's suitability for the job. Peter caused problems even before his departure from Rome, stealing two manuscripts from the Vatican Library.[50] Such actions perhaps contributed to the breakdown of relations between Peter and Widmanstetter, but it appears that their differences may have emerged from more fundamental causes. Widmanstetter's letter to Cervini shows that food was a particular problem for Peter, who objected to eating fish on certain days, and worried about consuming blood.[51] This letter therefore highlights the day-to-day problems faced by eastern Christians in adjusting themselves to life in Europe. While cities such as Rome that had large and established eastern communities likely posed fewer problems in this regard, in the mid-sixteenth century smaller towns like Landshut seem to have had less familiarity with eastern Christian visitors or how to accommodate them.[52] The result was friction over everyday events that could easily build up and explode. Peter may have done himself few favours with his thefts

68   *Eastern Christianity, Catholic Orientalism*

from the Vatican Library, but his disastrous stay in Landshut cannot be blamed on issues of character alone.[53]

However disastrous its conclusion, the experiment with Peter was not without its benefits for Cervini. It had expanded his network, connecting Rome to a potential centre of Catholic Orientalism in Bavaria. These lines of communication were travelled by another Syrian Jacobite who arrived in Rome five years later.

The Jacobite in question was Moses of Mardin. Unlike Peter, Moses appears to have travelled to Rome in an official capacity. He arrived in Rome in 1549, carrying a letter of obedience from his patriarch 'Abdullah I (1521–1557) to Pope Paul III.[54] But despite the importance of his mission, Moses was forced to wait for a reply. Pope Paul III was then on his deathbed, and it took three months for his successor Julius III to be elected. The manner in which Moses occupied himself in the meantime is shown in a manuscript that he copied in Rome in 1549, now housed in the British Library.[55] This manuscript is a copy of the Roman Mass transcribed into Syriac characters, a move between scripts that would have enabled a reader of Syriac to pronounce Latin-sounding words with no knowledge of the latter language.[56] The manuscript also contains an invocation of the Trinity in Arabic, Ge'ez, Greek, Latin, and Syriac.[57] These were the languages that Moses would have encountered when speaking to eastern Christians and Catholic Orientalists in Rome. Indeed, Moses listed the contacts that he had made in a colophon to this manuscript. He mentioned Pier Paolo Gualtieri, Mariano Vittorio, Reginald Pole, and Jean du Bellay, but credit for the execution of this manuscript was given to two figures above all: Tasfā Ṣeyon, and Marcello Cervini.[58]

Moses's manuscript is a microcosm of the interests and characters that we have encountered in this chapter, showing that this Jacobite deacon was quickly integrated into the network of eastern Christians and Catholic Orientalists that Cervini had created in Rome. However, a document recently analysed and edited by Giacomo Cardinali shows that Moses was a potentially destabilising newcomer in this network.[59] This document, a letter of 29 September 1549 addressed to Cervini by two Syrian Jacobites in Paris, provides a different account of Moses's mission and his conduct in Rome. First, these Jacobites denied that Moses was an official emissary from the Jacobite Patriarch 'Abdullah. Rather, they claimed that he had been excommunicated by 'Abdullah, and had fled to Cyprus. There, after forging letters from 'Abdullah, Moses was allegedly banned from celebrating Mass by the Jacobites of the island and ejected from their congregation, an act witnessed by the patriarch of the Armenians. This Armenian patriarch and his entourage, together with the senders of this letter, then encountered Moses in Rome, and reported his misdeeds to Tasfā Ṣeyon. Moses allegedly responded to this denunciation by attacking one of the Jacobites, but he was protected by Tasfā, whose threats against the Jacobites appear to have forced them to flee from Rome. It would seem that the Armenian patriarch and his company left soon afterwards, since the Jacobites reported that this party was also in France.[60]

Some recent studies have highlighted instances in which eastern Christians supported one another in Rome, despite coming from different Churches that often clashed in the Levant.[61] By contrast, this episode shows that conflict as well as collaboration was a part of this community's history. Moreover, such conflicts had the potential to redirect Catholic policy towards the eastern Churches. After this letter, Cervini was left with the problem of whether to trust Moses or his accusers. It seems that eastern Christians in Rome intervened at this point to resolve the cardinal's doubts.

The two Jacobites wrote to Cervini in the expectation that he would take their side in their conflict with Moses. Such expectations were misguided, as their letter shows that Moses had some influential allies in Rome. He was protected by Tasfā Ṣeyon, who was a natural ally of Moses. Like this Syrian emissary, Tasfā had travelled to Rome in order to seek greater Catholic involvement in his Church. Tasfā could then be relied upon to stress Moses's pro-Catholic credentials to cardinals like Cervini when disputes arose between eastern Christians in Rome. As such, this letter is a salutary reminder that not every node in a network is equal. In an alternative universe the two Jacobites might have proved close collaborators of Cervini. But as it turned out, Cervini instead favoured their opponents. His decision was probably guided by his trust in Tasfā as an interlocutor with the eastern Churches, as well as by Moses and Tasfā's utility to his plans of increasing Catholic influence among the eastern Churches. It appears therefore that this Ethiopian scholar can take some credit for saving Moses's mission, as well as for shaping Roman policy towards the Syrian Jacobites.

The favour that Moses enjoyed in Rome after this debacle is shown in the documents that he received in 1550 from the newly-elected Pope Julius III. Julius entrusted Moses with the task of carrying to Syria his reply to Patriarch 'Abdullah, in which he praised the patriarch's acknowledgement of papal supremacy, and communicated his blessings and an indulgence to 'Abdullah's flock.[62] Moses also received a commendatory letter from the pope to assist in this journey east.[63] Nonetheless, while praising 'Abdullah's loyalty to Rome, Julius did not accept the patriarch's obedience. Instead, acceptance of this obedience was made dependent upon the patriarch furnishing a profession of faith.

After travelling back to Syria, Moses returned to Rome in 1552 with a tranche of documents. One of these was a letter from Patriarch 'Abdullah to Cervini, which was recently discovered by Paolo Sachet.[64] In this letter, which was received in Rome on 15 October 1552, 'Abdullah asked Cervini to assist Moses in printing books in Syriac. He expressed his hope that the multiplication of copies through the printing press would save Syriac literature from destruction at the hands of time, and increase the faith of the Jacobites by expanding their access to books.[65]

This letter confirms the suspicions of historians as far back as Ignace Antoine II Hayek that Moses conceived of the plan to print books in Syriac during his first visit to Rome.[66] 'Abdullah's letter omitted to mention the books that Moses wanted to print, but a clue can be found in further

70 *Eastern Christianity, Catholic Orientalism*

documentation relating to Cervini. On 3 December 1552, the Vatican Library issued a payment of 13 gold *scudi* to Moses to print books in Syriac for its use. Since Cervini was then cardinal protector of the Vatican Library, this decision was likely made at his command to fulfil the request made by 'Abdullah.[67] Notably, 13 gold *scudi* was the same amount as that paid to the Ethiopians of Santo Stefano in 1549 to print the New Testament in Ge'ez.[68] Moses would have witnessed work on this project first-hand during his stay in Rome between 1549 and 1550, and it appears to have inspired in him a desire to print the New Testament in Syriac.[69]

Another of the documents that Moses carried to Rome was the profession of faith that Julius III had demanded from Patriarch 'Abdullah. This profession was translated in Rome by a Dominican named Ambrosio Buttigeg, as well as by the Maronite bishop of Beirut, Simeon. Simeon has now appeared multiple times in the past two chapters. We have seen him representing the Maronite patriarch Musa al-Akkari in Rome, assisting Cervini in his investigations of the Maronite Mass, and contributing to the development of Catholic Orientalism through his teaching of Arabic and Syriac to Widmanstetter. Simeon's involvement in the translation of 'Abdallah's confession of faith further emphasises that the Maronites were trusted intermediaries between Rome and eastern Christianity within Cervini's network. A Latin copy of 'Abdullah's profession indeed survives among Cervini's papers, annotated with manicules (pointing hands) that guide the reader's attention towards incriminating passages about Christ's natures, and to 'Abdullah's failure to mention his acceptance of Chalcedon. One wonders whether these manicules imply that the Maronite and Dominican translators of this profession of faith also sought to guide Cervini's interpretation of it.[70]

Despite the concerns highlighted in this profession of faith, Julius III accepted 'Abdullah's obedience, issuing a bull to that effect on 26 May 1553. From the perspective of Rome, the Syrian Jacobites had therefore returned to communion with the Catholic Church. As a result, both 'Abdullah and Moses of Mardin were subject to much greater scrutiny than had been the case before their union to Rome. In the bull of 26 May 1553, Julius III asked 'Abdullah to use more precise language about the *filioque* and about the two natures in Christ, threatening excommunication should these changes not be effected.[71] As for Moses, he had already provided his own unquestionably Catholic confession of faith in 1552.[72] Yet it would appear that his Catholic hosts wanted more from him after he had unified his Church to Rome. On 8 June 1553, two weeks after Julius' reply to 'Abdullah, Moses wrote a letter to Andreas Masius (1514–1573), a Flemish Orientalist whom he had taught Syriac.[73] In this letter Moses complained that he had been abandoned by prelates in Rome, after he had rejected their attempts to re-ordain him a Catholic priest.[74] Masius's doubts about this report have been echoed by later writers, but Moses may not have been lying.[75] Gian Pietro Carafa's Ethiopian chaplain, Yoḥannes, was for

Eastern Christianity, Catholic Orientalism 71

example re-ordained a Catholic in the reign of Julius III after admitting that he had been originally ordained by a Jacobite bishop in Cyprus.[76]

Once more, Moses' experience shows that eastern Christians in mid-sixteenth-century Rome who wanted to be treated as Catholic were forced to overcome growing suspicions about their orthodoxy by supplying ever-greater proofs of their fidelity to this Church. Given his confession of faith and unification of the Syrian Jacobites to Rome, Moses's Catholic contacts may not have understood why he would decline to be re-ordained a Catholic when given the option. Confidence in his true beliefs would appear to have been undermined when he refused, causing his former patrons to abandon him. When Moses wrote to Masius on 8 June 1553, he complained not only of attempts to re-ordain him, but also of the fact that prelates in Rome had done nothing with the Syriac types and a copy of the Syriac New Testament that he possessed.[77] Perhaps doubts about Moses's orthodoxy led to doubts about his competence to edit Scripture.

Having been abandoned by the Catholic hierarchy in Rome, Moses therefore decided to leave the city. It is possible that this decision emerged from fears that he would be become a target of the Roman inquisition. In a later letter to Masius, Moses expressed his dissatisfaction that the inquisitor Gian Pietro Carafa had been made pope. He stated that he held no hope of returning to Rome unless Carafa's enemies, Pole or Morone, obtained the papacy instead.[78] Once more, Moses's concerns should be taken seriously. Some eastern Christians were indeed charged with heresy by the Roman inquisition in the sixteenth century, for instance a Greek metropolitan named Macarius, who was executed as an 'obstinate heretic' in Rome during the night of 10 June 1562.[79]

Perhaps concerned about such dangers, Moses's original intention was to leave Rome for the Levant. However, Masius proposed an alternative plan to his Jacobite confidant. In a letter of 22 June 1553, he encouraged Moses to bring his books and the Syriac types that had been made in Rome to Augsburg, where he would attempt to arrange a meeting with the Fuggers, a wealthy family of bankers and bibliophiles.[80] Moses followed Masius's advice and travelled north. We find him in Venice, where he copied a Syriac Psalter for Ludovico Beccadelli (1501–1572), a former member of Cervini's household who was then serving as papal nuncio to that city.[81] On 15 July 1553 Moses informed Masius that he was on his way to Augsburg in the train of Cardinal Pole.[82] But during this journey he met Widmanstetter, who took him to Vienna instead. Over the next two years Moses, Widmanstetter, and the French Orientalist Guillaume Postel (1510–1581) brought to completion in Vienna the plans that Moses had originally devised in Rome. They edited the first edition of the Gospels in Syriac, which was printed in 1555 in Vienna by Michael Zimmermann with a dedication to the Archduke of Austria, Ferdinand I.[83] Despite not being directly involved in the planning of this edition, the Maronites were imagined as an audience for it. Moses reported that Ferdinand had given him 300 copies of the Syriac

72 *Eastern Christianity, Catholic Orientalism*

Gospels, which were meant for distribution to the Maronite as well as the Jacobite patriarch in the east.[84]

The paratextual material added to this edition by Widmanstetter makes it clear that the Gospels was not the only work that he and his collaborators aimed to print in Syriac. Instead, Widmanstetter claimed that he, Postel, and Moses intended to print the rest of the Old and New Testament as well.[85] Further funding was needed for this project, for which Moses aimed to interest the Count Palatine, Otto Heinrich (1505–1559). Otto was a good candidate, since he wanted to build a library containing books "in every language". However, the only money that Moses received from Otto Heinrich was when the count purchased his manuscripts, as well as a printed copy of the Syriac Gospels.[86] Having failed to secure sufficient investment, Moses was forced to abandon his editorial plans and to return to the east.[87] His later life in Syria, Egypt, as well as his career as a teacher of Syriac at the College of the Neophytes in Rome, all merit further investigation, but they are topics that sit beyond the scope of the present study.[88]

The exchanges between Rome and the Syrian Jacobites that are brought to light by the experiences of Moses of Mardin repeat the core elements of what is by now a familiar plot. An eastern Church takes the initiative in dispatching an envoy to Rome in order to address a matter of local concern, in this case church union and the preservation of its written heritage through the printing press. This envoy is received in Rome by the network of eastern Christians and Catholic Orientalists that had been constructed by Cervini, in which Maronites like Simeon and Ethiopians such as Tasfā Ṣeyon emerge as particularly authoritative interlocutors. Finally, Catholic policymakers come to suspect the orthodoxy of the given Church, leading on this occasion to the flight of the envoy from Rome.

Maronites, Ethiopians, and Jacobites are the eastern Christians most commonly encountered in Rome from sources produced during Cervini's cardinalate. However, some evidence also survives for contacts between Rome and two further Churches. After briefly summarising this material, the present chapter will conclude by reviewing the main developments in Catholic approaches to the eastern Churches in the period covered by this book.

VI. An Armenian catholicos and a Chaldean patriarch in Rome

As Ana Sirinian has recently underlined, from ancient times Armenians have come to Italy as merchants, pilgrims, soldiers, and more besides. The Armenian community of Rome was particularly well-established. In 1269, around 50 Armenians, men and women, religious and secular, were recorded as inhabitants of the Armenian 'hostel' then situated near St Peter's.[89] Rome also hosted the signing of a decree of union between the Catholic and the Armenian Churches on 22 November 1439, as part of the negotiations conducted at the Council of Ferrara-Florence.[90] But as is

Eastern Christianity, Catholic Orientalism 73

true in the history of other eastern Churches that we have encountered in this book, it is unclear how long either party preserved the memory of this event.[91]

Exchanges between Rome and Armenia during Cervini's cardinalate are equally obscure, coming as they do before the arrival in Italy of 'Abgar of Tokat in 1564 that established longer-lasting connections between them.[92] However, documents in the Vatican uncover some evidence of interaction in the decades leading up to 'Abgar's arrival. One such source notes that on 5 March 1545, Pope Paul III provided the Dominican archbishop of Nakhchivan with a safe conduct to travel to Rome in order to offer his obedience.[93] We can presume that this prelate arrived safely, as on 30 June 1546 Paul issued another letter that established Stefanos, archbishop of Nakhchivan, as papal legate to Georgia.[94]

In light of this material, it is perhaps not a coincidence that the Armenian Catholicos of Echmiadzin, Stefanos V Salmastesi, arrived in Rome just two years later.[95] It seems that Cervini and his network were again entrusted with hosting this eastern Christian prelate. Stefanos's arrival in Rome in 1548 was recorded by Pier Paolo Gualtieri, the Catholic scholar whom we have already encountered as a collaborator of Cervini and Tasfā Ṣeyon. Gualtieri noted that he had enjoyed conversing with Stefanos and his party about Persia and the Tartars. But at the same time, he also observed that their conversions had left him with no illusions about the doctrinal differences between the Armenian and Roman Church.[96] While these differences appear not to have harmed Gualtieri and Stefanos's affection for one another – Gualtieri wrote his notes about Stefanos in a Persian *Diatessaron* that the catholicos had gifted him – his acute awareness of these differences is another sign of Catholic disenchantment about the orthodoxy of eastern Christians during the mid-sixteenth century.[97]

Further proof of Cervini's responsibility for this patriarch is shown in the fact that he represented Stefanos V's suit in the consistory of cardinals in the year following this Armenian prelate's arrival in Rome. On 21 August 1549, he informed his colleagues that Stefanos had offered his obedience to the pope and sought confirmation of his election.[98] There is no mention of Stefanos in later consistories, but other sources show that he remained in Rome for another few months. He participated in the funeral of Paul III, attended the ceremonial opening of the Jubilee in 1550, and appears to have appointed Tasfā Ṣeyon as protector of Armenian pilgrims to Rome.[99] The new pope, Julius III, eventually provided Stefanos with letters of introduction to the Habsburg court in Vienna and Sigismund II of Poland. He may also have supplied Stefanos with vestments, including a mitre, which would suggest that his act of obedience was ultimately accepted.[100] With these letters and goods in hand, Stefanos left Rome in 1550, intending to return to Armenia via Vienna, Poland, and Muscovy. Nonetheless, it appears that he died in Poland before he was able to complete the journey home.[101]

There is much more to know about Stefanos V's travels in Italy and eastern Europe between 1548 and 1551. The route that he took back to

74 *Eastern Christianity, Catholic Orientalism*

Armenia, for example, might indicate that he aimed to raise alms or even military support from Christian monarchs who had an interest in the Caucasus. In contrast to the history of this Armenian catholicos, much has been recently written about another eastern Christian embassy to Rome, which will be the last example studied in this chapter.

On 18 November 1552, Yoḥannan Sullāqā arrived in Rome with letters from the people and clergy of the 'Nestorian' Church of the East. These letters claimed that he had been elected as the new patriarch of this Church, the confirmation of which Sullāqā now sought from the pope.[102] Sullāqā was not the first representative of the Church of the East to make contact with Rome. Two earlier patriarchs had sent embassies to Rome in the thirteenth century, and Metropolitan Timothy of Tarsus had abjured Nestorianism at the Council of Florence in 1445.[103] Nonetheless, Sullāqā was the first 'Nestorian' patriarch to make the journey to Rome in person, an unprecedented step that likely related to the circumstances of his election. While Sullāqā reassured his Catholic hosts that he had been elected after the death of Patriarch Simon VII Bar-Mama, Simon was very much alive when Sullāqā headed to Rome. Sullāqā was in fact Simon's rival rather than his successor, having been elected by a faction dismayed either at the Bar-Mama family's treatment of the patriarchate as a hereditary possession, or at the poor condition of the Church of the East in general.[104]

Four months later, on 15 February 1553, Sullāqā presented a profession of faith to Pope Julius III.[105] Here Sullāqā embraced Roman doctrine in key areas of difference with the Church of the East, for instance accepting the *filioque*, as well as the Council of Ephesus (431) that had condemned some aspects of Nestorius's theology. This profession of faith only survives in a Latin translation by Andreas Masius. However, another profession of faith attributed to Sullāqā also exists, preserved in a Syriac poem about his journey to Rome that was written by his successor 'Abd-Isho.[106] While it is as such probably more representative of 'Abd-Isho's beliefs than those of Sullāqā, this Syriac profession of faith omits many of the crucial elements that Sullāqā had declared to Julius III on 15 February 1553.[107]

As a result of these contradictions, Lucy Parker and Herman Teule have suggested that Catholic prelates and scholars likely assisted Sullāqā in crafting the profession of faith that he offered in Rome.[108] We can gain a sense of the network into which Sullāqā was integrated from a letter that he sent to Julius III after his return to the Levant. There, Sullāqā passed his greetings to a host of Catholic prelates, including Cervini, Rodolfo Pio da Carpi, and the Master of the Sacred Palace, Girolamo Muzzarelli.[109] Given the involvement of these cardinals in the Roman inquisition, and the fact that the Master of the Sacred Palace was the pope's official theologian, we can expect that theology was a subject of at least some of their meetings with Sullāqā. Indeed, the Master of the Sacred Palace also monitored the Ethiopian community of Rome in the mid-sixteenth century.[110] Such connections are a further indication of how personnel from the inquisition and prelates with interests in eastern Christianity often overlapped.

Eastern Christianity, Catholic Orientalism 75

Besides these inquisitors, Sullāqā may have received advice from other quarters when drafting his profession of faith. In his letter to Julius III, Sullāqā also greeted Yoḥannes, the Ethiopian chaplain of Gian Pietro Carafa, Simeon, the Maronite bishop of Beirut, as well as another Maronite named George.[111] Sullāqā thanked these three for their "teachings" and referred to himself as their "pupil".[112] Since such language establishes a pupil–teacher relationship, we might assume that these Christians from the east similarly assisted the patriarch in crafting a profession of faith that was acceptable to his Roman hosts.[113]

Sullāqā's embassy therefore offers additional proof of the privileged role of Maronites and Ethiopians as go-betweens for Rome and the eastern Churches in the mid-sixteenth century. Later events during Sullāqā's stay in Rome also reflect themes discussed throughout this chapter. On 20 February 1553, Bernardino Maffei represented Sullāqā's case to the consistory of cardinals. There, he alerted his colleagues to Sullāqā's report that copies "of the four [ecumenical] councils in huge tomes, as well as books by the ancient Church Fathers that we lack here, such as those by Ephrem [Syrus] and others" could be found in Syria.[114] Just as in Felice da Venezia's mission to the Maronites in 1543, and Cervini's collaborations with Tasfā Ṣeyon, prelates in Rome therefore saw their contacts with the Church of the East as an opportunity to expand Catholic knowledge of church history. The value of these conciliar and patristic texts to polemics against Protestantism was unlikely to have been far from their minds, not least given Bernardino Maffei's earlier collaborations with Cervini to use Ethiopic material to this end.[115]

After receiving his profession of faith, Julius III invested Sullāqā with the pallium on 28 April 1553, making him the first 'Chaldean' Patriarch of Mosul.[116] Sullāqā then returned to the Levant with two Dominicans, Ambrogio Buttigeg and Antonino Zahara, reaching Amida (Diyarbakir) by December 1553. There they set about announcing the union to Rome, with Buttigeg even preaching to the people of Aleppo in Latin and Arabic during the Advent of 1554.[117] As Lucy Parker has argued, Sullāqā's actions upon his return to the Levant contradict much earlier historiography about this patriarch. Most studies have claimed that he offered his profession of faith in Rome under duress, a claim that depends on regarding as more authentic the Syriac profession of faith that was written on Sullāqā's behalf by 'Abd-Isho. By contrast, Sullāqā's attempts to drum up support for union in the east, as well as what we might assume was his support for Buttigeg's preaching, instead suggest that Sullāqā was committed to Catholicising some aspects of his Church. It is simply that the Catholicism that Sullāqā sought to institute was a distinctively Chaldean, rather than Roman, understanding of what Catholicism meant, which saw no contradiction in balancing obedience to Rome with the observance of local customs, and the veneration of local saints such as Nestorius who had been condemned by Rome.[118]

Finally, it is worth noting that Sullāqā did not seek to conceal his new connections to Rome from the Ottomans. His return journey to the Levant was determined by attempts to seek approval of the union with Rome

76 *Eastern Christianity, Catholic Orientalism*

from Sultan Suleiman I (1520–1566). He attempted to find Suleiman first in Istanbul, and then travelled to meet him in Aleppo, apparently obtaining letters favourable to the new order that he had created.[119] As such, it appears that the Ottoman central government did not consider it a threat that a new church loyal to Rome had come into existence in the Levant. Instead, Sullāqā encountered fiercest resistance from other Christians in the east. Sullāqā's rival for the patriarchate, Simon VII, was less than pleased with his actions. In the evocative terms used by Ambrogio Buttigeg, Simon therefore "bought Sullāqā's blood" by bribing the local governor of Mosul, leading to Sullāqa's execution in 1555.[120] For his part, Buttigeg spent most of the rest of his life attempting to extend the Chaldean Church's reach into India, dying in Cochin in 1558.[121]

VII. Conclusion

Like many other figures encountered in this chapter, there is still much more to know about Ambrogio Buttigeg. Future studies will doubtless amend and eventually replace the panorama of collaborations between Maronites, eastern Christians, and Catholic Orientalists during the cardinalate of Marcello Cervini that has been offered here. However, I hope that the evidence presented in this chapter has shown the importance of the years between 1539 and 1555 to the history of exchanges between Rome and Churches from the Levant and Africa. With the exception of the Maronites and Ethiopians, there had been little, if any direct contact between Rome and the eastern Churches after the Council of Ferrara-Florence. But in this sixteen-year period, the Maronites cemented their ties to Rome, Ethiopian pilgrims convinced the Jesuits to send a mission to their homeland, and the patriarchs of two (the Syrian Orthodox and Chaldean), if not three (Armenian) eastern Churches agreed a union with the papacy. Events in Cervini's cardinalate therefore led to defining moments in the later histories of these Churches, such as the adoption of Catholicism as the state religion of Ethiopia between 1626 and 1632, the establishment of the Chaldean Church in Mesopotamia and India, and the collaboration of the Jacobite Patriarch Ignatius Ni'matallah on the reforms that led to the Gregorian Calendar.[122] Where the Maronites differ from these other Churches is that the Maronite hierarchy has maintained an unbroken union to Rome from the thirteenth century, through the early modern period, and into the present. The unions with other Churches negotiated during Cervini's cardinalate were rather more fleeting. That between Rome and the Chaldeans lasted for about a century, for example, while Catholicism was the state religion of Ethiopia for just six years. Over time, the preservation of union by the Maronites cemented their status as privileged interlocutors between Rome and the eastern Churches, a status that we have seen that they had previously shared with the Ethiopians in the mid-sixteenth century.

As such, the years between 1539 and 1555 can be regarded as a pivotal period in the strictest sense of that term. During these years exchanges

Eastern Christianity, Catholic Orientalism 77

between Rome and the eastern Churches departed in a new direction, after representatives of various Churches travelled to Rome for a wide variety of reasons. Tasfā Ṣeyon came to Rome to enlist Catholic support in the reconstruction of Ethiopia, for example, Moses of Mardin was sent to Italy to arrange a church union and to make use of the printing press, while Sullāqā headed west to obtain the pope's support in a contested election in Mesopotamia. As we have seen, the key to understanding these missions is to place them in the local context of each Church, and so, as far as is possible, to assess them through their eyes of their eastern Christian protagonists. Such a change of perspective not only allows for fresh interpretations of familiar material, but also encourages a search for new sources, both in western archives, and repositories in Africa and the Levant. The work of John-Paul Ghobrial, Verena Krebs, and Lucy Parker offer models in this regard.[123]

However, it is important to stress once more that incorporating eastern Christian perspectives ought not lead us to overlook Catholic views on these exchanges. Indeed, the years of Cervini's cardinalate were also a part of a pivotal time in Rome's perception of Christians from Africa in the Levant. In the first two chapters of this book, we saw how Catholics in Rome were willing to accept the orthodoxy of the Maronites despite significant evidence to the contrary. Then, in Chapter 3, we saw how this attitude changed between 1523 and 1550, when suspicion initially created by the Reformation led Catholics to doubt the orthodoxy of the Maronites, to insist on greater proofs of their faith, and to search Maronite history and literature for new tools in polemic against Protestantism. This chapter has provided many examples that show how preoccupations with Protestantism consistently pushed Catholic exchanges with eastern Christians in the same direction. These various strands can now be woven into a summary of how and why Roman approaches to non-Latin Christians changed between the opening of the Council of Ferrara-Florence in 1438 and Cervini's death in 1555.

The medieval Catholic Church had regarded non-Latin Christians as the principal enemies of the faith, as expressed in the vast body of anti-Greek polemic built up during that time. This attitude was challenged by the various unions negotiated at the Council of Ferrara-Florence, not least because Catholics in the early modern period may not always have known that many Churches soon defected from the unions that they had made there.[124] The Council of Ferrara-Florence therefore accumulated a stock of goodwill towards eastern Christianity in the Catholic world that lasted into the early sixteenth century, which does much to explain the rise of Oriental studies in Rome and the positive disposition towards the Maronites shown by Leo X. But the sources that we have just studied show that all of this changed with the Reformation. Through the ready possibility for exchange offered by places like Santo Stefano, and an unprecedented increase in eastern Christian embassies to Rome, a generation of Catholics that had been made more alert to the boundaries of orthodoxy by Protestantism quickly became aware that the rites and doctrines of the eastern Churches had

78   *Eastern Christianity, Catholic Orientalism*

less in common with Rome than they had been led to expect. This painful realisation led to deepening suspicion of eastern Christians and a growing demand for proof of their Catholicity, such as professions of faith and re-ordination, which were meant to determine whether pilgrims and travellers from the east who presented themselves as Catholics really deserved to be treated as such. We have seen this suspicion and the consequent demands for proof in the careers of Tasfā Ṣeyon, Yoḥannes the Ethiopian, and Moses of Mardin, as well as in the documents relating to the Maronites that were composed in Rome between 1542 and 1544. The shift in Catholic attitudes towards eastern Christians and their place in Christendom between Leo X and Paul III therefore suggests that the Reformation was a decisive factor in Rome's relations with Christians in the Middle East and Africa in the early modern period. Through these sources, we see that the multiplying definitions of orthodoxy and its rigorous enforcement that were sparked by the Reformation shaped Catholic exchanges with eastern Christians as well as with Protestants. This policing of the faith of eastern Christians inside and outside the Catholic world was paralleled by an increasing exploration of eastern Christian sources, which when vetted and approved were put to use in religious polemics against Protestantism. We see therefore that eastern Christians were firmly incorporated into the history of the Reformation, making them actors in a chapter in the history of Christianity that has largely been conceived on a western scale.

As has been stressed already, the inclusion of eastern Christianity into the Catholic world has largely been studied as a post-Trent phenomenon. This argument has been shaped by the huge archives that exist for this later period, especially that of Propaganda Fide. Cervini's correspondence as such provides a counterweight to these collections, demonstrating that trends that apparently define Catholic exchanges with eastern Christianity after Trent had been developed before and during this council. For example, it would be short-sighted to refer to the Maronite College as a Tridentine innovation when Musa al-Akkari had already sought such an educational programme in 1542, to regard the Medici Oriental Press as unprecedented in light of Roman patronage of Syriac and Ge'ez printing between 1546 and 1555, or to think that eastern Christians were only asked for confessions of faith after Trent, when these had been sought from Moses of Mardin in 1552 and Sullāqā in 1553. Rather than breaking from Rome's earlier approaches to the eastern Churches, the years between the Council of Trent and the foundation of Propaganda Fide (1622) instead mark the institutionalisation of policies that had been experimented with since the Council of Ferrara-Florence, most intensely between 1539 and 1555. Arguably, it could not be otherwise. The foundation of an institution tends not to mark the beginning of a policy or movement, but rather the moment of its acceptance after a much longer history of false starts and dead ends.

That said, it is also essential to be cautious of misconceptions that can generated by Cervini's correspondence. Using documents written by cardinals

Eastern Christianity, Catholic Orientalism 79

like Cervini might lead to the assumption that Maronite exchanges with Catholics were only concerned with confessional themes, such as the desire for papal confirmation on the part of the Maronites, or by anxiety about the Reformation for Catholics. The next chapter will outline the limitations of confession as an explanatory framework, drawing attention to how Musa al-Akkari sought to attract Habsburg interest in the Maronites as anti-Ottoman agents.

Notes

1 Giorgio Levi della Vida, *Ricerche sulla formazione del più antico fondo dei manoscritti orientali della Biblioteca Vaticana* (Vatican City: Biblioteca Apostolica Vaticana, 1939); Robert J. Wilkinson, *Orientalism, Aramaic and Kabbalah in the Catholic Reformation. The First Printing of the Syriac New Testament* (Leiden: Brill, 2007).
2 Most obviously Emily Michelson and Matthew Coneys, eds, *A Companion to Religious Minorities in Early Modern Rome* (Leiden: Brill, 2020); see also works by Pier Giorgio Borbone, Robert Clines, Aurélien Girard, András Mércz, Lucy Parker, and Matteo Salvadore listed in the Bibliography.
3 See Irene Fosi, "The Plural City: Urban Spaces and Foreign Communities," in *A Companion to Early Modern Rome, 1492–1692*, ed. Pamela M. James, Barbara Wisch, and Simon Ditchfield (Leiden: Brill, 2019), 169–83; and for a later period, eadem, *Convertire lo straniero. Forestieri e Inquisizione a Roma in età moderna* (Rome: Viella, 2011).
4 Matteo Salvadore, *The African Prester John and the Birth of Ethiopian-European Relations, 1402–1555* (London: Routledge, 2017); Sam Kennerley, "Ethiopian Christians in Rome, c.1400–c.1700," in *A Companion to Religious Minorities in Early Modern Rome*, 142–68; Verena Krebs, *Medieval Ethiopian Kingship, Craft, and Diplomacy with Latin Europe* (London: Palgrave, 2021).
5 Salvatore Tedeschi, "Etiopi e Copti al Concilio di Firenze," *Annuarium Historiae Conciliorum* 21 (1989): 400.
6 See below, Chapter 4:IV and 4:VII.
7 Matteo Salvadore, "African Cosmopolitanism in the early modern Mediterranean: the diasporic life of Yohannes, the Ethiopian pilgrim who became a Counter-Reformation bishop," *Journal of African History* 58 (2017): 61–83.
8 Kennerley, "Ethiopian Christians," 145.
9 Delio Vania Proverbio, "Santo Stefano degli Abissini: Una breve rivisitazione," *La parola del passato* 69 (2011): 50–68.
10 Kennerley, "Ethiopian Christians," 160–1.
11 Ibid., 149–57; Matteo Salvadore and James De Lorenzi, "An Ethiopian Scholar in Tridentine Rome: Täsfä Ṣeyon and the Birth of Orientalism," *Itinerario* 45 (2021): 17–46.
12 Kennerley, "Ethiopian Christians," 147–9.
13 CC 19, 28r.
14 "[Q]uel arcivescovo o vescovo Maronita". Ibid., 28r.
15 See above, Chapter 3:IV–V.
16 Simeon had also copied a "Kalendarium Sanctorum, per integrum annum, additis variis Hymnis, & Benedictionibus" in Rome on 12 April 1543. See Stefano Evodio Assemani, *Bibliothecae Mediceae Laurentianae et Palatinae codicum manuscriptorum orientalium catalogus* (Florence: ex Typographio Albiziniano 1742), 91–2.
17 Their translation of the Mass over June and July 1547 is discussed (in date order) in Vat.lat. 6177.2, 313r, 323r, 317r, 321r; Vat.lat.6178, 321r.

80 Eastern Christianity, Catholic Orientalism

18 *Modus baptizandi, preces et benedictiones quibus ecclesia Ethiopum utitur [...] orationes quibus iidem utuntur in sacramento Baptismi et confirmationis [...] Missa qua communiter utuntur, quae etiam Canon universalis appellatur* (Rome: Antonio Blado, 1549). Here the Ethiopic Mass is accompanied by a Latin version of the Ethiopic order of baptism translated by Tasfā and edited by another Catholic scholar named Bernardino Sander.

19 "Annotationes quaedam in praecedentes libros," in ibid., [sig]ci.r–cii.v. Tasfā's preface is edited in Renato Lefevre, "Documenti e notizie su Tasfā Ṣeyon e la sua attività romana nel sec. XVI," *Rassegna di Studi Etiopici* 24 (1969–1970): 94–6.

20 Lucy Parker, "The Ambiguities of Belief and Belonging: Catholicism and the Church of the East in the Sixteenth Century," *English Historical Review* 133 (2018): 1420–45.

21 *Modus baptizandi*, [sig]ci.v–[sig]cii.v.

22 Contrast with the chaplain Yoḥannes, who is the subject of Salvadore, "African Cosmopolitanism" as well as Samantha Kelly and Dennis Nosnitsin, "The Two Yoḥanneses of Santo Stefano degli Abissini, Rome: Reconstructing Biography and Cross-Cultural Encounter through Manuscript Evidence," *Manuscript Studies* 2 (2017): 392–426.

23 "[C]atholici sumus et esse volumus [...] tanquam scismatici ab omnibus fere europeis iudicamur". Lefevre, "Documenti e notizie su Tasfā Ṣeyon," 94–5.

24 Kennerley, "Ethiopian Christians," 156.

25 Andreu Martínez d'Alòs-Moner, *Envoys of a Human God: The Jesuit Mission to Christian Ethiopia, 1557–1632* (Leiden: Brill, 2015), 308–23.

26 Theobald Freudenberger, "Das Konzil von Trient und das Ehescheidungsrecht der Ostkirche," in *Wegzeichen: Festgabe von Prof. Dr. Hermengild M. Biedermann OSA*, ed. Ernst Chr. Suttner and Coelestin Patock (Würzburg: Augustinus-Verlag, 1971), 153–63; Vittorio Peri, "Il Concilio di Trento e la Chiesa greca," in *Il Concilio di Trento nella prospettiva del terzo millennio*, ed. Giuseppe Alberigo and Iginio Rogger (Brescia: Morcelliana, 1997), 403–41.

27 *Concilium Tridentinum Diariorum, Actorum, Epistularum Tractatum nova collectio*, ed. Theobald Freudenberger (Freiburg-im-Breisgau: Herder, 1974), 6/III:419–20, 452, 464, 466, 476, 502–3, 512, 514–15, 521.

28 Vat.lat. 6177.2, 328r. On him see now Benedetto Clausi and Santo Lucà, eds, *Il "sapientissimo calabro". Guglielmo Sirleto nel V centenario della nascita (1514–2014)* (Rome: Università degli Studi di Roma 'Tor Vergata', 2018).

29 On him see Santo Lucà, "Guglielmo Sirleto e Francisco Torres," in *Il "sapientissimo calabro"*, 533–602.

30 Vat.lat. 6177.2, 310r. For other manuscripts owned by Tasfā, see Rafał Zarzeczny, "Su due manoscritti etiopici della Biblioteca Casanatense a Roma," in *Aethiopia fortitude eius. Studi in onore di monsignor Osvaldo Raineri*, ed. Rafał Zarzeczny (Rome: Pontificio Istituto Orientale, 2015), 501–37.

31 Vat.lat. 6178, 116r and 117r. Unfortunately, I have been unable to find the correspondence between Tasfā and Cervini.

32 Vat.lat. 6177.1, 118r–119r.

33 These claims are noted, but not approved, in Levi della Vida, *Ricerche*, 140.

34 Ian Felce, *William Morris and the Icelandic Sagas* (Cambridge: D.S. Brewer, 2019), 11–12.

35 On this term, see John-Paul Ghobrial, "The Archive of Orientalism and its Keepers: Re-Imagining the Histories of Arabic Manuscripts in Early Modern Europe," *Past & Present* 230 (2016): 90–111. This other translator was Yoḥannes, the Ethiopian chaplain of Gian Pietro Carafa. See Lefevre, "Documenti e notizie," 85.

36 Vat.lat.6178, 118r, 119r, 122r; Vat.lat.6177.2, 313r. The canon is number 37 of the Ethiopic tradition, which is translated into Italian in Mauro Da Leonessa, "La versione etiopica dei canoni apocrifi del concilio di Nicea secondo i codici vaticani ed il fiorentino," *Rassegna di Studi Etiopici* 2 (1942): 76–7.

Eastern Christianity, Catholic Orientalism 81

37 Sylvain Grébaut and Eugene Tisserant, *Codices aetiopici Vaticani et Borgiani, Barbarinus orientalis 2, Rossianus 865* (Vatican City: Biblioteca Vaticana, 1935), 2:15.

38 "Ego interim cum magno adhuc desiderio tenerer priorem interpretationem cum alio si possem aliquando recognoscere, et conferre, incidi in Paulum Vrsinum neophytum natione Turcam, qui quia erat studiis Arabicae, et aliarum linguarum imbutus, et Latine, atque Italice mediocriter loqui didicerat, effeci quod volebam. Recognita, et collata sunt omnia, et correcta non pauca. Accessit ad hanc recognitionem aliud exemplar Arabicum vetustum ex Bibliotheca pontificis Marcelli 2. quod ita cum Alexandrino conueniebat, vt plane videretur vtrumque ex eodem exemplari descriptum, licet in exemplari Marcelli aliquot paginas anteriores vetustas consumpsisset". *Apostolicarum constitutionum et Catholicae doctrinae Clementis Romani libri VIII [...] Accesserunt Canones Concilii Nicaeni LXXX ex Arabico in Latinum conuersi et Responsa Nicolai 1 ad consulta Bulgarorum*, ed. and trans. Francisco Torres and Paolo Orsini (Antwerp: Christophe Plantin, 1578), 2. Further information about Paolo Orsini can be found in Robert Jones, *Learning Arabic in Renaissance Europe (1505–1624)* (Leiden, Brill, 2020), 66–8. For later interest in these Arabic canons, see also Aurélien Girard, "Was an Eastern Scholar Necessarily a Cultural Broker in Early Modern Europe? Faustus Naironus (1628–1711), the Christian East, and Oriental Studies," in *Confessionalisation and Erudition in Early Modern Europe: An Episode in the History of the Humanities*, ed. Nicholas Hardy and Dmitri Levitin (Oxford: Oxford University Press, 2019), 251–3.

39 Lefevre, "Documenti e notizie su Tasfā Ṣeyon," 91.

40 "Ego sane habui cum eo, & omnibus suis magnam familiaritatem, & varios saepe sermones de rebus Persarum, & Tartarorum, quibus valde me delectavit; sed plura fuerunt & gravia, quae de Religione inter nos disseruimus [...] Magna animo agitabat, non sine gravibus rationibus; sed tempora impediebant eius conatus. Deus Omnipotens eum comitetur". Assemani, *Bibliothecae Mediceae Laurentianae et Palatinae codicum manuscriptorum orientalium catalogus*, 56–7.

41 *Chaldeae seu Aethiopicae linguae institutiones: Omnium Aethiopiae regum [...] libellus* (Rome: Valerio Dorico, 1552), [sig.]ii.r–iii.r.

42 Bent Juel-Jensen, "Potken's *Psalter* and Tesfa Tsion's *New Testament, Modus baptizandi* and *Missal*," *Bodleian Library Record* 15 (1996): 480–96; Kennerley, "Ethiopian Christians," 152–7; Sachet, *Publishing for the Popes*, 174–9.

43 Rome: Biblioteca Casanatense, Rari 947, as identified in Sachet, *Publishing for the Popes*, 178 n.104.

44 Heleen Murre-van den Berg, "Syriac Christianity," in *The Blackwell Companion to Eastern Christianity*, ed. Ken Parry (Oxford: Basil Blackwell, 2007), 252–6; Joseph Gill, *The Council of Florence* (Cambridge: Cambridge University Press, 1959), 307–35.

45 Giacomo Cardinali, "Ritratto di Marcello Cervini *en orientaliste* (con precisazioni alle vicende di Petrus Damascenus, Mose di Mardin ed Heliodorus Niger)," *Bibliotheque d'Humanisme et Renaissance* 80 (2018): 79–83. Cardinali edited Widmanstetter's letters to Cervini and Massarelli, in which the events recounted here are described, in ibid., 338–9.

46 Wilkinson, *Orientalism, Aramaic and Kabbalah*, 137–69, esp. 143–4.

47 Widmanstetter's copy of the Syriac Gospels picks out Simeon's name with the note "Symeon Episcopus Libani, praeceptor meus", Munich: Bayerische Staatsbibliothek, Rar. 155, [sig]a***3.v.

48 Wilkinson, *Orientalism, Aramaic and Kabbalah*, 145–6.

49 *Liber sacrosancti Evangelii de Iesu Christo Domino & Deo nostro* (Vienna: Michael Zimmerman, 1555), [sig]a****1r.

50 Cardinali, "Ritratto di Marcello Cervini *en orientaliste*," 79–82, 338.

82 Eastern Christianity, Catholic Orientalism

51 Ibid., 338.
52 For a later period when these visitors were more common, see Renate Dürr, "The World in the German Hinterlands: Early Modern German History Entangled," *Sixteenth Century Journal* 50 (2019): 148–55.
53 Which was the charge adduced by Widmanstetter in his letter to Massarelli. See Cardinali, "Ritratto di Marcello Cervini *en orientaliste*," 339.
54 Ignace Antoine II Hayek, *Le relazioni della Chiesa Siro-giacobita con la Santa Sede dal 1143 al 1656*, ed. Pier Giorgio Borbone and Jimmy Daccache (Paris: Geunther, 2015), 62–5; Cardinali, "Ritratto di Marcello Cervini *en orientaliste*," 84–6 and 341.
55 London: British Library, Harley 5512. Studied in J. Leroy, "Une copie syriaque du Missale Romanum de Paul III et son arrière-plan historique," *Mélanges de l'Université Saint-Joseph*, 46 (1970–1971): 355–82.
56 As observed in Wilkinson, *Orientalism, Aramaic and Kabbalah*, 67.
57 Leroy, "Une copie syriaque du Missale Romanum de Paul III," 359–60.
58 Ibid., 361–2.
59 Cardinali, "Ritratto di Marcello Cervini *en orientaliste*," 87–9 and 340.
60 Ibid., 340.
61 Parker, "Ambiguities of Belief and Belonging," 1431–2; Lucy Parker, "The Interconnected Histories of the Syriac Churches in the Sixteenth Century," forthcoming in *The Journal of Ecclesiastical History*.
62 This letter of 22 April 1550 is printed in Hayek, *Le relazioni della Chiesa Siro-giacobita con la Santa Sede*, 176.
63 Printed in Cardinali, "Ritratto di Marcello Cervini *en orientaliste*," 341. Might the lacuna observed in this letter be "[harum litterar]um exhibitor"?
64 Sachet, *Publishing for the Popes*, 179.
65 CC 48, 53r–53v. Quoted in Sachet, *Publishing for the Popes*, 179 n.108.
66 Hayek, *Le relazioni della Chiesa Siro-giacobita con la Santa Sede*, 65; see now Cardinali, "Ritratto di Marcello Cervini *en orientaliste*," 90–8; Sachet, *Publishing for the Popes*, 180.
67 Cardinali, "Ritratto di Marcello Cervini *en orientaliste*," 93–4.
68 Sachet, *Publishing for the Popes*, 178 n.103.
69 Hayek, *Le relazioni della Chiesa Siro-giacobita con la Santa Sede*, 65.
70 CC 34, 120r–129v. The manicules can be found in ibid., 127v and 128r.
71 This letter of 26 May 1553 is printed in Hayek, *Le relazioni della Chiesa Siro-giacobita con la Santa Sede*, 177–83.
72 Studied in ibid., 72–3.
73 On him, see Wim François, "Andreas Masius (1514–1573): Humanist, Exegete, and Syriac Scholar," *Journal of Eastern Christian Studies*, 61 (2009): 199–244. The letter is printed in Andreas Müller, *Symbolae syriacae* (Berlin: ex officina Rungiana, 1673), 6–8.
74 Ibid., 6–7.
75 For instance Wilkinson, *Orientalism, Aramaic and Kabbalah*, 89–90 and 90 n.102.
76 Salvadore, "African Cosmopolitanism," 73–4.
77 Müller, *Symbolae syriacae*, 7–8. From Moses's later work as a copyist during his second sojourn in Europe, it would appear that he also carried other books with him besides this New Testament that would have served as exemplars. Manuscripts copied by Moses are listed in Pier Giorgio Borbone, "Monsignore Vescovo di Soria, also Known as Moses of Mardin, Scribe and Book Collector," *ХРИСТІАНСКІЙ ВОСТОКЪ* 8 (2017): 99–113.
78 András Mércz, "The Coat of Arms of Moses of Mardin," *Hugoye* 22 (2019): 373.
79 "[E]retico pertinace". For Macarius's execution, see Domenico Orano, *Liberi pensatori bruciati in Roma dal XVI al XVIII secolo* (Livorno: Bastogi, 1904), 13. For other examples of eastern Christians tried by Catholic inquisitions, see

Stathis Birtachas, "Religious dissent and its repression in Venice's Maritime State: the case of Cyrpus (mid-sixteenth century)," in *Le fonti della storia dell'Italia preunitaria: casi di studio per la loro analisi e 'valorizzazione'*, ed. Gerassimos D. Pagratis (Athens: Papazissis Publishers, 2019), 575–600; Vincenzo Lavenia, "*Quasi hereticus*. Lo scisma nella riflessione degli inquistori dell'età moderna," *Mélanges de l'École française de Rome. Italie et Méditerranée modernes et contemporaines*, 126:2 (2014), accessible online at: https://doi.org/10.4000/mefrim.1838; José M. Floristán, "Atanasio Rasia: Atanasio de Acrida? Proceso ante el Santo Oficio," in *Aspetti e momenti dell'albanologia contemporanea*, ed. Matteo Mandalà and Gëzim Gurga (Tirana: Naimi, 2019), 83–118; José M. Floristán, "Clero griego ante el Santo Oficio (I): Anastasio Ventura (1577), Nicéforo de Esfigmenu (1621) y Dionisio Condilis de Patmos (1657)," *Erytheia* 40 (2019): 267–305; José M. Floristán, "Clero griego ante el Santo Oficio (II): Manuel Accidas (1542) e Hilarión Cuculis (1699)," *Erytheia* 41 (2020): 159–81.
80 Müller, *Symbolae syriacae*, 10.
81 Borbone, "Monsignore Vescovo di Soria," 100–1. Beccadelli was also interested in Ethiopia, see Gabriele Natta, "L'enigma dell'Etiopia nel Rinascimento Italiano: Ludovico Beccadelli tra inquietudini religiose e orizzonti globali," *Rinascimento* 55 (2015): 275–309.
82 Borbone, "Monsignore Vescovo di Soria," 85–6.
83 *Liber sacrosancti Evangelii de Iesu Christo Domino & Deo nostro* (Vienna: Michael Zimmerman, 1555). The making of this book is the subject of Wilkinson, *Orientalism, Aramaic and Kabbalah*.
84 Mércz, "The Coat of Arms of Moses of Mardin," 353.
85 See Widmanstetter's letter to Georg Gienger and Jacobus Jonas in *Liber sacrosancti Evangelii*, [sig]KK3.r–KK4.v.
86 Masius to Postel, 13 April 1554. "Is habet in animo bibliotecham instituere insignem, atque eam ad rem conquirit undequaque libros in omni lingua, etiam arabicos". Quoted in Borbone, "Monsignore Vescovo di Soria," 86 n.35.
87 Ibid., 88.
88 See in general ibid., 79–98.
89 Anna Sirinian, "La presenza degli Armeni nella Roma medievale: Prime testimonianze manoscritte ed epigrafiche (con un'iscrizione inedita del XVI secolo)," *Atti della Pontificia Accademia romana di archeologia. Rendiconti* 86 (2013/14): 7–9.
90 Gill, *The Council of Florence*, 307.
91 For visits of Armenian prelates to Europe between 1439 and 1548, see also L.B. Zekiyan, "Le colonie armene del medio evo in Italia e le relazioni culturali italo-armene," in *Atti del primo Simposio internazionale di arte armene*, ed. Giulio Ieni and Levon B. Zekiyan (Venice: Toplitografia armena, 1975), 905–7 and 921–2.
92 Gabriella Uluhogian, "Il *Salterio* di Abgar T'oxat'ec'i (a. 1565) e l'avvio degli studi armenistici presso la Biblioteca Ambrosiana di Milano," in *Collectanea Armeniaca*, ed. Rosa Bianca Finazzi and Anna Sirinian (Milan: Biblioteca Ambrosiana, 2016), 321.
93 Francesca Di Giovanni, Sergio Pagano and Giuseppina Roselli, eds, *Guida delle fonti per la storia dell'Africa del Nord, Asia e Oceania nell'Archivio Segreto Vaticano* (Vatican City: Archivio Segreto Vaticano, 2005), 222.
94 Ibid., 266.
95 Assemani, *Bibliothecae Mediceae Laurentianae et Palatinae codicum manuscriptorum orientalium catalogus*, 59–61.
96 "Ego sane habui cum eo, et omnibus suis magnam familiaritatem, et varios saepe sermones de rebus Persarum, et Tartarorum, quibus valde me delectavit; sed plura fuerunt & gravia, quae de religione inter nos disseruimus". Ibid., 60.

84 *Eastern Christianity, Catholic Orientalism*

97 Ibid., 59–61. The manuscript has been edited and analysed in Giuseppe Messina, *Notizia su un diatessaron persiano* (Rome: Pontificio Istituto Biblico, 1943); Giuseppe Messina, *Diatessaron persiano* (Rome: Pontificio Istituto Biblico, 1951). My thanks to Dr Tim Greenwood (University of St Andrews) for alerting me to the existence of this evidence.

98 "Eadem die R.[mus] Marcellus tituli Sancte Crucis in Hierusalem presbiter Cardinalis fecit uerbum de quodam patriarca Armeno qui superioribus diebus ad vrbem uenerat et qui se offerebat praestare obedientiam S.[ti] S. et S.[te] R. Ecclesiae petens electionem de persona sua in patriarcham Armenie a populo celebrata per S.[tem] S. approbari. Et fuit commissum negocium eidem R.[mo] Marcello Car.[li] nec non R.[mis] de Crescentio et Sfrondato ad cogitandum quid super hoc esset agendum et Ste S. referendum". AAV: Arch. Concist., Acta Vicecanc. 7, 28v.

99 Gregorio Petrowicz, "Il Patriarca di Ecimiazin Stefano V Salmastetzì (1541?–1552)," *Orientalia Christiana Periodica* 28 (1962): 365–7.

100 Ibid., 375–6.

101 Ibid., 373–401; Assemani, *Bibliothecae Mediceae Laurentianae et Palatinae codicum manuscriptorum orientalium catalogus*, 60.

102 Giuseppe Beltrami, *La Chiesa Caldea nel secolo dell'Unione* (Rome: Pontificium Institutum Orientalium Studiorum, 1933), 2–5.

103 Herman Teule, "Les professions de foi de Jean Sullaqa, premier patriarche chaldéen, et de son successeur 'Abdisho d-Gazarta," in *L'Union a l'épreuve du formulaire. Professions de foi entre églises d'Orient et d'Occident (XIIIe–XVIIIe siècle)*, ed. Marie-Helene Blanchet and Frederic Gabriel (Leuven: Peeters, 2016), 259–63.

104 For the former (the received opinion), see, for instance, Beltrami, *La Chiesa Caldea*, 2; for the latter, see Parker, "Ambiguities of Belief and Belonging," 1427.

105 Teule, "Les professions de foi de Jean Sullaqa," 264–5.

106 On him, see now too Margherita Farina, "A New Autobiograph by 'Abdīšō Marūn. Renaissance Rome and the Syriac Churches," *Journal of Eastern Christian Studies* 70 (2018): 241–56.

107 Teule, "Les professions de foi de Jean Sullaqa," 266–8; Parker, "Ambiguities of Belief and Belonging," 1421.

108 Teule, "Les professions de foi de Jean Sullaqa," 265–6; Parker, "Ambiguities of Belief and Belonging," 1430–2.

109 The letter is printed in Beltrami, *La Chiesa Caldea*, 146–8, and its personalities identified in Parker, "Ambiguities of Belief and Belonging," 1430–2.

110 Kennerley, "Ethiopian Christians in Rome," 151 n.45.

111 This might be the same George who communicated Musa al-Akkari's letter of 19 September 1543 to Cervini, see above Chapter 3:IV.

112 "[V]ostro discepolo […] tuoi buoni ammaestramenti". Beltrami, *La Chiesa Caldea*, 148.

113 Parker, "Ambiguities of Belief and Belonging," 1431–2 is more reserved in this regard.

114 "Addit etiam [Sullāqā] illic quattuor concilia magna magnis volumnibus haberi atque ea et alios etiam libros veterum doctorum, quibus hic caremus, quales sunt Ephrem etc". W. van Gulik, "Die Konsistorialakten über die Begründung des uniert-chaldäischen Patriarchates von Mosul unter Papst Julius III," *Oriens Christianus* 4 (1904): 277.

115 See above, Chapter 4:III.

116 van Gulik, "Die Konsistorialakten," 277.

117 Beltrami, *La Chiesa Caldea*, 150.

118 Parker, "Ambiguities of Belief and Belonging," 1429–45.

119 Beltrami, *La Chiesa Caldea*, 147.

Eastern Christianity, Catholic Orientalism 85

120 "[E]mit sanguinem eius Simonis Sulachae magna pecuniarum quantitate, plusquam ter mille ducatos aureos dans gubernatori Musal". Ibid., 149.

121 Ibid., 27–58.

122 d'Alòs-Moner, *Envoys of a Human God*, 308–23; Beltrami, *La Chiesa Caldea*, 27–137; Giorgio Levi della Vida, *Documenti intorno alle relazioni delle chiese orientali con la S. Sede durante il pontificato di Gregorio XIII* (Vatican City: Biblioteca Apostolica Vaticana, 1948), 1–113; Pier Giorgio Borbone, "From Tur 'Abdin to Rome: The Syro-Orthodox Presence in Sixteenth-Century Rome", in *Syriac in its Multi-Cultural Context*, ed. Herman Teule et al (Leuven: Peeters, 2017), 277–88; Pier Giorgio Borbone and Margherita Farina, "New Documents concerning Patriarch Ignatius Na'matallah (Mardin, ca. 1515– Bracciano, near Rome, 1587)," *Egitto e Vicino Oriente* 37 (2014): 179–89.

123 See the Bibliography for works by these authors.

124 The Greek Orthodox Church formally rejected Florence in 1484, see Gill, *The Council of Florence*, 410–11. The reception of Florence among the Jacobites is still unclear. Hayek, *Le relazioni della Chiesa Siro-giacobita con la Santa Sede*, 43–5 was unsure of the reception of Florence, but cites examples of Jacobite patriarchs who claimed to follow the union in the later sixteenth century. In one of his polemical works, al-Qilāʿi accused the Jacobites of detaining the legates who returned from Florence and having them murdered. See Joseph Moukarzel, *Gabriel Ibn al-Qilāʿi († c. 1516). Approche biographique et etude du corpus* (Jounieh: PUSEK, 2007), 265.

5 The Maronites as anti-Ottoman agents

Their correspondence with Emperor Charles V (1519–1556)

I. Introduction

Consistent with most recent research, the previous chapters of this book have explored the place of the Maronites in the religious history of the early modern Mediterranean. However, the following chapter will concentrate on a different theme. It will argue that the Maronites not only sought ever-closer religious union with Rome during the early Reformation, but that they even attempted to form military alliances with Catholic rulers like Charles V (1519–1556). As such, this chapter proposes a more capacious interpretation of eastern Christian contacts with Europe, in which eastern Christians appear not only as alms-collectors, scholars, pilgrims, and clerical envoys, but also as soldiers, spies, and saboteurs.

The key source for this argument is the last letter that Patriarch Musa al-Akkari is known to have sent to Cervini. This chapter will first investigate the characters and context of this letter, tackling themes such as western knowledge of Persia, and Maronite contacts with Latin agents in Syria and Lebanon. Discussion of these topics will set the stage for an analysis of Musa's correspondence with Emperor Charles V, and so of the political as well as religious connections that the Maronites established with Catholic powers in the mid-sixteenth century.

II. The letter of 1550: Characters and context

The last letter that Patriarch Musa al-Akkari is known to have sent Cervini is dated to 1 January 1550. The New Year of 1550 marked the end of a miserable two months for the patriarch, who had spent this period imprisoned at the behest of the *sanjakbey* of Tripoli.[1] Musa informed Cervini that he had been detained by this Ottoman official on the charge of receiving a brocade garment from Emperor Charles V (1519–1556), and letters addressed to the Persian shah Tahmasp I (1524–1576). He stressed that these accusations were not only false but unjust, since the local judge, the *qadi*, had certified that this brocade had been sent to him from Venice on behalf of the pope.[2] As for the letters, he knew nothing about them. Despite the injustice

DOI: 10.4324/9781003165392-6

of these charges, Musa claimed that he been forced to raise 500 gold ducats in alms from his people in order to secure his freedom.[3]

Although it is not mentioned explicitly, the hope that Cervini and other benefactors in Rome might reimburse this fee was the likely cause of this letter. We have seen that Rome was a source for largesse for the Maronite patriarchs throughout the fifteenth and sixteenth centuries, and the city was also an important stop on the alms collection routes trodden by Maronites and other eastern Christians throughout the early modern period. Like them Musa seems to have looked west for funds to liberate captives, with the exception that he sought to raise money for himself rather than for family members or friends.[4]

However, Musa only made one explicit demand in this letter, which is also familiar from his earlier correspondence with Cervini. The patriarch reiterated his desire that Franciscans be sent to Mount Lebanon to teach his people the "rites and customs" of Rome.[5] But he added to this the qualification that Cervini should first get the Venetian *bailo* in Istanbul to secure from the sultan a commendatory letter addressed to the *sanjakbey* of Tripoli, which would ensure that the friars avoided any trouble on arrival. Musa closed his letter by observing that it would be carried to Rome by the Franciscan Hugo of Aquitaine, whose reports of Musa's good faith would be supported by the commissioner of the Maronites in Rome, another Franciscan named Cornelio Divo. A colophon to this letter states that it had been copied for Musa by a Venetian priest named Heliodorus Niger.

This letter was edited and assessed in a recent article by Giacomo Cardinali.[6] A reader familiar with that article will note how it differs from the account just provided. Cardinali understood this letter to state that Heliodorus Niger, rather than Musa, had been imprisoned by the *sanjakbey* and forced to pay the fee of 500 ducats for his release. By contrast, I have understood Musa to have suffered these indignities. This is because the 'I' and 'we' of this letter seem to refer to Musa rather than to Heliodorus. The first hints in this direction are provided by the content of this letter. It is unlikely that a western priest visiting the Levant would have had a flock in Mount Lebanon and his own commissioner in Rome, whereas we have seen that Maronite patriarchs like Musa had both. As just noted, the request for Franciscans to teach the Maronites was also a long-standing request in Musa's correspondence with Rome.[7] These internal pointers towards Musa are reinforced in the colophon to this letter, which states that Heliodorus wrote it on Musa's behalf and at his command.[8] Such an instruction to Heliodorus is clear in the letter, which is copied in a fine western hand, and in a fluent Italian that suggests it was written by a native speaker in collaboration with the patriarch.[9] However, if Heliodorus was the scribe and even co-author of this letter, this does not mean that he was its subject. Early readers noted this distinction, as the envelope for this letter survives among Cervini's correspondence, where it has been marked by a secretary as from "the Patriarch of Mount Lebanon".[10]

88 *The Maronites as anti-Ottoman agents*

If we have to partially remove Heliodorus from one document, we can however add another signalled in P.O. Kristeller's *Iter Italicum*.[11] Vat. lat.5270 is a historical and geographical miscellany that carries the name "Eliodoro Negro" at the top of the first recto.[12] The hand of this manuscript is similar to that of the letter copied by Heliodorus, and the text was clearly composed by a citizen of Venice, as it refers to this city as "our republic".[13] Both of these factors suggest that Heliodorus may have been behind its composition. The creation of this manuscript appears to have been prompted by the Turkish invasion of Corfu in 1537, and it would seem to have been completed around 1540/1, since it refers to John Zapolya (d.1540) as King of Hungary and makes no mention of events later than that year.[14]

As noted, this manuscript is a miscellany of geographical and historical material. The first part of the text is taken up with a survey of the known world and its rulers, which draws on Ptolemy, medieval histories, and contemporary events.[15] This survey is followed by a collection of documents about Venice and Florence, before coming to perhaps the most interesting section: a history of the first two Safavid Shahs, Ismail and Tahmasp. The history of Ismail in this manuscript is dependent on the 1508 account by the Venetian merchant Giovanni Rota, from which the author's knowledge of Arabic and Turkish terms also derives.[16] By contrast, the account of Tahmasp appears to have been based on interviews with Persians in Venice, since two such interlocutors are mentioned as sources in the treatise.[17] These interlocutors seem to have played to the pro-Persian sentiments of the author of this tract, a stance common among Venetian writers who regarded the Safavids as natural allies against the Ottomans.[18] Indeed, in the reign of Leo X, two Venetian monks, Paolo Giustinian and Vincenzo Querini, even expressed the hope that the Persian shah and the Mamluk sultan could be converted to Christianity, a step that they made essential to their grand plan of re-unifying the eastern Churches to Rome.[19] This history of Persia in Vat.lat.5270 is followed by a study of the Circassians, based on the Genoese author Giorgio Interiano's account of this people, which had been printed in 1502 by Aldo Manuzio.[20]

If the attribution to Heliodorus is correct, Vat.lat.5270 is a valuable witness to his intellectual development. His reading of books about the Levant and interviews with travellers indicate his fascination with the languages and history of the east long before he is attested in Lebanon and Istanbul in 1550.[21] Heliodorus's life after this trip is however obscure, an adjective that can equally be applied to the bearer of Musa's letter to Cervini, Hugo of Aquitaine. Besides this letter, Hugo can perhaps be associated with a friar of the same name who copied a manuscript of sermons and tracts by Bernardino of Siena and Giovanni Capistrano that is now in Jerusalem.[22]

By contrast, the other Franciscan mentioned in this letter, Cornelio Divo, is quite well-attested. This Venetian friar was greeted in Paolo Manuzio's letters to friends in Padua during the mid-1530s. Later in life he became an important figure in Franciscan affairs in the Veneto.[23] Divo is not, however, known to have had any contact with the Levant, so this letter in Cervini's

The Maronites as anti-Ottoman agents 89

correspondence adds a new chapter to his life. Musa noted that Divo had served two years as chaplain to the Venetian merchants in Tripoli, a detail that perhaps allows us to be more precise about when and why he was in the Levant. Besides the *bailo* in Istanbul, the Venetians maintained a network of consulates that looked after communities of their merchants in other cities of the Ottoman Empire.[24] Among them was a consulate in Syria, whose officers served for two years with a staff that included a chaplain. Following the movement of Levantine trade in this period, the Venetian consulate in Syria relocated from Damascus to Tripoli on 11 December 1545, and then from Tripoli to Aleppo on 10 December 1548.[25] From this information, we can speculate that Divo was named in Musa's letter as chaplain to the community of merchants in Tripoli by virtue of his attachment to the Venetian consul, and that he was in that city for two years in the period that the consulate was there between 1545 and 1548.

Tripoli was an important city for the Maronites as well as for Venice. We have seen that it functioned as a point of departure for emissaries heading to Rome, but the Maronites also maintained a more permanent presence there. They visited Tripoli to trade, and resided in the city during winter when their villages in Mount Lebanon were made inaccessible by snow.[26] Musa may then have gotten to know Divo in Tripoli, and his awareness of the Venetian *bailo*'s influence in this letter perhaps drew on knowledge and connections that he had acquired through this Franciscan. Musa was correct to assert that the *bailo* would be a useful ally for the Maronites, since this official had a record of success in acquiring privileges for Christians in the Ottoman Empire.[27] Previous explorations in Ottoman archives for documents relating to Lebanon have failed to turn up any letters from Suleiman I (1520–1566) concerning the Maronites, but further excavation into collections in Istanbul and Lebanon may unearth such texts.[28]

Musa's 1550 letter therefore demonstrates a much deeper experience of the functioning of the Ottoman state than his previous letters to Paul III and Cervini, in which the Ottomans appear as faceless enemies. But while he perhaps gained experience of Ottoman central government from well-connected Venetians like Divo, he needed little assistance in getting to know the empire's provincial administrators. This letter indicates that rumours flew around Musa as a result of the patriarch's relations with western powers, attracting the attention of Ottoman officials in Tripoli. Musa could do little to deny his contacts with two periodic enemies of the Ottomans, the papacy and Venice. His correspondence with Rome has been the subject of previous chapters, while a letter sent to Musa on 28 April 1540 by a Franciscan named Cherubino, who had been imprisoned in Damascus, indicates that Musa had been in contact with the Venetian consulate even before its move to Tripoli.[29] However, the boldest accusation made against Musa was that which caused his imprisonment. Musa had been detained on suspicion of passing letters between the two greatest foes of the Ottomans, the Habsburg Empire of Charles V in the west, and the Safavid Empire of Tahmasp I in the east, charges that he vehemently denied. Nonetheless, other documents

90 *The Maronites as anti-Ottoman agents*

indicate that Musa and the Maronites were much more active on the grandest political stage of the Mediterranean than the patriarch wanted to admit.

III. The Maronites as anti-Ottoman agents

In order to understand the severity of the accusations that were mentioned in Musa's letter, it will be useful to briefly recapitulate the political context in which this letter was set. Lebanon entered the Ottoman Empire with the conquests of Selim I (1512–1520). His defeat of Shah Ismail at the battle of Caldiron in 1514 ejected the Safavids from eastern Anatolia, causing the Mamluk Sultan Qansuh (1501–1516) to march from Egypt to confront the growing Ottoman threat on the northern border of his empire. Qansuh was defeated and killed by Ottoman forces near Aleppo on 24 August 1516, and his successor Tumanbay (1516–1517) was executed by Selim the following year after his defeat by the Ottomans near Cairo. Lebanon therefore became part of a new Ottoman province governed from Damascus.[30] However, the Ottomans' latest acquisitions proved to be restive. The new sultan Suleiman's reign was marked by revolts in Syria and Egypt between 1520 and 1524, and pro-Safavid risings in eastern Anatolia between 1526 and 1528.[31] Mount Lebanon was embroiled in similar conflicts during this transition from Mamluk to Ottoman rule. The Venetians instigated Druze and Bedouin revolts around Beirut in 1518, and may even have attempted to capture this city in 1520. The Ottomans responded with raids against the Druze in 1523.[32] Five years later, a Turcoman chief named Mansur Assaf ordered the assassination of an Ottoman tax-farmer in Tripoli, becoming the real power in this irregularly administered area until his death in 1579.[33]

This war-torn region was criss-crossed by an unlikely traveller named Peter the Maronite. Peter first appears as a messenger transporting letters from the King of Hungary to the Persian Shah Ismail. In these letters the king, who was likely Louis II (1516–1526), invited Ismail to make a co-ordinated attack against the Ottoman Empire. In 1523, Ismail responded by sending Peter west with a letter to Charles V, which sought to attract this ruler's interest in a similar venture for April 1524.[34] Peter found Charles in Nuremberg, but suspicion about his credentials meant that April 1524 came and went without a response from the emperor. However, the following year Charles prepared a campaign against the Ottomans, which would have made the Safavids a valuable ally. He therefore sent Peter back to Persia to announce his plans for invasion to Ismail. As such, it appears that news of Ismail's death in May 1524 had yet to reach Charles's court a year later.[35]

That Charles and his advisors were ignorant of the death of one of the most powerful rulers in the Middle East indicates the difficulty of communication between Spain and Persia at this time.[36] It is also unclear in which language these letters were carried to their intended readers, as Charles could only understand the letter he received from Ismail once its contents had been translated for him in Rome.[37] Equally unclear is the extent to which Peter's journey to Charles V was conducted with the knowledge of

The Maronite patriarchs. Peter may be identifiable with the emissary of that name who was sent from Mount Lebanon to Leo X in 1513, and perhaps the 'Petrus Cavalarius' whom, in a letter to Charles of 25 March 1527, Musa claimed to have sent to the emperor, without however receiving a reply from this emissary.[38]

While it cannot provide concrete proof about Musa's involvement in the initial exchanges between Charles and Shah Ismail, this letter of 25 March 1527 demonstrates that the patriarch conducted his own correspondence with the emperor. In this letter Musa invited Charles to liberate the Holy Land from the Turks, promising Maronite assistance for an invasion that he claimed would fulfil a prophecy about the emperor that he had found in an ancient manuscript. Moreover, he requested 15,000 ducats from Charles, a sum that he had allegedly been forced to pay the Turks in order to stop them turning his monastery into a mosque.[39] Musa's letter to Charles was supported by another of the same date from his bishops. As well as exhorting Charles to liberate the Holy Land, these bishops sketched a blueprint of the world that they wanted to see after his conquest. They requested that Charles banish the Jews from Syria as recompense for the aid that they had provided the Ottomans, and punish non-Maronite Christians for their historic treachery by denying them any position of honour or power.[40]

Charles pursued both the avenues for undermining Ottoman rule in the Levant that had been presented to him by the Maronites. On 15 February 1529, he wrote another letter to the long-deceased Shah Ismail, asking him to join an attack on their mutual foe, Suleiman. Charles sent this new letter with a member of his court, a Knight of St John named Pietro Balbi. Balbi's updates to Charles between 30 August 1529 and 13 May 1530 record how he travelled east into Persian territory with the help of an Englishman named Robert 'Brensitur' and a Venetian merchant in Aleppo, Andrea Moresini. Balbi's letters to Charles stop with a final note of 13 May 1530, in which he recorded his reception by Safavid officials.[41] Letters sent to Charles by the Spanish ambassador in Venice confirm that Balbi had received a warm welcome from Shah Tahmasp.[42] However, they also show that Moresini suffered terrible punishment for his part in this plot. The Ottomans discovered the assistance that he had provided to Balbi, leading them to execute him in Aleppo.[43]

At around the same time as Balbi's mission to Persia, Patriarch Musa continued to propose to his western contacts the notion of military resistance against the Ottomans. A Spanish pilgrim to the Holy Land, Antonio de Aranda, recalled that on his visit to the Maronites in 1531, Musa had confided in him that he would be able to raise an army in Mount Lebanon, given the right circumstances.[44] These hopes were still alive six years later. In another letter to Charles of 8 October 1545, Musa mentioned that eight years previously – so in 1537 – the Maronites had received a letter from Charles, in which the emperor suggested a combined operation against the Ottomans, with the Spanish attacking by sea, and the Maronites by land. Charles had perhaps sought to enlist the Maronites as part of preparations

92 *The Maronites as anti-Ottoman agents*

for the Holy Alliance, an anti-Ottoman coalition of Spain, France, Venice, Austria, and the papacy formed in 1538. But two years later this alliance had been broken without the fleet reaching the Lebanese coast.[45] Abandoned by his allies in the west, Musa claimed that the Turks had launched raids against the Maronites and cast him into prison with a bail of 4000 gold ducats. Even after these tribulations Musa continued to exhort Charles to liberate the Christians of the Levant from the Turks, but the military aid that the patriarch hoped for failed to materialise.[46]

This correspondence between Musa and Charles puts paid to claims that there was no direct contact between the Maronites and the Habsburg emperors.[47] Instead, we see that the Maronites were viewed by some Catholic rulers as a potential fifth column within the Ottoman Empire.[48] In this respect they were treated in the same manner as Christians in the Balkans, who were armed and encouraged by western powers in a wide range of anti-Ottoman activities.[49] The Habsburgs were particularly active in this regard. They promoted rebellions among Greeks and Albanians to accompany their military campaigns in the Balkans, such as during their seizure of the strategic city of Corone (1532), and around the time of battle of Lepanto (1571).[50] The Venetians also employed Greeks, Albanians, and even local Turks in their operations against the Ottomans, for instance in a meticulously-planned, but ultimately unsuccessful attempt to capture the city of Clissa in 1572.[51] The Ottomans similarly cultivated potential fifth columnists in the west. Documents in Turkish archives show that they sought to provide weapons and ammunition to Muslims in the south of Spain during their rebellion against the Spanish crown in 1568.[52] Nonetheless, religious affinity was not the only reason for fifth columnists to contact another state. Political dissatisfaction could also be a factor, such as when a group of Dominicans, including the philosopher Tommaso Campanella, sought to enlist the Ottomans in a plan to eject the Habsburgs from southern Italy.[53]

When coupled with Musa's correspondence with Charles V, these examples suggest a potential expansion of historiography about contacts between eastern Christians and the Latin west. Eastern Christians have generally been studied within the history of religion and scholarship, with attention focusing on scribes, intellectuals, and other figures who facilitated contact between different Churches. But parallel to this religious world was a political realm, in which eastern Christians served as spies, soldiers, and saboteurs for every empire of the early modern Mediterranean. This topic has yet to receive much attention in Anglophone historiography, despite outstanding work in other languages.[54] It may well be that this is because most work in English has concentrated on contacts between eastern Christians and the papacy, whom Christians in the Ottoman Empire do not seem to have regarded as a military power. For example, there is no evidence that the Jacobite envoy Moses of Mardin sought to interest the papacy in a crusade. By contrast, the colophons to the manuscripts that he copied for Ferdinand I of Austria are full of direct appeals for Ferdinand to liberate the Christians of the east from Ottoman rule.[55]

IV. Conclusion

This chapter has explored the political as well as religious ties that bound Catholic Europe and the Levant, analysing Heliodorus Niger's knowledge of Persia, the history of the Venetian consulate in Syria, and Charles V's correspondence with the Safavids and Maronites. However, the survival of Musa's letters has also made it possible to assess the Maronite as well as the western perspective in this exchange. In the previous two chapters, we saw how the Catholic Church placed ever-growing demands on eastern Christians to demonstrate their Catholicity after the Reformation. We have now seen that Catholic republics and monarchies could prove unreliable or even irresponsible allies for the Christians of the east, whose invitations to armed rebellion placed these peoples at risk of reprisal by the Ottomans. Faced with these demands and dangers, it is perhaps unsurprising that some eastern Christians cut the ties that had been painfully woven by Catholics and their allies in the east. Over half a century of missionary work by the Jesuits in Ethiopia was capped by the conversion of the Emperor Susenyos in 1626. But just six years later, Susenyos was deposed when the Ethiopian elite decided to reject Catholicism as the religion of their state, expelling the Jesuit missionaries and persecuting Catholics in their empire.[56]

Musa's letters to Paul III, Cervini, and Charles V indicate that the Maronites trod a different path. We have seen that exchanges between Rome and Mount Lebanon were instigated by Musa's repeated requests for cardinal protectors and Franciscan missionaries, and it appears that it was the patriarch who took the initiative to establish correspondence with Charles V. These letters therefore show that Musa pursued a coherent and sustained policy of integrating the Maronites ever more closely into the religious and political worlds of Catholic Christendom. Indeed, Musa appears to have been much more interested in Catholics of the west than they were in him. His patriarchate was a story of frustration, which saw popes, emperors, and cardinals largely decline the religious and military assistance that he either requested or proffered. It is as such understandable that Musa's policy of integration into the Catholic west was not followed by all the Maronites of Mount Lebanon in the sixteenth century. The chief advisors to the nominal ruler of Mount Lebanon for much of this period, Mansur Assaf, were members of the Maronite Hubays family, whose privileged status at Mansur's court precipitated a migration of Maronites away from the patriarch's base the north. These Maronites chose a future conducted within the Ottoman Empire, rather than one in dialogue with the west.[57]

Despite the disappointments that he had faced, Musa persevered in his aim to integrate the Maronites into the Catholic world. After Julius III's death on 23 March 1555, and that of Marcellus II just over a month later, he sent his obedience to Pope Paul IV (1555–1559) together with a request for a new cardinal protector.[58] The office vacated by Cervini was filled by two new protectors, Rodolfo Pio da Carpi (1500–1564) and Gianbernardino Scotti (1493–1568).[59] Musa passed away in 1567. The new patriarch

94 *The Maronites as anti-Ottoman agents*

Michael ar-Ruzzi (1567–1581) continued his predecessor's policies, finding in Rome an active supporter in the shape of the next cardinal protector of the Maronites, Antonio Carafa (1538–1591).

However, the world that we have traced in this study began to change towards the end of the sixteenth century. The Franciscan monopoly on missions to the Maronites was challenged by the loss of its possessions in Jerusalem and the rise of the Jesuits.[60] After Antonio Carafa's death in 1591, the cardinal protector's importance faded, their role taken over by institutions of the post-Tridentine Church such as the Maronite College (found 1584) and Propaganda Fide (founded 1622).[61] For their part, later generations of Maronites took their Catholicity so much for granted that the hesitations of the patriarchs of the late fifteenth and early sixteenth century were overwritten by a history of perpetual fidelity to Rome.[62] Musa's patience had been rewarded.

Notes

1 For the function of this official, see in general Colin Imber, *The Ottoman Empire, 1300–1650*, 3rd ed. (London: Red Globe Press, 2019), 151–2; for the *sanjak* of Tripoli, Abdul-Rahim Abu-Husayn, *The View from Istanbul. Lebanon and the Druze Emirate in the Ottoman Chancery Documents, 1546–1711* (London: I.B. Tauris, 2004), 11.

2 The duties of the *qadi* are explained in Douglas A. Howard, *A History of the Ottoman Empire* (Cambridge: Cambridge University Press, 2017), 114.

3 CC 45, 3r. Text printed in G. Cardinali, "Rittrato di Marcello Cervini en orientaliste (con precisazioni alle vicende di Petrus Damascenus, Mose di Mardin ed Heliodorus Niger)," Bibliothèque d'Humanisme et Renaissance 80 (2018): 342.

4 John-Paul Ghobrial, "Migration from Within and Without: In the Footsteps of Eastern Christians in the Early Modern World," *Transactions of the Royal Historical Society* 27 (2017): 153–73.

5 "[A]ffini d'instituirci secondo il rito et consuetudine della S.ta madre Chiesa Romana". Cardinali, "Rittrato di Marcello Cervini *en orientaliste*," 342.

6 Ibid., 326–8 and 342.

7 As in the letter of February 1542: Tobias Anaissi, ed., *Collectio documentorum Maronitarum* (Livorno: Fabbreschi, 1921), 46.

8 "De mandato R.mi D. Patriarchae montis Libani [...] Ego Presbyter Heliodorus Niger Venetus [...] Manu mea eius nomine". CC 45, 3r; Cardinali, "Ritratto di Marcello Cervini *en orientaliste*," 342.

9 Musa only knew a little Italian. The pilgrim Antonio de Aranda reported "habla vn poco Italiano". See Antonio de Aranda, *Verdadera Informacion dela tierra sancta* (Alcala: Francisco de Cormellas y Pedro de Robles, 1563), 260r.

10 "Il Patriarca del Monte libano". Like most envelopes in the Carte Cerviniane this is unfoliated, but it is the verso of fifth folio after CC 45, 3r.

11 Paul Oskar Kristeller, *Iter italicum* (Leiden: Brill, 1967), 2:332.

12 "D'Eliodoro Negro Car". Vat.lat.5270, 1r.

13 "La nostra Republica Vinitiana". Ibid., 2r.

14 "Il Re Giouani domina la rouinata Ongaria". Ibid., 2r.

15 Ibid., 1r–6r.

16 Compare ibid., 32r and Giovanni Rota, *La vita: costumi: et statura de Sofi: Re di Persia et di Media et de molti altri Regni et paesi* ([Rome: Eucharius Silber, 1508]), 1v.

The Maronites as anti-Ottoman agents 95

17 "Et per quanto mi disse uno Mola qual trouai a Venetia che era uenuto con gioie et era nato in Ardueli prima patria de questi sophi. È grandissimo homo et dottissimo qual parti di persia l'anno .1533. et trouò Imbraim bassa in Alepo. Vnde hauendo io contratto amicitia con lui qual mi ha informato si de l'ordinanza come de li costumi del paese hauendone io confirmatione da diuersi altri che sono stati et hanno practicato in quelli lochi ho deliberato de scriuer questa opera [...] Diro una cosa admiranda che ho inteso a uenetia da un Mercatante de Tauris homo degno di fede che in quattro mutatione che furono in Thauris non fu saccheggiata pur una casa sola. Cosa che non so se li nostri christiani l'haueriano potuto fare". BAV: Vat.lat.5270, 37v, 43r–43v.
18 Margaret Meserve, *Empires of Islam in Renaissance Historical Thought* (Cambridge, MA: Harvard University Press, 2008), 231–7; Giorgio Rota, *Under Two Lions: On the Knowledge of Persia in the Republic of Venice* (Vienna: Verlag der Österreichischen Akademie der Wissenschaften, 2009). The papacy maintained similar hopes that Persia could serve as an ally against the Ottomans, see Angelo Maria Piemontese, *La Persia istoriata in Roma* (Vatican City: Biblioteca Apostolica Vaticana, 2014), 289–307.
19 Paolo Giustinian and Vincenzo Querini, "Libellus ad Leonem X," in *Annales Camaldulenses*, ed. Giovanni-Benedetto Mittarelli and Anselmo Costadoni (Venice: Pasquali, 1773), 9:632–54.
20 Vat.lat.5270, 43v–50r; Giorgio Interiano, *La vita: & sito de Zichi: chiamati Ciarcassi: historia notabile* (Venice: Aldo Manuzio, 1502).
21 For Heliodorus's visit to Istanbul, see the letter from Postel to Maes (10 June 1550), mentioned in Cardinali, "Ritratto di Marcello Cervini *en orientaliste*," 325, and printed in Jacques George de Chaufepie, *Nouveau dictionnaire historique et critique* (Amsterdam: Chatelain et al, 1753), 3: letter P, 216–17.
22 Jerusalem: Biblioteca Generale della Custodia di Terra Santa, Fondo latini, MS 81.
23 *Epistolarum Pauli Manutii libri XII* (Trnava: Typis Collegii Academici Societatis Jesu, 1752), 171–2 (IV.43), 313–14 (VIII.24), 314 (VIII.26), 316 (VIII.29). For his later career, see Riccardo Varesco, "I frati minori al Concilio di Trento," *Archivum Franciscanum Historicum*, 42 (1960): 108, 158.
24 Maria Pia Pedani, *Venezia porta d'Oriente* (Bologna: Il Mulino, 2010), 78–87.
25 Guglielmo Berchet, *Relazioni dei Consoli Veneti nella Siria* (Turin: G.B. Paravia, 1866), 19.
26 Kamal S. Salibi, "The *muqaddams* of Bsarri: Maronite Chieftains of the Northern Lebanon, 1382–1621," *Arabica* 15 (1968): 65.
27 See "Catalogo dei Firmani ed altri documenti legali [...] conservati nell'Archivio della [...] Custodia in Gerusalemme," in *L'Archivo Storico della Custodia di Terra Sancta (1230–1970)*, ed. Andrea Maiarelli (Bari: Edizioni Terra Santa, 2012), 1:15–26.
28 See Abu-Husayn, *The View from Istanbul*.
29 "Hauendo in questi giorni pasati (signor mio obseruandissimo) visto una di V.S.R. escrita al clarissimo console". Portugal: National Library of Lisbon, 303, 333r–335v (at 333r). My thanks go once more to Dr Joseph Moukarzel for alerting me to the existence of this source. Dr Roberto Khatlab is preparing a French translation of this manuscript, a dossier of texts about historical ties between Rome and the Maronites that was originally compiled by the Franciscan Antonio Soares da Albergaria at Musa's insistence.
30 Abu-Husayn, *The View from Istanbul*, 11. For Selim's campaigns, see Ebru Boyar, "Ottoman Expansion in the East," in *The Cambridge History of Turkey. Volume III: The Ottoman Empire as a World Power, 1453–1603*, ed. Suraiya N. Faroqhi and Kate Fleet (Cambridge: Cambridge University Press, 2013), 96–114.
31 Boyar, "Ottoman Expansion in the East," 114–16.
32 Abu-Husayn, *The View from Istanbul*, 14–15.

96 The Maronites as anti-Ottoman agents

33 Kamal S. Salibi, "Northern Lebanon under the Dominance of the Gazir (1517–1591)," *Arabica* 14 (1967): 156–7.

34 Karl Lanz, ed., *Correspondenz des Kaisers Karl V. aus dem königlichen Archiv und der Bibliothèque de Bourgogne zu Brüssel* (Leipzig: Brochaus, 1844), 1:52–3; I follow the dating of this letter in Rudolf Neck, "Diplomatische Beziehungen zum Vorderen Orient unter Karl V," *Mitteilungen des österreichischen Staatsarchivs* 5 (1952): 67–8 n.25.

35 Lanz, *Correspondenz des Kaisers Karl V*, 1:168; Neck, "Diplomatische Beziehungen," 67–8.

36 Similarly, it took eleven days for news of Lepanto to reach Venice, and three months before the death of Charles V was known in Istanbul – a reminder of just how slowly information moved in the sixteenth century. See respectively Paolo Preto, *I servizi segreti di Venezia. Spionaggio e controspionaggio ai tempi della Serenissima*, 2nd ed. (Milan: Il Saggiatore, 2016), 312; Josef Žontar, "Michael Černović, Geheimagent Ferdinands I. und Maximilians II., und seine Berichterstattung," *Mitteilungen des österreichischen Staatsarchiv* 24 (1971): 180.

37 Neck, "Diplomatische Bezeigungen," 68.

38 "[…] in diebus elapsis duos nuntios sive ambasciatores tibi misi quorum nomina sunt haec, Petrus Cavalarius, et Iohannes archdeaconus de meo Castro de quibus aliquod responsum non habui, neque eos amplius vidimus". Musa al-Akkari to Charles V, 25 March 1527, printed in Antoine Rabbath, ed., *Documents inédits pour server a l'histoire de Christianisme en orient (XVI–XIX siècle)* (Paris: A. Picard et Fils, 1910), 2:617. Contrary to ibid., 2:618 n.2, the Maronite Archbishop of Damascus, Antonius, who is named as the bearer of this letter is unlikely to be the same Antonius who carried Musa's letter to Clement VII in 1527, as this latter Antonius is named as the bishop of a different see ("Caserontum") in Clement's reply, and had in any case died by the time that Musa wrote his letter to Charles V. See Appendix V.

39 "[…] invenimus in libro quodam antiquissimo compilato anno Dominicae Incarnationis 965, videlicet quod [hoc?] anno Dominicae Incarnationis venturus sit Carolus Imperator natione alemanus, et quod ingressurus sit sanctam Civitatem cum magno gaudio, sicut Helena mater Constantini Imperatoris. Quod de tua Ces. M^{te} intelligendum et per eam implendum esse nemo nostrum dubitat". Ibid., 2:617–18. Rabbath's transcription seems to skip in what year Charles was expected, hence speculative addition of *hoc*; "anno Dominicae Incarnationis" could also be an unnecessary repetition.

40 "Volumus tamen, veniente tua Ces. Maiestate, ut omnes Judei de Sorya expellantur, eo quod ipsi Turchos fortificant faciendo illis sclopeta et bombardas atque alia arma contra nos Soryanos. Volumus etiam, ut nullus alienae Nationis a nostra tuae Ces. Maiestati servire volens possit alicuius dignitatis uti Comitis et Equitis aurati seu prefecturarum gradus ascendere, quia Greci ut plurimum traditores et proditores reperiuntur". Ibid., 2:621.

41 Lanz, *Correspondenz des Kaisers Karl V*, 1:293–6, 329–30, 355–6, 379–80, 385; Neck, "Diplomatische Bezeigungen," 70–1. Adel Allouche, *The Origins and Development of the Ottoman-Safavid Conflict (906–962 / 1500–1555)* (Berlin: Klaus Schwarz, 1983), 129–30 does not add to what is known from Lanz's edition.

42 *Espias. Servicios secretos y escritura cifrada en la Monarquía Hispánica* (Madrid: Secretaría General Técnica, 2018), 86–7; see however Neck, "Diplomatische Bezeigungen," 71–2, which regards Balbi's mission as fruitless.

43 *Espias. Servicios secretos y escritura cifrada*, 86–7.

44 Antonio de Aranda, *Verdadera Informacion dela tierra sancta*, 260r–260v.

The Maronites as anti-Ottoman agents 97

45 Gaetano Cozzi, "Venezia dal Rinascimento all'Eta barocca," in *Storia di Venezia dalle origini alla caduta della Serenissima*, vol. 6, ed. Gaetano Cozzi and Paolo Prodi (Rome: Istituto della Enciclopedia Italiana, 1994), 29–34.

46 Musa's letter of 1545 to Charles is partially translated into Italian in Noujaim, *I Francescani e i Maroniti*, 2:41–2. C.C. Casati, "Extraits de dépêches diplomatiques inédites des empereurs Maximilien Iᵉʳ et Charles-Quint," *Bibliothèque de l'École des Chartes* 31 (1870): 70–1 states that what is likely Charles's reply, a letter of "pure courtoise" to Musa of 2 June 1546, exists in a Venetian archive. However, Casati does not name that archive there, nor in his later *Lettres royaux et lettres missives inédites* (Paris: Librarie Académique, 1877).

47 William Harris, *Lebanon: A History, 600–2011* (Oxford: University Press, 2012), 86.

48 A conception that some Catholics extended to other Christians in the Middle East and Africa too: see Paolo Giustinian and Vincenzo Querini, "Libellus ad Leonem X," 9:651–2.

49 Noel Malcolm, *Agents of Empire: Knights, Corsairs, Jesuits and Spies in the sixteenth-century Mediterranean World* (London: Allen Lane, 2015), 123–50, 178–80, 406–12; Maria Antonietta Visceglia, "Il contesto internazionale della incorporazione di Ferrara allo Stato ecclesiastico (1597–1598)," in eadem, *La Roma dei papi. La corte e la politica internazionale (secoli XV–XVII)*, ed. Elena Valeri and Paola Volpini (Rome: Viella, 2018), 293–322.

50 J.K. Hassiotis, "La comunità greca di Napoli e i moti insurrezionali nella penisola balcanica meridionale durante la seconda metà del XVI secolo," *Balkan Studies* 10 (1969): 279–88. For the activity of Albanians and Greeks as spies for the Habsburgs, see moreover the works of Gennaro Varriale, such as Gennaro Varriale, "Liricas secretas: los espías y el Gran Turco (siglo XVI)," *Hispania* 76 (2016): 37–66; Gennaro Varriale, "Lo spionaggio sulla frontiera mediterranea nel XVI secolo: La Sicilia contro il sultano," *Mediterranea* 13 (2016): 477–516; Gennaro Varriale, "Un covo di spie: il quartiere greco di Napoli," in *Identità e frontiere. Politica, economia e società nel Mediterraneo (secc. XIV–XVIII)*, ed. Lluis J. Guia Marín, Maria Grazia Rosaria Mele and Gianfranco Tore (Milan: FrancoAngeli, 2014), 47–62.

51 Preto, *I servizi segreti di Venezia*, 307.

52 Emrah Safa Gürkan, "Espionage in the 16th-century Mediterranean: Secret diplomacy, Mediterranean go-betweens and the Ottoman-Habsburg Rivalry" (PhD diss., Georgetown University, 2012), 390–1.

53 Ibid., 393.

54 José M. Floristán Imízcoz, *Fuentes para la política oriental de los Austrias. La documentacíon griega del Archivo de Simancas (1571–1621)* (Leon: Universidad de León, 1988); Gennaro Varriale, *Arrivano li Turchi. Guerra navale e spionaggio nel Mediterraneo (1532–1582)* (Novi Ligure: Città del Silenzio Edizioni, 2014).

55 See the colophons in Pier Giorgio Borbone, "Monsignore Vescovo di Soria, also Known as Moses of Mardin, Scribe and Book Collector," *ХРИСТІАНСКІЙ ВОСТОКЪ* 8 (2017): 79–114.

56 Andreu Martínez d'Alòs-Moner, *Envoys of a Human God: The Jesuit Mission to Christian Ethiopia, 1557–1632* (Leiden: Brill, 2015), 308–23.

57 Salibi, "Northern Lebanon under the Dominance of the Gazir," 156–8; Harris, *Lebanon: A History*, 90–1.

58 See Appendix XII and XIII.

59 Matteo Al Kalak, 'Pio, Rodolfo," *DBI*, 84, 2015; Andrea Vanni, "Scotti, Bernardino," *DBI* 91, 2018.

98 *The Maronites as anti-Ottoman agents*

60 Ammon Cohen, "The Expulsion of the Franciscans from Mount Zion: Old Documents and New Interpretation," *Turcica* 18 (1986): 147–57. For Carafa and the famous missions to the Maronites of the Jesuit Giovanni Battista Eliano, see now Robert John Clines, *A Jewish Jesuit in the Eastern Mediterranean: Early Modern Conversion, Mission, and the Construction of Identity* (Cambridge: Cambridge University Press, 2019), 90–149; Robert John Clines, "Between hermits and heretics: Maronite religious renewal and the Turk in Catholic travel accounts of Lebanon after the Council of Trent," in *Travel and Conflict in the Early Modern World*, ed. Gábor Gelléri and Rachel Willie (London: Routledge, 2020), 108–26.

61 Aurélien Girard, "Le Collège maronite de Rome et les langues au tournant des XVIᵉ et XVIIᵉ siècles: éducation des chrétiens orientaux, science orientaliste et apologétique catholique," *Rivista Storica Italiana* 132 (2020): 272–99; Giovanni Pizzorusso, "Le lingue a Roma: studio e practica nei collegi missionari nella prima età moderna," in ibid., 248–71.

62 See above, Chapter 1:III.

Conclusion

This book has attempted to reconstruct contacts between Rome and the Maronites in an understudied period of this history. It began with the Council of Ferrara-Florence, where the Maronite patriarch Johannes al-Ghagi pursued a different course from other eastern prelates by requesting confirmation of his place within the Roman Church rather than union to it. But as we saw, the rise of Jacobite influence among the Maronites dissuaded Johannes's immediate successors from following his example. It was therefore left to Franciscans of the Holy Land to fight for the Catholic identity of the Maronites. Gryphon's mission to Mount Lebanon bore fruit, not least in the shape of Gabriel ibn al-Qilāʿī, whose letters and poems popularised a Catholic past for the Maronites that was later honed into a history of perpetual orthodoxy by Counter-Reformation writers like Stefanos al-Duwayhi. The efforts of Franciscans like Gryphon and al-Qilāʿī were rewarded when Patriarch Simon al-Hadathi dispatched emissaries to Pope Leo X in 1513. The exchanges in the reign of this pope proved to be transformational for Rome and Mount Lebanon. In Rome, the Maronite emissary Elias established the scholarly study of Arabic and Syriac through his teaching and copying of manuscripts. For their part, the Maronite patriarchs were won over by Leo's light touch and largesse, stimulating a policy of active contact with the papacy and other Catholic powers that was pursued by Simon's successors.

The trust and co-operation built up from the Council of Ferrara-Florence to the reign of Leo X were however challenged by events in the north. The outbreak of the Reformation was followed by stricter demands for orthodoxy and its demonstration, which were applied to eastern Christians as well as to Catholics and Protestants. In Rome, Catholic scholars and their patrons delved into the past and present faith of the Armenians, Copts, Ethiopians, Greeks, Jacobites, 'Nestorians', and Maronites, causing them to discover useful sources for confessional polemic against Protestantism, but more often leading them to lose their faith in the Catholicity of the Churches of Africa, the Balkans, and the Middle East. The leading figure in this difficult absorption of eastern Christianity into the Reformation was the third cardinal protector of the Maronites, Marcello Cervini. Cervini's correspondence shows that he orchestrated a wide range of collaborations

DOI: 10.4324/9781003165392-7

100   *Conclusion*

between eastern Christians and western Orientalists in which the struggle against Protestantism was never far from sight. The Maronites were a key part of Cervini's network and its plans. He helped to launch investigations into the textual heritage of the Maronites in Mount Lebanon, while Maronites in Rome like Bishop Simeon of Beirut put their skills to use in copying texts useful to contemporary religious polemic and in translating documents that had been dispatched to Rome from the Middle East.

The long history of contact between the Maronites and Rome ultimately conditioned how Catholic prelates like Cervini responded to representatives of other eastern Churches. But where these other Churches sometimes baulked after learning the full implications of union with Rome, the Maronites sought ever-closer integration into the politicial and religious world of Catholic Christendom. Patriarch Musa al-Akkari followed his predecessors by fostering educational exchanges between Rome and Mount Lebanon, and supported this cultural policy with overtures to Emperor Charles V that sought to attract armed intervention in the Holy Land. Ultimately the popes and emperors were unable or unwilling to fully satisfy Musa's desire for integration into the Catholic world.

A number of conclusions can be drawn from this account of exchanges between Rome and the Maronites. The first relates to periodisation. The years surveyed in this study are punctuated by a number of important events: the conquest of Constantinople in 1453; the outbreak of the Reformation in 1517; the expansion of the Ottoman Empire into the Holy Land between 1516 and 1520; the Council of Trent between 1545 and 1563. Often, these events are treated as historiographical caesura, with studies either beginning or ending at each point. Studies of the Franciscans in the Holy Land commonly end in 1516, for example, whereas analysis of Catholic missions to the eastern Churches have typically explored the period after the Council of Trent. As a result, it has been overlooked that the period between the Council of Ferrara-Florence and the reign of Pope Gregory XIII can be treated as a distinct period in the history of relations between Rome and the eastern Churches.[1]

After Ferrara-Florence and the conquest of Constantinople in 1453, eastern Christians entered the Catholic imagination less as enemies of the faith, and more as persecuted co-religionists and potential allies against the real threat to the Church, the Turks. Eastern Christians in the west were happy enough to play to these Catholic expectations when asked, until the questions that they were meant to answer changed in the Reformation. At this point challenges to Rome's past were joined by the scrutiny of the past of other Churches. The ensuing disillusionment led to a policy of conversion and standardisation that characterised Catholic dealings with the eastern Churches in the late sixteenth-century, until disasters like the loss of Ethiopia encouraged the formulation of a different approach. However, these later events and trends cannot be understood without reference to the history of contact between Catholics and eastern Christians during the Renaissance and the Reformation. It is difficult to fully comprehend the foundation of

Conclusion 101

the Maronite College in 1584 without considering the preceding century of educational exchanges between Rome and the Maronites, for instance, or to understand the intransigence of the later sixteenth century without reference to disillusionment about the Catholicity of eastern Christians that is manifest in Cervini's correspondence.

Studying the longer history of relations between Rome and the eastern Churches therefore helps to define how and why the Catholic Church developed between 1439 and the late sixteenth century. It also contributes to our knowledge of the religious history of the Maronites. Chapter 1 of this study showed how a Catholic identity for the Maronites was built up over the late fifteenth and early sixteenth century. Yet this history was written in the Levant by Gryphon and al-Qilāʿi, and accepted only through the decisions of actors in Lebanon. Here, Musa's persistence in establishing and maintaining contact with the Catholic world in the face of the apathy or limitations of his western correspondents was essential to ensuring that missionaries like Giovanni Battista Eliano were well-received when the Roman hierarchy finally took interest in the Maronites in the late 1570s. As stressed in Chapter 2, decision-makers in Rome as such depended on their partners in peripheries to achieve their goals in Europe and Middle East. The fact that the Maronites arrived so early on the scene made them essential to how Rome conceived of its relations to other Christians in Africa and the Levant. The success of Maronite missions of Leo X's reign, for example, was instrumental to shaping how later Catholics reacted to other Churches who looked west after a century of separation from Rome, such as the Jacobites and 'Nestorians'.

Similarly, the discovery of Musa's letters to Cervini open out a new way of understanding this cardinal. Research in the past few years has established beyond doubt that this cardinal had serious interests in eastern Christianity, and has offered some suggestions for why that was the case. However, there is a risk of affording too much credit to Cervini. Cervini could be treated as omniscient because he was apparently omnipresent, which would be to exaggerate his importance to the detriment of his contemporaries. This study has therefore drawn on Cervini's correspondence to provide a different interpretation of this cardinal. In his contacts with eastern Christians, Cervini appears as a supremely competent fixer and administrator, whose strength was drawn from his ability to build and sustain a network that he guided towards well-defined goals, if with varying degrees of success.

As noted, this revision of Cervini has been based on a study of his correspondence. Yet this study is inevitably incomplete, due to the present impossibility of accessing his correspondence in its entirety. A digital edition of Cervini's correspondence is therefore a major desideratum, since an edition open to forms of digital analysis promises to add a significant new resource to the study of the early Reformation. Such a project would be based at first on the letters that Cervini received, now stored mainly in the Vatican and the Archivio di Stato in Florence, but would also need to perform the

102 *Conclusion*

arduous task of finding the letters that he sent in order to avoid the myopia that has just been been descried. With such an edition we would learn a great deal about Cervini and about correspondents whose voices are at present hard to recover, such as Pier Paolo Gualtieri or Johann Albrecht von Widmanstetter.

Nonetheless, it is not only the western side of this story that needs to be developed. In a period so alert to the movement of people and ideas between Europe and the Levant, it is scandalous that Gabriel ibn al-Qilāʿī has yet to receive a biography in English. Such a project would be an excellent topic for a PhD, as would a study of the later Maronite patriarch and historian Stefanos al-Duwayhi, who is currently missing from many accounts of seventeenth-century Maronite history. These studies would need to draw on archives in Lebanon and the Middle East as well as Europe, since they possess autograph documents that would say a great deal about the methods and aims of these Maronite historians. But the reader may come away with different ideas for future paths for research. I hope that the present study has at least provided signposts to guide them along their way.

Note

1 A similar periodisation is promoted in Elise Andretta, Antonella Romano, and Maria Antonietta Visceglia, "Introduzione. Le lingue nella Roma del Cinquecento," *Rivista Storica Italiana* 132 (2020): 87–111, whose rich footnotes gather much recent research on the papacy's contacts with peoples beyond Europe.

Appendices

I. 1514–1515? Francesco Suriano's two reports on the Maronites to Leo X

Summary:

The former Franciscan Custodian of the Holy Places, Francesco Suriano, probably drafted the following reports about Maronite customs in Lebanon in 1514–1515. The first report answers a questionnaire that Leo X had originally sent to the superior of the Franciscan monastery in Beirut, Marco da Firenze. Here Suriano informs the pope of how the patriarch of the Maronites is elected (point 1), where his patriarchal seat can be found (2), what sort of vestments he wore (3), from whom he received these vestments and holy orders (4), and how long the current patriarch had served in his office (5). Although Suriano's description of patriarchal elections in particular differed from what the Maronites had themselves told Leo about their customs, he concludes by recommending their orthodoxy to Leo.

The second report is instead a list of customs in which Suriano believed that the Maronites were not in complete union with Rome. These are: the blessing of the Sacrament (1), the fact that Maronite priests could marry, and celebrated the sacraments at different times to Latins (2), uses of vestments that differed from Roman practice (3), what Suriano appears to have regarded as superstitions around participation in Communion (4) and baptism (5), the lack of confessors among the Maronites (6), marriages carried out at uncanonical degrees of relation (7), and finally practices of divorce (8).

See Chapter 2:II–III.

Text:

AAV: Misc., Arm. VI, 39, 18v–19v[1]

[18v] Morum Maronitarum relatio per fratrum Franciscum Surianum ad S.D.N. Leoni .PP. X.[2]

Beatissime pater alias S.V. per suas in forma breuis litteras humili eius seruo fratri Francisco Suriano tunc loci sancti Montis Syon in Hierusalem immerito guardiano, nunc vero ad pedes S.V. humiliter prostrato commisit

104   *Appendices*

ac mandauit, ut quedam circa mores ac consuetudines Patriarche Maronitarum examinaret, que sic hec[3]

> Primo quomodo eligitur, iste Patriarcha, et qui sunt electores.
> Secundo que est sedes sua Metropolitana
> Tertio que insignia pontificalia gestat
> Quarto a quo sollitus sit suscipere ordines sacros et etiam pontificalia
> ornamenta et insignia
> Quinto quanto tempore stetit in dignitate

Ad primum quomodo eligitur, cum omni humilitate respondeo Quod licet
iste modernus patriarcha ob ipsius vitae laudabilis morumque integritate
fuerit acclamatibus cunctis clero et populo electus tamen stilus ordinarie
electionis hic est Tempore igitur faciende electionis huiusmodi conueniunt
sex archiepiscopi et episcopi [, archiepiscopi][4] duo, et episcopi quattuor,
quia plures inibi non sunt qui inter se de hac creatione tractant virum nominant ex se ipsis quem sic nominant expectante clero et populo proponunt
quem si recipit ille absque vlla questione intronisatur Si autem dissentiunt
astantes et non recipiantur electus seu nominatus [19r] Illi idem sex ad hoc
deputati ad alterius nominationem procedunt Cumque electus et a clero
populoque acceptatus fuerit consuetudo regionis illius habet quod ad dominum Ciuitatis Tripolitanum Syriae Impissime secte Maumete subiectum
mittunt, vt electum patriarcham regnare permittat pro quo etiam ducati
.60. eidem domino pro munere donantur Quod si facere recusaret electus
et clero et populo vt Patriarcha minime habetur et hic ritus in patriarchae
creationis seruatus ab illis.

Ad secundum que eius sit sedes, Respondeo quod illius sedes est Antio-
chie quod satis probant Bulle summorum ponticifium .S.V. predecessarium
quem ipsum Antiochenum patriarcham vocitant.

Ad tertium que insignia pontificalia gestat, Respondeo que tantum Infu-
lam siue Mitram et annullum aureum sine sigillo consueuit habere et hiis
tantumodo et cum peragit misteria vtitur.

Ad quartum a quo consueuit suscipere ordines sacros Respondeo quod
ab vno Illorum sex eligentur antiquiori videlicet et sanctiori pontificalia
ornamenta suscipere consueuit et sermonem exhortatorium ille facit coram
omni clero et uniuerso populo Regionis illius, nomine omnium cum illo
protestando quod quotiens deuiauerit a catholicorum et orthodoxorum
patrum dogmatibus et fidelis S. sedi Apostolice non fuerit aut simonia-
cam prauitatem in se admiserit quod totiens[5] infidelitatem contra fidem et
sanctam sedem Apostolicam et ex tunc prout ex nunc si dignitate patriarchali priuatus eo ipso, ipse autem patriarcha ore proprio se condemnat
quod totiens incurrerit et de Symonia fuit conuictus se ipsum exuit illa dignitate et sic protestando iurat sollemni iuramento astantibus cunctis deinde
procedunt ad altare et astantibus electoribus supradictis in girum inuocant
gratiam spiritus sancti vt dirigatur electus ad laudem et gloriam diuine Maiestatis et populi directionem et vtilitatem et ibi faciunt planctum[6] maximum

Appendices 105

propter onus graue illi impositum et sic Remanet in officio patriarchali, et est adeo hic actus sollemnis quod vniuersi Maronitarum populi illo die simul conueniunt ad actum huiusmodi.

Ad sextum et vltimum quanto videlicet tempore stetit in patriarchate quod hic Modernus patriarcha xxx Annos vel circa residit.

Hec sunt pater Sancte que inueni inter deuotos .S.V. filios Maronitarum populos de partiarche institutione, et aliis supra dictiis semper paratus S.V. obedire mandatis Cuius Beatos pedes ore humiliter ac fide pio osculo adoro debitoque honore veneror.

Frater franciscus Surianus prouincie S.ti Francisci S.V. seruus ordinis minorum obseruantie

[19v] Mores cleri ac populi Maronitarum quos ego Inueni in .216. 2228.[7]

Primo conficiunt sacramentum die Iovis more grecorum de quo per totum annum communicant infermos decedentes etiam si non confiteantur.

Secundo sacerdotes sunt vxorati et non celebrant tempore quadragesime et aduentus nisi post horam vespertinam aliis tamen temporibus autem nonam et communicant omnes clericos astantes altari sub vtraque specie seculares vero sub specie vna tantum.

Subdiaconi non vtuntur manipulo sed stola super humerum sinistrum vidi tamen archipiepiscopum celebrantem cum manipulo in ambabus manibus.

Quarto tenet esse peccatum spuere die illo quo acceperunt communionem similiter Impeditus est qui a communione obluendo os cum aqua pura aut si pilus barbe intrauit in os die illo similiter, si naturaliter sanguis de dentibus vel de naribus exierit.

Quinto differunt baptizare baptizandos post 4° dies vt mater post purificationem possit introducere puerum vel puellam baptizandos in ecclesiam, dicunt enim quod si baptizaretur ante 4° diem lac maternum esset sibi in peccatum et quod oporteret conducere nutricem ad prolem alendam.

6° In tota Moronia sunt tres aut quattuor tantum qui audiunt confessiones, et ex hoc veniunt multa scandala et mala ordinetur igitur si placet S.V. quod quilibet sacerdos parochianus audiat suos parochianos vt possint scire mala ista et procurare salutem saltem tempore mortis populi sibi commissi.

Septimo Matrimonium contra sunt in gradu tertio inclusive qui numerant gradus sic frater et soror faciunt secundum gradum quia ponunt stipitem pro primo gradu filius et filia tertium nepos et neptes faciunt quartum et in isto gradu [blank] in tertio gradu ac quarto

Octavo quando mulier aut vir insaniatur aut quis mox infirmatur, infirmate incurabile alter eorum qui sanus est al[t]erum nubit dimisso consorte aut steriles.[8]

Nemo fuit multum ignoranter circa gradus affinitatis et spiritualis cognationis in Matrimoniis contrahendis.

Humilis seruus S.V. frater Franciscus Surianus.

106 *Appendices*

II. 20 August 1515, Indulgentia plenaria pro ecclesia Maronitarum in Monte Libano

Summary:

This document offers a plenary indulgence to any Christian who each year, having confessed, visited and gave alms at an unnamed Maronite church in Mount Lebanon on a certain number of holy days (Christmas, Nativity of John the Baptist, Circumcision, Epiphany, Ascension, Pentecost, Ascension of Mary, Feast of Peter and Paul, Invention of the Cross). To facilitate this process, Leo X permits the Maronite patriarch (Simon al-Hadathi) to appoint as many confessors as he saw fit from the regular and secular clergy, who were provided with the power to absolve even sins for which recourse to the Roman curia would otherwise be required. By increasing the number of confessors among the Maronites, Leo perhaps responded to the dearth of confessors that Francesco Suriano had brought to his attention (Appendix I). The request for alms as part of the indulgence may also have helped the Maronite patriarch to raise funds, a constant theme of their correspondence with the papacy.

See Chapter 2:IV.

Text:

AAV: Misc. Arm. VI, 39, 15r–16r[9]

[15r] Leo etc. Universis Christi fidelibus presentes litteras inspecturis. salutem. etc. De salute gregis Dominici curae nostrae Domino disponente commissi, prout ex debito pastoralis officii astringimur, solicite cogitantes, fideles singulos, etiam in remotissimis regionibus constitutos, gregis eiusdem, ad pia et meritoria opera exercenda quibusdam spiritualibus muneribus, indulgentiis videlicet et remissionibus libenter inuitamus, ut per eorundem operum exercitium aeternam salutem ab omnibus desideratam, ualeant facilius promereri. Cupientes igitur ut Ecclesia Maronitarum in monte libano consistens, cui Venerabilis frater noster Petrus patriarchae Maronitarum praeesse dinoscitur, quique et illius clerus saepe saepius oppressiones ab infidelibus patiuntur, ac diuersis grauaminibus afficiuntur: Et aliae ecclesiae inibi ad honorem Dei constitutae in suis aedificiis, ac paramentis, et ornamentis diuino cultui necessariis, quibus indigere dinoscitur, reparentur, manuteneantur, et conseruentur, congruisque frequentur honoribus, ipsique fideles eo libentius ad Ecclesiam ipsam Maronitarum deuotionis causa confluant, et ad praemissa manus [15v] promptius porrigant adiutrices, quo ex hoc ibidem dono coelestis gratiae uberius conspexerint se refectos, de omnipotentis Dei misericordia, ac beatorum Petri et Pauli Apostolorum eius autoritate confili, omnibus et singulis utriusque sexus Christifidelibus uere poenitentibus et confessis, qui dictam ecclesiam Maronitarum, in Domini nostri Jesu Christi, et Sancti Johannis Baptistae natiuitatem, ac Circumcisionis, necnon Epiphaniae, et Ascensionis, et Pentecostes, et assumptionis Beatae Mariae de mense Augusti, et in Sanctorum Petri et Pauli Apostolorum, necnon inuentionis Sanctae Crucis, festiuitatibus annuatim deuote uisitauerint, et ad praemissam manus porrexerint adiutrices, seu pias heleemosynas inibi erogauerint, plenariam omnium peccatorum suorum, de

Appendices 107

quibus corde contriti, et ore confessi fuerint, indulgentiam et remissionem elargimur. Et ut fideles ipsi ad consequenda huiusmodi indulgentem gratiam aptiores reddantur, praefato Petro, et pro tempore existenti Patriarchae Maronitarum tot presbyteros seculares, uel cuiusuis ordinis regulares, quot ad id idoneos et necessarios cognouerit, deputandi, qui omnium, et singulorum Christifidelium ad huiusmodi ecclesiam pro dicta indulgentia consequenda confluentium confessiones audire. Et ipsos ab omnibus et singulis eorum criminibus excessibus et delictis commissis, etiam si talia forent, super quibus esset Apostolica Sedes merito consulenda, a censuris ecclesiasticis, etiam quarum legitur in coena Domini, absoluere, eisque paenitentiam salutarem iniungere, ac emissa per eos uota quaecunque, ultramarino, uisitatione liminum Beatorum Apostolorum Petri et Pauli, et Sancti Jacobi Compostella, ac castitatis, et Religionis uotis duntaxat [16r] exceptis, in alia pietatis opera commutare, libere et licite ualeant, licentiam et facultatem concedimus. Non obstantibus constitutionibus et ordinationibus Apostolicis, necnon suspensione quibusdam similium uel dissimilium Indulgentiarum, praesertim propter fabricam Basilicae Principis Apostolorum de Vrbe, factis et faciendis, caeterisque in contrarium facientibus quibuscunque, praesentibus perpetuis temporibus ualituris. Datae Romae ap. S. Pet. Anno etc. M.D.XV. xiii kl. Septembris. Pont. Nostri anno. iii.º

III. 3 July 1526, Clement VII to 'Peter' patriarch of the Maronites [Musa al-Akkari]

Summary:
Here Clement VII explains how, once news had reached him of the election of the new patriarch of the Maronites (Musa al-Akkari), he decided to send the Franciscan Bernardino da Udine as his nuncio to provide confirmation of this election. Bernardino was also charged with carrying other documents, perhaps indulgences, that Clement hoped would be welcome to the Maronites. The document ends with an exhortation that Musa preserve his flock in the faith.
See Chapter 3:II.
Text:
AAV: Arm. XL, 12, 7r–7v
[7r] Venerabili fratri moderno Patriarchae Maronitarum
Venerabilis frater Salutem etc. Cum ad nos de obitu bonae memoriae Petri Patriarchae Maronitarum et suffectione tue fraternitatis in illius locum[10] esset allatum, sane nos qui antea ex nostro etiam officio et nostrorum predecessorum cunctos ^{consuetudine} istorum locorum christifideles per Nuntium et literas ^{visitare} institueramus, desyderium hoc nostrum ^{aliquanto} maturauimus, vt tuae fraternitatis electionem apostolica autem ^{de more} confirmaremus quo nihil tibi in regendis spiritualiter istis populis ad autoritatem deesset.[11] Itaque delegimus dilectum filium Bernardinum de Vtino ordinis minorum et sacre Theologie professorem nostrum et huius Sancte Sedis Nuntium, per quem

108   *Appendices*

confirmationem ipsam ad te mitteremus, teque cum populis tue cure commissis in dei omnipotentis seruitio confortaremus. Addidmus Breuia aliquot in commendationem tue fraternitatis et populorum eorundem ^ad dominos temporales^ precipueque ^Macchademum vestrum ac^ facultates eidem Nuntio nos concessimus ^nonnullas^ vt erga tuam fraternitatem tuosque populos nomine huius Sante Sedis gratiosum se reddere posset. Nunc etsi ^te minime^ indigere ^vllius^ adhortationis arbitramur, teque tuo officio et electioni de te facte digne responsum speramus, tamen ex abundantia caritatis qua te et populos tuos paterniter prosequimur[12] et ^affectu te^ hortamur in domino,[13] vt te ipsum [7v][14] tuosque ^[populos]^ in catholicae fidei puritat[e e]t in ea cu[m] Romana ecclesia unione que[15] [vo]biscum iam inde ab Inno. iii. et Eugenii iiii. pred[eces]sorum nostrorum temporibus sancita est ^conserues, et^ In pressuri[s] gentium Diuinam misericordiam et ^consolationem^ proximam ^fore^ speretis. Id enim nos agimus (te[ste] domino) et ad eum finem nostre cognitationes dirigunt[ur] vt rebus inter christianos ^principes^ quacunque ratione compositis, ad vestram et aliorum christifid[e]lium in seruitute infidelium degentium liberation[em] ^nos^ conuertamus. Id quod ^non pro[cul]^ per Dei [mi]sericordiam confidimus. Ita[que] ^venerabilis frater^ quando ad tuo[rum] spiritualium filiorum regimen a Deo vocat[us] es, incumbe in eam cura[m] vt tuae oues spirituali pabulo a te assidue foueantur, et ^intra^ fidei sancte cancellos ^et septa^ custodiantur ne hereticorum aut infidelium morsibus [p]ateant.[16] Nostrum enim erit, v[t] post Deum omnipotentem tibi et tuis ^nulla in re et^ nunquam desim[us]. Quemadmodum hec ex eodem Nuntio nostro cui fide[m] habebis plenissime intelliges. Datum Romae iii. Iulii. 1526. Anno tertio.

IV. 7 July 1526, Clement VII to the Custodian of Holy Places in Jerusalem

Summary:
This is a letter of introduction for Bernardino da Udine to the Franciscan Custodian of the Holy Places in Jerusalem. It certifies Bernardino's mission to the Maronites and Armenians, and asks that the Custodian support this Franciscan, particularly in replacing members of his party who may have been lost along the way.
  See Chapter 3:II.
Text:
AAV: Arm. XL, 12, 17r
  Dilecto filio Guardiano domus Hierosolimitanum
  Dilecto filio salutem. Cum mittamus in presentia Nuntium nostrum ad Maronitas et Armenos dilectum filium ^Bernardinum^ de Vtino tui ordinis minorum de obseruantia et sacrae Theologiae professorem exhibitor praesentium pro nonnullis nostris et huius Ste Sedis ac catholicae fidei negotiis, nos etsi pro certo atque exploratum habemus deuotionem tuam ei cum sua tum nostra etiam causa de benigna charitate non defuturam, tum te hortamur in domino, ac praecipuis etiam tibi in virtute Sanctae obedientiae, vt ipsi ^Bernardino^

Appendices 109

Nuntio nostro quacumque in re poteris, caritatem et hospitalitatem exhibeas. Et si quo casu sociorum eius numerus iminutus, et ei opus aliis iis ad hoc ministerium de vno vel pluribus sociis ex ista domo amanter prouideas. vt munus fuerit nostrae commisionis ad Dei laudem exequi ipse [Bernardinus] hoc posset. Datum Romae vii. Iulii. 1526 anno tertio.

V. 19 March 1527, Clement VII to the Patriarch of the Maronites [Musa al-Akkari]

Summary:
Patriarch Musa al-Akkari had sent two ambassadors, an archbishop named Antonius, and a monk named Elias, to Rome with a declaration of obedience to the papacy. Antonius died in a shipwreck during this journey, but Elias reached Rome safely. Clement therefore appoints Elias as his nuncio to Musa, charging him to deliver confirmation of his obedience, and so of his election as patriarch. Musa's later attempts to acquire confirmation, however, suggest that Elias was unable to complete the return journey to Lebanon. At the very end of this letter Clement informs Musa of the difficulties that he was himself facing, doubtless a reference to the events that would soon lead to the sack of Rome on 6 May 1527.

See Chapter 3:II.

Text:
AAV: Arm. XL, 17, 70r–70v

[70r] Venerabilis frater salutem. Postquam superiore anno memores fraternitatis tue quam in Patriarcham dilectorum in Christo filiorum vniuersorum Maronitarum in Syria degentium [nouiter] electam audiebamus, et tam illam quam ipsos Maronitas paterna charitate visitare et in domino consolari[17] cupientes dilectum filium Bernardinum de Vtino ordinis minorum et sacre Theologiae professorem Nuntium ad te nostrum cum nostris literis et facultate electionem de te factam confirmandi[18] miseramus, venit ad nos [nuper] is qui has nostras tue fraternitati reddet dilectus filius Helias monachus nec sine [graui] nostri animi dolore nobis exposuit, bonae memoriae Antonium Archiepiscopum Caserontum vnacum ipso Helia obedientiam nobis tuo nomine prestandam a te[19] missus naufragio perisse [antequam ad nos peruenire potuit]. De eius viri casu sicut debuimus intime doluimus, Tue autem fraternitatis affectum et pietatem[20] perinde suscepimus et admissimus[21] per dominum Archiepiscopum obedientiae praestationis effect[am] aliter adimpleuisses. [Quare ipsum] Heliam pedes deosculatum cum nostra ad te et omnes Maronitas benedictione remittentes, cum iam ipsum Nuntium nostrum cetera quae ei mandauimus tecum egisse, et electionem de tua fraternitate factam confirmasse credamus [70v] [...][22] nomine domini Iesu Christi virtute sancte obedientie,[23] Tua fraternitas populusque tibi comissus assidue precatur[24] vt in pressuris et persecutionibus, quibus dignum sua persona animum et constantiam serue[s] salutemque animarum gregis tibi comissi inc[es]santer inuigiles, premium a Deo multiple[x] pro multiplicia labore relaturus. Nos

110   *Appendices*

enim ne ipsi quidem ᵗᵒᶜ ᵗᵉᵐᵖᵒʳᵉ experti sumus fluctationum et erumnarum, petrique cymbam ᵃᵈᵛᵉʳˢᵃⁿᵗⁱᵘᵐ ᵛᵉⁿᵗᵒʳᵘᵐ colluctatione ᵠᵘᵃˢˢᵃᵗᵃᵐ vix r[e]gimus, nunquam fraternitati tue neque nostris precibus neque ope [...]²⁵ poterimus deerimus. Dat[um] Rome die xviiij. Martij. 1527. anno 4.

VI. 25 January 1531, Clement VII to the *muqaddam* 'Abd al-Mun'im III

Summary:
A letter of consolation and exhortation from Clement VII to the *muqaddam*, or governor, of Bsharri, 'Abd al-Mun'im III. As in Appendix V above, Clement remarks upon recent persecutions that he had himself faced, but promises to assist the *muqaddam* in so far as he is able.

See Chapter 3:II.

Text:
AAV: Arm. XL, 41, 40r

Dil. Fili salutem. Superiori anno literas Nobilitatis tuae recepimus nobis summe gratas. Te enim in ista longinqua regione nomen sanctum Christi adorantem et vexillum Sanctae Crucis cum popularibus tuis gerentem dilecti in Christo filii loco habemus precipuaque charitate prosequimur. Quamobrem cum haberemus idoneum nuntium per quem literas ad te daremus, non duximus praetermittendum quin paterne salutaremus te, et in Deo Domino consolaremur, siquidem non ignoremus quas pro Dei nomine sufferas cum tuis pressuras de quibus cum compatimur vobis, tum etiam congaudemur. Illis enim mediis ut nosti ad celestia peruenitur, et fides credentium coronatur. Nam etiam ipsi quod tibi notum credimus quamque in medio Christianitatis totius constituti, tamen per hos annos nihil non passi simul a nostris, quid mirum si haec vos suffertis ab alienis. Proinde fili dilecte perseuerandum est, et contra humanas accerbitates pro diuino honore fortibus animis et constanti voluntate persistendum. Quamquam haec charitate potius adducti loquimur, quam ut relligionem Nobilitatis tuae adhortatione agere putemus, de cuius inclyta constantia et in Dio Dei seruitio uoluntate assidue audimus quae cupimus. Nos hinc si qua in re aut consolari, aut iuuare Nobilitatem tuam possemus. Uolumus esse tibi paratam huius Sanctae Sedis benignitatem, sicut pro communi relligione et mutua dilectione facere debemus et semper faciemus. Dat. Romae etc XXV Januarii 1531 anno 8°.

VII. 30 August 1535, Paul III to Joseph Peter the Maronite, archbishop elect of Tripoli

Summary:
Paul III appoints Joseph Peter, a Maronite priest and monk 'of the order of St Basil', to the see of Tripoli in Lebanon. The new pope also provides a special license for Joseph Peter to reside in Antioch rather than in his see.

Appendices   111

Text:
Bkerké: Bibliothèque de la Résidence patriarcale maronite, 113, 278–84.

[278] Paulus Epicopus seruus seruorum Dei Dilecto filio Joseph Petri de Monte Libano electo Tripolensis salutem et Apostolicam Benedictionem. Apostolatus officium meritis licet imparibus nobis ex alio communicatum, quo ecclesiarum omnium regimini praesidemus utiliter exequi, adiuuante Domino cupientes solliciti cordis reddimur [280] et solertes, ut cura de Ecclesiarum ipsarum regiminibus agitur committendis, tales illis in Pastores praeficere studeamus, qui populum suae curae creditum scians non solum doctrina uerbi, sed etiam exemplo boni operis informare, commissaque Ecclesias uelint et ualeant, duce Domino salubriter regere, et feliciter gubernare; Dudum siquidem prouisiones Ecclesiarum omnium hinc uacantium, et in antea uacaturum ordinationi, et dispositioni nostrae reseruauimus, decernentes ex tunc irritum et inane, si secus super his aliis quoque quauis auctoritate scienter uel ignoranter contingeret attemptari. Postmodum uero Ecclesia Tripolitanum cui bonae memoriae Simon Episcopus Tripolensis dum uiueret praesidebat, per obitum eiusdem Simonis Episcopi qui extra Romanam Curiam debitum naturae persoluit, Pastoris solatio destituta nos uacatione huiusmodi fide dignis relatione intellecta ad prouisionem eiusdem Ecclesiae celerem et felicem, de quas nullius praeter nos hac uice se intromittere potuit, siue potest, ne Ecclesia quae longae uacationis exponatur incommodis; Paternis, et sollicitis studiis intendentes post deliberationem, quam de praeficiendo eidem Ecclesiae personam utilem, et fructuosam, cum fratribus nostris habuimus diligentem, demum ad te Monachum Ordinis S. Basilii ordinem ipsum expresse professum in Praesbiteratus ordine constitutum litterarum scientia praeditum, uitae ac morum honestate decorum in spiritualibus prouidum, et temporalibus circumspectum, aliisque [282] multiplicum uirtutum meritis, prout fide dignorum testimoniis accepimus insignitum, direximus oculos nostrae mentis, quibus omnibus debita meditatione pensatis, te a quibusuis excommunicationis suspensionis, et interdicti, aliisque Ecclesiasticis sententiis, censuris et poenis, a iure uel homine quauis occasione, uel causa latis, si quibus quomodolibet innodatus existis ad effectum praesentium dumtaxat consequendum, harum serie absoluentes, et absolutum fore censentes de persona tua nobis, et eisdem fratribus ob tuorum [ex]igentiam[26] meritorum acceptam praefatae Ecclesiae de ipsorum fratrum consilio auctoritate Apostolica prouidimus, teque illi in Episcopum praeficimus, et Pastorem, curam et administrationem ipsius Ecclesiae tibi in spiritualibus et temporalibus plenarie committendo in illo, qui dat gratias et largitur praemia confidentes, quod dirigentes Domino actus tuos, praefata Ecclesia sub tuo felici regimine regetur utiliter, et prospere dirigetur, ac grata in eisdem spiritualibus et temporalibus suscipiet incrementa. Iugum igitur Domini tuis impositum humeris prompta deuotione suscipiens, curam et administrationem praedictas sic exercere studeas sollicite fideliter et prudenter, quod Ecclesia ipsa gubernatori prouido, et fructuoso administratori gaudeat se commissam. Tuque praeter aeternae retributionis praemium, nostram et Apostolicae benedictionem et gratiam

112 *Appendices*

exinde uberius consequi merearis, et insuper cum sicut accepimus, tu ad dictam Ecclesiam, quae in partibus infidelium consistit omnimode nequias te conferre [284] uotis tuis fauorabiliter annuentes, Tibi quod ad dictam Ecclesiam Tripolensis accedere et apud illam personaliter residere minime tenearis, quodque postquam munus consecrationis susceperis in Ciuitate et Dioecesi Antiochenae dummodo ad id per venerabilem fratrem nostrum Petrum Modernum et pro tempore existentem Patriarcham Antiochenam requisitus fueris, et de eorum speciale licentia Pontificalia officia exercere libere et licite ualeas, constitutionibus et ordinationibus Apostolicis, caeterisque contrarijs nequaquam obstantibus, auctoritate praedicta, tenore praesentium de speciali gratia indulgemus. Datum Romae apud. S. Nazareum anno Incarnationis Domini 1535 .3. Kl. Septemb. Pontificatus nostri anno primo.

L. de Torres

VIII. 21 September 1542, Paul III to the Maronite clergy and people

Summary:

Paul III announces to the Maronite clergy and people that he has sent the Franciscan Felice da Venezia to Lebanon with letters to Patriarch Musa al-Akkari, the *muqaddam* 'Abd al-Mun'im III, as well as the present letter to the wider Maronite community. The pope then exhorts the Maronites to keep the faith, which he defines by reference to earlier papal bulls to the Maronites.

See Chapter 3:IV.

Text:

Bkerké: Bibliothèque de la Résidence patriarcale maronite, 113, 294–6.[27]

[294] Paulus Episcopus seruus seruorum Dei Venerabilibus Fratribus Archiepiscopis, et Episcopis, ac dilectis filiis Clero, et populo Maronitarum Salutem et Apostolicam Benedictionem. Fili redeunti istuc dilecto filio Fratre Felici de Venetiis Commissario, et Procuratori Guardiani domus Montis Sion litteras ad Venerabilem fratrem Petrum Patriarcham, et ad dilectum filium nobilem virum Ioannem Abdelmenem Dominum temporalem uestros dedimus; perpetua tamen erga uos Charitate impulsi etiam ad uos separatim alias dare litteras ei uoluimus, ad uestrum omnium spiritualem consolationem, sumus enim cum de omnium Christi fidelium ubique consistentium salute solliciti, tum de uobis aliquanto curiosius, quos longo Maris et terrarum spatia a nobis separant, et hostes infideles duro praemunt seruitio, quo magis uestra fides ac pietas laudanda est, quod seiuncti a nobis, ab infidelibus opressi; Deo tamen inconcussam tanto iam tempore seruastis, et seruaturos uos pollicemini; Pergite igitur Venerabilis fratres et dilecti filij, sicut cepistis, ut uos decet, obedite huic Sanctae Apostolicae sedi et mandatis eius per uestros Praedecessores, praecipue per felice recordationis Innocentium 4: Eugenium 4: et Leonem X. uobis traditis, mutuam

Appendices 113

inter uos Charitatem seruare; praessuras propter Iesum Domnium fortiter [296] sustinete, expectantes Beatam spem, et eam, quae in Euangelio talibus repromissa est a Domino, consolationem aeternam, et copiosam mercedem in Coelis, qui uos sua omnipotenti dextera benedicat et protegat, Datum Romae apud S. Petrum Anno Dominicae Incarnationis. 1542 11. Kl. Xbrio Pontificatus nostri anno nono.

Blo. El. Fulgin.

IX. 5 April 1544 [=1543], Musa al-Akkari to Marcello Cervini[28]

Summary:

See the discussion of this document in Chapter 3:IV. This letter has been translated from the karshuni original by Rosemary Maxton (Oxford) and Lucy Parker (Oxford).

Text:

ASF: Carte Cerviniane, 41, 99r–99v

[99r] I kiss [your] pure, immaculate hands after prostrating to [your] brotherly Eminence, beloved and revered brother, most reverend brother, cardinal of Santa Cruz, protector of [me] the despicable one. And [I] the despicable one two years ago sent some students to offer obedience before the Holy Father and before our brothers the cardinals in the apostolic see. They were the brother monk Fra Felizio [Felice] and the boy deacon Butrus [Peter] the Maronite. As we have not heard [any] news from them, on this date we have sent this boy, Deacon Sarkīs, from among the students of the despicable one, so that [you] the brother will watch over him, just as the deceased cardinal of Santa Cruz [Bernardino López de Carvajal] watched over students during the time of the deceased Father [Pope] Adrianus the Sixth. In this way [you] the brother can watch over this boy, so that he can be established in the [papal] see, and learn speech and reading and writing. And what we wish of you is that he should inform us of [any] news and continue to send us blessed letters from the Holy Father and from [you] the brother. May your brotherhood always remind the Holy Father to not continue to forget we despicable ones, because we are striving intensely for our faith and we are greatly oppressed. We hope for aid and salvation through your prayers, Amen, Amen.

Sent from Dayr Qannubin in the blessed Mount Lebanon in the district of Ṭrāblūs [Tripoli].

Written on the fifth day of the blessed month of Nīsān [April] in the year 1544 from the divine incarnation.

The letter of the most wretched of patriarchs, Butrus [Musa al-Akkari], in the monastery of our Lady the Virgin of Qannubin.

[99v] To be given to the brotherly hand of the brother the cardinal of Santa Cruz, protector of the Maronites in the city of Rome, as a pledge of love.

114 *Appendices*

X. 5 April 1543, Musa al-Akkari to Marcello Cervini

Summary:
In this letter to Cardinal Marcello Cervini, the Maronite Patriarch Musa al-Akkari complains of how he had yet to receive news from previous emissaries he had sent to Rome. This included the Maronite bishop of Beirut, Simeon, whom Musa had sent to Rome, with the aim that he would then return to Lebanon to teach what he had learned there to the Maronites. As a result, Musa was now sending new messengers with letters to Paul III and Cervini, by which the Maronite deacon Sarkis and the Franciscan Felice da Venezia are doubtless intended (see Appendix IX).

See Chapter 3:IV.

Text:
ASF: Carte Cerviniane, 41, 101r–101v

[101r] Tradutione   IC   XC

Dopo la debita R.ᵗⁱᵃ humiliter et deuote accetto et baso le Mani Mondi et Purj di V.S.R.ma dounque sera la veneranda Presentia del Mons.ᵒʳ mio R.ᵐᵒ Car.ˡᵉ di S.ᵗᵃ Croce, Per mera benignita sua Protetor di tutta la Natione di Maruniti figlioli della chiesia catholica Romana, alla quale, io humil discipulo Pietro Patriarca di monte libano mandai per il Passato al quante lettere al summo Pontefice Romano, basando et rendendo debita obedientia a sua Beatitudine secondo il solito, delle qual lettere non habiamo hauuta risposta ancora, ne manco habbiamo hauuto notitia del R.ᵈᵒ vescouo di Baruti nominato Simeon Marunita, qual habbiamo mandato agli Piedi di sua santtita in loco nostro, accioche impari gli Riti et santti costumi della chiesia catholica di Roma, per poter poi canonicamente instruir questi Populi nostri di qua Autoritate accepta a Pontefice, se il nominato [vescovo è ancora][29] in Roma (come credo che sia) supplico humilmente V.S.R.ma gli habbia per riccomandato et tenghi spesso gli occhij suoi sopra di luj. Il Presente latore e il Diacono Cerchis Marunita nostro Discipulo homo dabene et catholico, per il quale etiam scrissi vna al summo Pontefice in caldeo con propria mia mano et altra feci scriuere in lengua Taliana per il predetto cerchis, la qua cosa V.S.R.ma legendo la lettera che feci scriuere intendera la materia contiene. Per il che humilmente suppli et Prego la S.V.R.ma per la charita et amore di Christo saluator del Mondo habbia chariteuolemente per ricommandate et il [...][30] Sercis Marunita et il presente lator cerchis Diacono, qual, spero, V.S.R.ma presentara al summo Pontefice et fara per amor mio tutto quello domandara detto cerchis iuste et oneste, cosi credo V.S.R.ma fara alla quale [101v] Humilmente me ricommando et baso le man et la Prego mi perdoni se sono stato fastedioso con V.S.R.ma. Data in Monte libano in la Prouincia di Tripoli di Suria adi, 5, April 1543.

L'humil seruitor di V.S.R.ma
Pietro Patriarca di Monte Libano

Appendices 115

XI. 19 September 1543, Musa al-Akkari to Marcello Cervini

Summary:

Musa al-Akkari notifies Cervini that he had received letters from him and from Pope Paul III. However, he had not received the vestments and insignia of office (mitre, chalice, and episcopal staff) that he expected to find with those letters. Musa therefore sends to Rome the Maronite deacon George, in order to request these items and to offer obedience to Paul III, asking Cervini that he present this emissary to the pope.

See Chapter 3:IV.

Text:

ASF: Carte Cerviniane, 41, 102r–102v

[102r] Benedictio diuina, et gratia celestis que quieuit super discipulos mundos, et apostolos sine macula congregatos in monte syon sancto, et in Monte Oliuarum mundo, sit quiescens et multiplicet, et stet super fratrem meum reuer.^{mam} car.^{lem} Ste Crucis curatorem nostre calamitatis in sede maiestatis, et coram patre sancto, et coram nostris fratribus cardinalibus in congregatione letitiae. Preterea idesse [sic: adesse?] fratribus sanctis nos desiderio magno tenemur uidere tuam benignitatem, Deus ostendat nobis faciem tuam in probitate et letitia, cito et sine tarditate amen. Idem nouimus de fratribus per litteras quas scripsisti et missisti ad nos, et intelleximus singule, et benignitas tua peruenit ad nos, et fuit multe super nos a principio, Deus magnificet caritatem tuam, et faciat super te misericordiam suam, nec impediat nos quin te uideamus, o lex nostra, et o ossa nostra, o, fortitudo nostra, Tu robur et stabilitor legis nostrae, et nos quiescimus sub tua probitate et benignitate, idem faciunt mitte a nobis, Deus, et Domina nostra custodiant te, sicut tu custodis pauperes, recepi quod mitit ad me sanctus papa Paulus per manus fratris felicis qui est frater Hierosolemitanum, et diaconi Petri Maronitae, et ea omnia integra, sine tamen mithra, et sine calice, et sine baculo pastorali, vos uero fratres pro mea consolatione orate patrem sanctum, ut mittat mithram, calicem et baculum pastoralem, quoniam monasterium hec non habet, alloquere patrem sanctum ut curam suscipiat montis, et eius paupertate sua benigna prouidentia subueniat, nec obliuiscatur pauperum ob eius misericordiam [102v] Ego pauper, fidelis in deo, et in sanctitate patris, sit oculus fratris nostri super filium nostrum Georgium diaconum, portitorem nostrae litterae qui pro me reuerentiam praestabit et obedientiam coram patre sancto, papa paulo, et coram omni cetero fratrum nostrorum cardinalium, frater mi comple desiderium meum, uade ad patrem sanctum cum nostro nuntio, et sis auxiliator ei quoniam tu frater protector noster es in omnibus nostris necessitatibus, et comples nobis necessaria super tuam consuetudinem et benignam prouidentiam pro tuo singulari amore tuo, diximus multa uerba ut ostendamus fratribus tuis, similiter sit oculus noster super filium episcopum Simonem ipse de discipulis meis est pauper nuntiatum est nobis quod ipse manet sub oculo patris

116   *Appendices*

sancti ipse meus discipulis erit sub obedientia et manu fratrum nostrorum singulorum Datum in monasterio Canuben Sanctae Mariae in Monte Libano sub prouincia Tripolis anno 1543 post humanatum Christum, 19 die Septembris.

XII. 19 September 1555, Musa al-Akkari to Paul IV

Summary:
Patriarch Musa al-Akkari notifies the newly-elected Pope Paul IV (elected 23 May 1555) that the ambassador of the Maronites, Galeazzo della Balle, as well as the Maronite bishop of Beirut, Simeon, would deliver the obedience of the Maronites to him, and inform him of their condition. Moreover, Musa asks for a blessing from Paul IV, and a new cardinal protector of the Maronites to take the place of Marcello Cervini, whose brief reign as Pope Marcellus II had come to an end with his death on 1 May 1555.

Text:
AAV: A.A. Arm. I–XVIII, 5406, 1r–2r
[1r] In Nome di Dio Eterno
Al Padre mio, Il padre santo, sedente nella sedià Apostolica
Di poi basciati gli piedi, et Inclinatomi alla Terra con ogni inclinatione et reuerentia, del mio Padre santo, Noi humil Patriarcha et seruo peccatore Petro patriarcha della Nation Maronità, hauemo mandato Il portatore di questa litera Il nostro diletto Figlio in Christo, M. Galeazzo dalle balle dalla città di Bologna, accio che lui uengha a dare obbedientia a .V.S.ᵗᵃ insieme col Episcopo Simeone Maronita che di li si truoua, et loro daranno obbedienza da parte del discepolo et di tutto Il populo Maronità, et hauemo eletto questo nostro Figlio sopranominato per esser da bene et non hauemo uoluto mandare altro Amb.ᵗᵉ della Sorià, saluo questo, Accio che la .S.ᵗᵃ.V. l'accetti fauoreuolmente, et gli diciamo come ci habiamo rallegrati et consolati, et massime gli spiriti nostri dell'assumption fatta della S.ᵗᵃ.V. alla Sedià Apostolica Ancor ne ha doluto della morte dell'Antecessore suo Marcello, perche lui era Protettore della Nation nostra, Ma maggiormente ci habiamo confortati et allegrati della assuntion sua al luogo della sedià di Pietro, et delli predecessori di quella; Iddio l'ha elettà desiderata et uoluta et l'ha assumta a questa sedià honorata et magna, speriamo in Iesu Christo, che lui la confirmara In quel stato, et gli dara longa vita, et molti anni, si come Feci à San Pietro, Et accio che noi humili uiuiamo sotto Il Gouerno di V.S.ᵗᵃ et viuino gli animi nostri In gaudio, Pero non desieriamo altro, noi peccatori, se non che ci habiate per racc.ᵗⁱ, et ne assoluerete con la benignità uestra, et ne mandiate la benedition della uestra bocca santa, si come hanno fatto la buona memoria delli Antecessori suoi sotto la misericordia di Dio; Et accio che noi ci [1v] essaltiamo et allegriamo, perche la benedition di V.Sᵗᵃ è la benedition di Iesu christo, et ne solua delli peccati et offese nostre, Et perche noi speriamo et crediamo et siamo stabili a quel che crede la

Romana chiesa, et da molto tempo fino al presente giorno mai n'è mancato la benedittioni delli Pontifici passati, come V.S.ᵗᵃ uedrà per Breui et altre patenti bollate in piombo, doue V.S.ᵗᵃ ne mandara vna simile, accio possiamo hauer memoria ancor di lei, Ancor ne habiamo vna cassa piena delli altri Pontefici, come la S.V. potrà intendere dall'apportatore di questa, et come le vediamo, ci rallegriamo et godemo della benedition loro, et domandiamo dalla S.V. il comfortò a quel che hoggi siamo, sotto le cattiuità et Tirannide di quelli che non hanno misericordia di Noi, Et gia sonno infastiditi gli animi nostri, et gli cori nostri delli Tribulationi che dentro h[ab]iamo, la S.ᵗᵃ V. orara per noi, et [do]mand[a]ra à Dio la liberatione et saluatione delle mani delli auuersarii nostri Infideli, Et se la. S.V. si uorrà Informare et certificare delle cose nostre, potra domandare al sopradetto nostro Ambasciatore, perche lui sa Il tutto come passano, al quale gli potra dare piena Fede et credenza; Et per Tanto domandiamo à Iesu Christo et alli prieghi di V.S.ᵗᵃ, che tutte queste Tribulation discacci da noi, perla misericordia sua et della Vergine Maria et de suoi santi: Et se V.S.ᵗᵃ ordenara cosa alcuna, della sua benedittione ò altro le mandi per Il nostro Ambasciatore M. Galeazo dalle balle, accio le vediamo inanzi la morte, et la S.ᵗᵃ V. l'haura per racc.ʳᵒ, perche è sotto l'ombra sua.

Voliamo da V.S.ᵗᵃ vn Protettore in luogho del nostro, che era la buona memoria di Marcello, ch'el signore Iddio gli perdoni; Et come habiamo ditto à V.S.ᵗᵃ, [2r] potra informarsi di tutte le cose nostre, dal sopradetto M. Galeazo, dechiarando che Tutto Il Fauore ch'ella Fara à lui, reputaremo farsi à noi humil seruo di V.S.ᵗᵃ, et cosi di nuouo humilmente Inclinomi alla Terra due et tre fiate alli piedi di V.Sᵗᵃ, et bascio quelli con molti basci, domandando à Iesu Christo, che si come ho basicato gli piedi del Padre santo Adriano buona memoria, cosi non mora che possa basicar' gli piedi et mani di V.Sᵗᵃ, alla quale nostro signore Iddio doni longa Vita, nel tempo del suo Felicissimo Pontificato,

Questa è l'Epistola del Humil Pietro Patriarcha della Nation Maronità del Monasterio di Canobin del Monte Libano Santo nel paese di Tripoli di Soria, fatta alli XIX di settembre 1555.

XIII. 23 September 1555, Bonifacio da Ragusa to Paul IV[31]

Summary:
This is a letter of recommendation for the Maronites, sent to Paul IV by the Franciscan custodian of the Holy Places, Bonifacio da Ragusa. Bonifacio asks that Paul bless the Maronites and provide them with the gifts that other popes had granted. However, like Francesco Suriano 40 years earlier (see Appendix I), Bonifacio alerts Paul to areas of custom in which the Maronites differed from Rome, asking that the Maronites abstain from meat on the Sabbath and wear shoes while administering the sacraments, just as Roman Catholics did. Finally, Bonifacio informs Paul of his efforts to repair the holy places in Jerusalem, commending them to the pope's care.

118 *Appendices*

Text:

AAV: AA. Arm. I–XVIII, 6542, 52r–53v

[52r] Mirabitur forsitan tua Beatissima paternitas mi pater Sancte quid me nunc potissimum prouocet ad eam literas dare verum nouerit ipsa me nullam prorsus cum sim insufficiens et indignus scribendi habere causam Nisi et facilitatem tuam que passim vulgo et per totam vniuersam orbem de ipsa (et merito) predicatur Nam et Religioni Christiane a tempore quo adhuc in minoribus erat, semper suis preclaris meritis profuit, suo itaque Immo Christi sacro ordine auxit et fidem in vniuerso periclitantem solus dei uirute sustentauit Quapropter tuam Beatitudinem supplex oro et supplico vt tuum gregem Montis Libani, quos Maronitas appellamus eo amore, eaque Charitate suscipias, qua predicessores tue Beatitudinis eos suscipere ac fauere Nunc ad pedes tue Beatitudinis tamquam ueri Christiani humiles accedunt Benedic igitur eis et nobis omnibus colesti benedictione Donesque iisdem donis quibus felicis Memorie et Recordationis Eugenius 4s Alexander 4s Innocentius 8s Nicolaus 5s Sixtus 4s Leo 8s leoque decimus Clemens etiam 10s et Paulus 3s eos donarunt Quorum fidei et Religionis ego frater Bonifacius de Ragusio immeritus Montis Syon Guardianus, ac aliorum s.^{te} terre locorum tua tuorumque predicessorum Auctoritate Gubernator optimum do testimonium.

Vellem tum si tue beatitudini luberet, cordi quoque esset vt ipsi Maronite Sabbatum eo ordine seruarent quo et nos seruamus sine esu carnium sacraque facerent calceatis pedibus sicut et nos facimus Ceterum tue etiam Beatitudi Domini nostri Yesu Christi Sepulchrum aliaque sanctuaria tam in Ciuitate Hierusalem quam extra commendamus Nam his elapsis diebus ereximus nostra paupertate a fondamentis Domini Sepulchrum, quod totaliter minabatur Ruina Tue Beatitudinis pedes humiliter sanctissime facientes osculamus Ex Hierosolimis 23 Septembis [sic] Anno Domini 1555

Tue Beatitudinis

Humilis seruus et obediens filius Guardianus sacri Montis syon

[53v] Beatissimo patri et Christi vicario

Diuina prouidentia

Pape Paulo Quarto

Notes

1 A now-incomplete sixteenth-century transcription of this document (up to *omnes clericos astantes* on 19v) can be found in AAV: Misc., Arm. VI, 39, 23r–24v.

2 This title has been copied in a later hand to that of the text that follows.

3 The transcription in AAV: Misc., Arm. VI, 39, 23r suggests "quae sic se habent".

4 This expansion is suggested in AAV: Misc., Arm. VI, 39, 23r.

5 AAV: Misc., Arm. VI, 39, 24r inserts here 'et ex tunc prout ex nunc sit dignitate patrialchali priuatus, eo ipso; ipse autem patriarcha ore proprio se condemnat. quod totiens...', which is found later in AAV: Misc., Arm. VI, 39, 19r, but with 'si' instead of 'sit'.

Appendices 119

6 AAV: Misc., Arm. VI, 39, 19r reads 'plantum'; my transcription follows the reading on AAV: Misc., Arm. VI, 39 24r.
7 This title is also present at end of AAV: Misc., Arm. VI, 39, 19r. The text in ibid., 19v is in the same hand as the main text of ibid., 18v–19r.
8 "Aut steriles" follows on this line without any break, but it may perhaps be understood with "aut insaniatur [...] aut infirmatur" in the line above.
9 Another copy of this indulgence is to be found in AAV: Misc., Arm. VI, 39, 25r, which is written in the same hand as Appendix I above – perhaps that of D.T. Comitibus who signs off this copy.
10 "et suffectione tue fraternitatis in illius locum" added in margin.
11 "quo nihil tibi in regendis spiritualiter istis populis ad autoritatem deesset" added in margin.
12 "teque tuo officio et electioni de te facte digne responsum speramus, tamen ex abundantia caritatis qua te et populos tuos paterniter prosequimur" added in margin.
13 From here this letter is published in *Bullarium Maronitarum*, 53, with minor variations from what follows.
14 The right margin of 7v is mutilated, hence the loss of some letters in what follows.
15 "conserues" in margin.
16 "ne hereticorum aut infidelium morsibus [p]ateant" in margin.
17 "et in domino consolari" in margin.
18 "cum nostris literis et facultate electionem de te factam confirmandi" in margin.
19 "vnacum ipso Helia obedientam nobis tuo nomine prestandam a te" in margin.
20 Four lines follow that have been rendered illegible through deletion.
21 "et admissimus" in margin.
22 The top line of 70v is mutilated.
23 "nomine domini Iesu Christi virtute sancte obedientie" in margin.
24 "Tua fraternitas populusque tibi comissus assidue precatur" in margin.
25 Deleted word illegible.
26 The first two letters have been partly scratched away. 'I[n]gentiam' may be intended.
27 See also Portugal: National Library of Lisbon, 303, 337r–337v.
28 This letter has been redated to April 1543 due to Appendix XI, which shows that Felice and Peter had returned to Mount Lebanon by September 1543. Since George rather than Felice or Peter then carried Musa's reply to Rome in late 1543, this letter would make little sense if it were sent in 1544.
29 Words erased – the transcription in square brackets is a guess at the possible content.
30 Two words destroyed.
31 For this Franciscan Guardian of the Holy Places, see Agustín Arce, "Bonifacio de Stephanis (c.1504–1582). Ultimo guardian de Monte Sion y obispo de Ston," *Archivium Franciscanum Historicum* 76 (1983): 296–341.

Bibliography

Bibliographies

A Comprehensive Bibliography on Syriac Christianity, n.d. http://www.csc.org.il/db/db.aspx?db=SB

Di Giovanni, Francesca, Sergio Pagano, and Giuseppina Roselli, eds. *Guida delle fonti per la storia dell'Africa del Nord, Asia e Oceania nell'Archivio Segreto Vaticano*. Vatican City: Archivio Segreto Vaticano, 2005.

Gualdo, Germano, ed. *Sussidi per la Consultazione dell'Archivio Vaticano*. Vatican City: Archivio Vaticano, 1989.

King, Margaret, ed. *Oxford Bibliographies Online: Renaissance and Reformation*, n.d. https://www.oxfordbibliographies.com/page/renaissance-and-reformation

Kristeller, Paul Oskar. *Iter Italicum*, vol. 2. Leiden: Brill, 1967.

Manuscript sources

Bkerké: Bibliothèque de la Résidence patriarcale maronite, MS 113.

Florence: Archivio di Stato, Carte Cerviniane, 19, 20, 23, 41, 42, 44, 45, 48.

Jerusalem: Biblioteca Generale della Custodia di Terra Santa, Fondo latini, MS 81.

Lisbon: National Library of Portugal, MS 303.

Vatican City: Archivio Apostolico Vaticano

    A.A. Arm. I–XVIII, 5406.

    A.A. Arm. I–XVIII 6542.

    Arch. Concist., Acta Vicecanc. 3.

    Arch. Concist., Acta Vicecanc. 5.

    Arch. Concist., Acta Vicecanc. 7.

    Arm. XL, 11.

    Arm. XL, 12.

    Arm. XL, 17.

    Arm. XL, 41.

    Misc. Arm. VI, 39.

Vatican City: Biblioteca Apostolica Vaticana, Vat.lat. 5270, 6177, 6178.

Bibliography 121

Printed primary sources

Analecta Franciscana, sive Chronica aliaque varia documenta ad historiam Fratrum Minorum spectantia, vol. 2. Quaracchi: ex Typographia Collegii S. Bonaventurae, 1887.

Chaldeae seu Aethiopicae linguae institutiones: Omnium Aethiopiae regum [...] libellus. Rome: Valerio Dorico, 1552.

Concilium Tridentinum Diariorum, Actorum, Epistularum Tractatum nova collectio. 19 vols. Freiburg-im-Breisgau: Herder, 1901–2001.

Epistolarum Pauli Manutii libri XII. Trnava: Typis Collegii Academici Societatis Jesu, 1752.

Liber sacrosancti Evangelii de Iesu Christo Domino & Deo nostro. Vienna: Michael Zimmerman, 1555.

Modus baptizandi, preces et benedictiones quibus ecclesia Ethiopum utitur [...] orationes quibus iidem utuntur in sacramento Baptismi et confirmationis [...] Missa qua communiter utuntur, quae etiam Canon universalis appellatur. Rome: Antonio Blado, 1549.

Anaissi, Tobias, ed. *Bullarium Maronitarum*. Rome: Bretschneider, 1911.

Anaissi, Tobias, ed. *Collectio documentorum Maronitarum*. Livorno: Fabbreschi, 1921.

de Aranda, Antonio. *Verdadera Informacion dela tierra sancta*. Alcala: Francisco de Cormellas y Pedro de Robles, 1563.

di Calahorra, Giovanni. *Historia cronologica della provincia di Syria, e Terra Santa di Gierusalemme*. Translated by Angelico di Milan. Venice: Antonio Tiuani, 1694.

Casati, C. C. *Lettres royaux et lettres missives inédites*. Paris: Librarie Académique, 1877.

de Chaufepie, Jacques George. *Nouveau dictionnaire historique et critique*, vol. 3. Amsterdam: Chatelain et al, 1753.

Ghobaïra Al-Ghaziri, Bernard. *Rome et l'Eglise Syrienne-Maronite: Théses, Documents, Lettres*. Beirut: Khalil Sarkis, 1906.

Gill, Joseph, ed. *Epistolae pontificiae ad Concilium Florentinum spectantes*, vol. 3. Rome: Pontificium Institutum Orientalium Studiorum, 1946.

Giustinian, Paolo, and Vincenzo Quirini. "Libellus ad Leonem X." In *Annales Camaldulenses*, edited by Giovanni-Benedetto Mittarelli and Anselmo Costadoni, vol. 9, 612–719. Venice: Pasquali, 1773.

Golubovich, Girolamo, ed. *Biblioteca bio-bibliografica della Terra Santa e dell'Oriente francescano*. Florence: Quaracchi, 1906–1939.

Golubovich, Girolamo, ed. *Il Trattato di Terra Santa e dell'Oriente di Frate Francesco Suriano*. Milan: Tipografia editrice Artigianelli, 1900.

Interiano, Giorgio. *La vita, et Sito de Zichi, Chiamati Ciarcassi: historia notabile*. Venice: Aldo Manuzio, 1502.

Lanz, Karl, ed. *Correspondenz des Kaisers Karl V. aus dem königlichen Archiv und der Bibliothèque de Bourgogne zu Brüssel*, vol. 1. Leipzig: Brochaus, 1844.

Lefevre, Renato. "Documenti e notizie su Tasfā Ṣeyon e la sua attività romana nel sec. XV." *Rassegna di Studi Etiopici* 24 (1969–1970): 74–133.

Lefevre, Renato. "Documenti pontifici sui rapporti con l'Etiopia nei secoli XV e XVI." *Rassegna di Studi Etiopici* 5 (1946): 17–41.

122 Bibliography

Mansi, Girolamo et al, eds. *Sacrorum Conciliorum nova et amplissima collectio*, vol. 32. Paris: Welter, 1901.

Müller, Andreas. *Symbolae syriacae*. Berlin: ex Officina Rungiana, 1673.

Olazarán, Jesús. *Documentos inéditos tridentinos sobra la justificación*. Madrid: Ediciones Fax, 1957.

Rabbath, Antoine, ed. *Documents inédits pour server a l'histoire de Christianisme en orient (XVI–XIX siècle)*, vol. 2. Paris: A. Picard et Fils, 1910.

Rota, Giovanni. *La vita: costumi: et statura de Sofi: Re di Persia et di Media et de molti altri Regni et paesi*. Rome: Eucharius Silber, 1508.

Torres, Francisco, and Paolo Orsini, ed. and trans. *Apostolicarum constitutionum et Catholicae doctrinae Clementis Romani libri VIII [...] Accesserunt Canones Concilij Nicaeni LXXX ex Arabico in Latinum conuersi et Responsa Nicolai I ad consulta Bulgarorum*. Antwerp: Christopher Plantin, 1578.

Secondary literature

Abouzayd, Shafiq. "The Maronite Church." In *The Syriac World*, edited by Daniel King, 731–750. London: Routledge, 2018.

Abu-Husayn, Abdul-Rahim. *The View from Istanbul. Lebanon and the Druze Emirate in the Ottoman Chancery Documents, 1546–1711*. London: I. B. Tauris, 2004.

Abulafia, David. *The Great Sea: A Human History of the Mediterranean*. London: Allen Lane, 2011.

Ágoston, Gábor. "Information, Ideology, and the Limits of Imperial Policy: Ottoman Grand Strategy in the Context of Ottoman–Habsburg Rivalry." In *The Early Modern Ottomans: Remapping the Empire*, edited by Virginia H. Aksan and Daniel Goffman, 75–103. Cambridge: Cambridge University Press, 2007.

Al Kalak, Matteo. "Pio, Rodolfo." *DBI* 84 (2015). https://www.treccani.it/enciclopedia/rodolfo-pio_(Dizionario-Biografico)

Allouche, Adel. *The Origins and Development of the Ottoman–Safavid Conflict (906–962 / 1500–1555)*. Berlin: Klaus Schwarz, 1983.

Andretta, Elisa, Antonella Romano, and Maria Antonietta Visceglia. "Introduzione. Le lingue nella Roma del Cinquecento." *Rivista Storica Italiana* 132 (2020): 87–111.

Aoun, Michel. "Le mariage dans l'église Maronite d'après un rituel manuscrit du XVI siècle (Vat. Syr. 52)." *Parole de l'Orient* 23 (1998): 111–165.

Arce, Agustín. "Bonifacio de Stephanis (c.1504–1582). Ultimo guardian de Monte Sion y obispo de Ston." *Archivium Franciscanum Historicum* 76 (1983): 296–341.

Aslanian, Sebouh David, Joyce E. Chaplin, Ann McGrath, and Kristin Mann, "AHR Conversation. How Size Matters: The Question of Scale in History." *American Historical Review* 118 (2013): 1431–1472.

Assemani, Stefano Evodio. *Bibliothecae Mediceae Laurentianae et Palatinae codicum manuscriptorum orientalium catalogus*. Florence: ex Typographio Albiziniano, 1742.

Assemani, Stefano Evodio, and Giuseppe Simone Assemani. *Bibliothecae Apostolicae Vaticanae codicum manuscriptorum catalogus*, vol. 1. Rome: Typographia linguarum orientalium, 1758.

Baroudi, Fady. "Jacobites, Ethiopians and Mount Lebanon." *Liban Souterrain 5* (1998): 75–160.

Bibliography   123

Beltrami, Giuseppe. *La chiesa caldea nel secolo dell'unione*. Rome: Pontificium Institutum Orientalium Studiorum, 1933.

Berchet, Guglielmo. *Relazioni dei Consoli Veneti nella Siria*. Turin: G. B. Paravia, 1866.

Bilaniuk, Petro B. T. *The Fifth Lateran Council (1512–1517) and the Eastern Churches*. Toronto: Central Committee for the Defence of Rite, Tradition and Language of the Ukrainian Catholic Church in USA and Canada, 1975.

Birtachas, Stathis. "Religious Dissent and Its Repression in Venice's Maritime State: The Case of Cyprus (Mid-Sixteenth Century)." In *Le fonti della storia dell'Italia preunitaria: casi di studio per la loro analisi e 'valorizzazione'*, edited by Gerassimos D. Pagratis, 575–600. Athens: Papazissis Publishers, 2019.

Birtachas, Stathis. "Tendenze filoprotestanti a Venezia al tempo di Gabriele Severo." In *Gavriil Seviros, arcivescovo di Filadelfia a Venezia e la sua epoca*, edited by D. G. Apostolopulos, 45–58. Venice: Istituto Ellenico di Studi Bizantini e Postbizantini di Venezia, 2004.

Borbone, Pier Giorgio. "From Tur 'Abdin to Rome: The Syro-Orthodox Presence in Sixteenth-Century Rome." In *Syriac in Its Multi-Cultural Context*, edited by Herman Teule et al, 277–288. Leuven: Peeters, 2017.

Borbone, Pier Giorgio. "Monsignore Vescovo di Soria, also Known as Moses of Mardin, Scribe and Book Collector." *ХРИСТІАНСКІЙ ВОСТОКЪ* 8 (2017): 79–114.

Borbone, Pier Giorgio, and Margherita Farina. "New Documents Concerning Patriarch Ignatius Na'matallah (Mardin, ca. 1515-Bracciano, Near Rome, 1587)." *Egitto e Vicino Oriente* 37 (2014): 179–189.

Bossy, John. *Under the Molehill: An Elizabethan Spy Story*. New Haven: Yale University Press, 2001.

Boyar, Ebru. "Ottoman Expansion in the East." In *The Cambridge History of Turkey. Volume III: The Ottoman Empire as a World Power, 1453–1603*, edited by Suraiya N. Faroqhi and Kate Fleet, 96–114. Cambridge: Cambridge University Press, 2013.

Breydy, Michael. *Geschichte der Syro-Arabischen Literatur der Maroniten vom VII. bis XVI. Jahrhundert*. Opladen: Westdeutscher Verlag, 1985.

Brunelli, Giampiero. "Marcello II, papa." *DBI* 69 (2007). https://www.treccani.it/enciclopedia/papa-marcello-ii_(Dizionario-Biografico)

Bucci, Onorato. "La Chiesa Maronita al Concilio Lateranese V." In *Alla ricerca di soluzioni: Nuova luce sul Concilio Lateranese V*, edited by Nelson H. Minnich, 335–345. Vatican City: Libreria Editrice Vaticana, 2019.

Buzi, Paola. "Roma e la riscoperta della 'perduta e morta lingua egizia dei Cofti' tra il Concilio di Firenze e la pubblicazione di *Lingua aegyptiaca restituta*." *Rivista Storica Italiana* 132 (2020): 158–179.

Calis, Richard Alexander. "Martin Crusius (1526–1607) and the Discovery of Ottoman Greece." PhD diss., Princeton University, 2020.

Cardinali, G. "Rittrato di Marcello Cervini *en orientaliste* (con precisazioni alle vicende di Petrus Damascenus, Mose di Mardin ed Heliodorus Niger)." *Bibliothèque d'Humanisme et Renaissance* 80 (2018): 77–98 and 325–346.

Carlson, Thomas A. *Christianity in Fifteenth-Century Iraq*. Cambridge: Cambridge University Press, 2018.

Casari, Mario. "Vecchietti, Giovanni Battista." *DBI* 98 (2020). https://www.treccani.it/enciclopedia/giovanni-battista-vecchietti_(Dizionario-Biografico)

Casati, C. C. "Extraits de dépêches diplomatiques inédites des empereurs Maximilien Iᵉʳ et Charles-Quint." *Bibliothèque de l'École des Chartes* 31 (1870): 68–71.

124 Bibliography

Catlos, Brian A. "Why the Mediterranean?" In *Can We Talk Mediterranean? Conversations in an Emerging Field in Medieval and Early Modern Studies*, edited by Brian A. Catlos and Sharon Kinoshita, 1–17. Basingstoke: Palgrave Macmillan, 2017.

Catlos, Brian A. "Ethno-Religious Minorities." In *A Companion to Mediterranean History*, edited by Peregrine Horden and Sharon Kinoshita, 361–377. Chichester: John Wiley & Sons, 2014.

Cenci, Cesare. "Il martirio di fra Ginepro da Catania secondo il codice Canoniciano italiano 203." *Archivum Franciscanum Historicum* 55 (1962): 378–381.

Chrysostomides, Julian. "The Byzantine Empire from the Eleventh to the Fifteenth Century." In *The Cambridge History of Turkey. Volume I: Byzantium to Turkey*, edited by Kate Fleet, 6–48. Cambridge: Cambridge University Press, 2010.

Clausi, Benedetto, and Santo Lucà, eds. *Il "sapientissimo calabro". Guglielmo Sirleto nel V centenario della nascita (1514–2014)*. Rome: Università degli Studi di Roma 'Tor Vergata', 2018.

Clines, Robert John. *A Jewish Jesuit in the Eastern Mediterranean: Early Modern Conversion, Mission, and the Construction of Identity*. Cambridge: Cambridge University Press, 2019.

Clines, Robert John. "Between Hermits and Heretics: Maronite Religious Renewal and the Turk in Catholic Travel Accounts of Lebanon after the Council of Trent." In *Travel and Conflict in the Early Modern World*, edited by Gábor Gelléri and Rachel Willie, 108–126. London: Routledge, 2020.

Clines, Robert John. "The Converting Sea: Religious Change and Cross-Cultural Interaction in the Early Modern Mediterranean." *History Compass* 17 (2019): 1–15.

Clines, Robert John. "Pope as Arbiter. The Place of Early Modern Rome in the Pan-Mediterranean Ecumenical Visions of Eastern Rite Christians." In *A Companion to Religious Minorities in Early Modern Rome*, edited by Matthew Coneys Wainwright and Emily Michelson, 55–88. Leiden: Brill, 2020.

Clines, Robert John. "Wayward Leadership and the Breakdown of Reform on the Failed Jesuit Mission to the Maronites, 1577–1579." *Journal of Early Modern History* 22 (2018): 215–237.

Cohen, Ammon. "The Expulsion of the Franciscans from Mount Zion: Old Documents and New Interpretation." *Turcica* 18 (1986): 147–157.

Cozzi, Gaetano. "Venezia dal Rinascimento all'Eta barocca." In *Storia di Venezia dalle Origini alla Caduta della Serenissima*, vol. 6, edited by Gaetano Cozzi and Paolo Prodi, 3–125. Rome: Istituto della Enciclopedia Italiana, 1994.

Da Leonessa, Mauro. "La versione etiopica dei canoni apocrifi del concilio di Nicea secondo i codici vaticani ed il fiorentino." *Rassegna di Studi Etiopici* 2 (1942): 29–89.

Da Leonessa, Mauro. *Santo Stefano Maggiore degli Abissini e le relazioni romano-etiopiche*. Vatican City: Tipografia Poliglotta Vaticana, 1929.

Davis, Natalie Zemon. *Trickster Travels: A Sixteenth-Century Muslim between Worlds*. London: Faber & Faber, 2007.

De Troeyer, B. "Gryphon, Griffoen van Vlaanderen, Griffo." In *Dictionnaire d'histoire et de géographie ecclésiastiques*, vol. 22, edited by R. Aubert, 453–455. Paris: Letouzey et Ané, 1988.

de Vries, Wilhelm. "Einladung nicht-römisch-katholischer Orientalen zum Konzil von Trient." *Catholica* 15 (1961): 134–150.

Del Col, Andrea. *L'Inquisizione in Italia. Dal XII al XXI secolo*. Milan: Mondadori, 2006.

Bibliography 125

Delsere, Ilaria, and Osvaldo Raineri. *Chiesa di S. Stefano dei Mori: Vicende edilizie e personaggi*. Vatican City: Edizioni Capitolo Vaticano, 2015.

Dib, Pierre. *History of the Maronite Church*. Translated by Seely Beggiani. Washington, DC: Maronite Apostolic Exarchate, 1971.

Ditchfield, Simon. "Catholic Reformation and Renewal." In *The Oxford Illustrated History of the Reformation*, edited by Peter Marshall, 152–185. Oxford: Oxford University Press, 2015.

Ditchfield, Simon. "The 'Making' of Roman Catholicism as a 'World Religion'." In *Multiple Reformations? The Many Faces and Legacies of the Reformation*, edited by Jan Stievermann and Randall C. Zachman, 189–203. Tübingen: Mohr Siebeck, 2018.

Douaihy, Hector. *Un Théologien Maronite: Gibra'il ibn al-Qalā'i, Evêque et Moine Franciscain*. Kaslik: Université Saint-Esprit, 1993.

Dürr, Renate. "The World in the German Hinterlands: Early Modern German History Entangled." *Sixteenth Century Journal* 50 (2019): 148–155.

Dursteler, Eric R. "On Bazaars and Battlefields: Recent Scholarship on Mediterranean Cultural Contacts." *Journal of Early Modern History* 15 (2011): 413–434.

El-Hage, Fouad. *Kitâb al-Nâmûs d'ibn al-Qilâ'î dans l'histoire juridique du marriage chez les Maronites*. Kaslik: Université Saint-Espirit, 2001.

El-Hāyek, Elias. "Struggle for Survival: The Maronites of the Middle Ages." In *Conversion and Continuity: Indigenous Christian Communities in Islamic Lands, Eighth to Eighteenth Centuries*, edited by Michael Gervers and Ramzi Jibran Bikhazi, 407–421. Toronto: PIMS, 1990.

Eliav-Feldon, Miriam. *Renaissance Impostors and Proofs of Identity*. London: Palgrave, 2012.

Espias. Servicios secretos y escritura cifrada en la Monarquía Hispánica. Madrid: Secretaría General Técnica, 2018.

Fabre, Pierre-Antoine, and Ines Županov, eds. *The Rites Controversies in the Early Modern World*. Leiden: Brill, 2018.

Falconi, Carlo. *Leone X, Giovanni de' Medici*. Milan: Rusconi, 1987.

Farina, Margherita. "A New Autobiograph by 'Abdīšō Marūn. Renaissance Rome and the Syriac Churches." *Journal of Eastern Christian Studies* 70 (2018): 241–256.

Farina, Margherita. "La circulation de manuscrits syriaques en Orient et entre Orient et Occident entre la fin du XVe et le XVIe siècle." In *Les chrétiens de tradition syriaque à l'époque ottoman*, edited by Bernard Heyberger, 93–120. Paris: Geuthner, 2020.

Feghali, Joseph. *Histoire du droit de l'Église Maronite. Tome I: Les Conciles des XVIe et XVIIe siècles*. Paris: Letouzey et Ané, 1962.

Felce, Ian. *William Morris and the Icelandic Sagas*. Cambridge: D. S. Brewer, 2019.

Fenoy, Laurent. "Refuge et réseaux: les chrétiens orientaux en Chypre entre 1192 et 1473." In *Espaces et réseaux en Méditerranée VIe-XVIe siècle. Volume 2: La formation des réseaux*, edited by Damien Coulon, Christophe Picard, and Dominique Valérian, 187–206. Saint-Denis: Bouchène, 2007.

Firpo, Massimo. *La presa di potere dell'Inquisizione romana*. Rome-Bari: Laterza, 2014.

Fleet, Kate. "The Ottomans, 1451–1603: A Political History Introduction." In *The Cambridge History of Turkey. Volume 2: The Ottoman Empire as a World Power*, edited by Suraiya N. Faroqhi and Kate Fleet, 19–43. Cambridge: Cambridge University Press, 2013.

126 Bibliography

Floristán, José M. "Atanasio Rasia: Atanasio de Acrida? Proceso ante el Santo Oficio." In *Aspetti e momenti dell'albanologia contemporanea*, edited by Matteo Mandalà and Gëzim Gurga, 93–118. Tirana: Naimi, 2019.

Floristán, José M. "Clero griego ante el Santo Oficio (I): Anastasio Ventura (1577), Nicéforo de Esfigmenu (1621) y Dionisio Condilis de Patmos (1657)." *Erytheia* 40 (2019): 267–305.

Floristán, José M. "Clero griego ante el Santo Oficio (II): Manuel Accidas (1542) e Hilarión Cuculis (1699)." *Erytheia* 41 (2020): 159–181.

Floristán Imízcoz, José M. *Fuentes para la política oriental de los Austrias. La documentacíon griega del Archivo de Simancas (1571–1621)*. Leon: Universidad de León, 1988.

Fosi, Irene. *Convertire lo straniero. Forestieri e Inquisizione a Roma in età moderna*. Rome: Viella, 2011.

Fosi, Irene. "The Plural City: Urban Spaces and Foreign Communities." In *A Companion to Early Modern Rome, 1492–1692*, edited by Pamela M. James, Barbara Wisch and Simon Ditchfield, 169–183. Leiden: Brill, 2019.

François, Wim. "Andreas Masius (1514–1573): Humanist, Exegete, and Syriac Scholar." *Journal of Eastern Christian Studies* 61 (2009): 199–244.

Freudenberger, Theobald. "Das Konzil von Trient und das Ehescheidungsrecht der Ostkirche." In *Wegzeichen: Festgabe von Prof. Dr. Hermengild M. Biedermann OSA*, edited by Ernst Chr. Suttner and Coelestin Patock, 153–163. Würzburg: Augustinus-Verlag, 1971.

Fussenegger, Geroldus. "De vita et scriptis Fr. Alexandri Ariosti." *Archivum Franciscanum Historicum* 49 (1956): 143–165.

Gattoni, Maurizio. *Leone X e la geo-politica dello Stato Pontificio (1513–1521)*. Vatican City: Archivio Segreto Vaticano, 2000.

de Ghantuz Cubbe, Mariam. "I rapporti fra Leone X e i Maroniti." *Studi e ricerche sull'Oriente Cristiano* 9 (1986): 149–173.

de Ghantuz Cubbe, Mariam. "La lettre du Patriarche Maronite Šamūn Butros de Hadet au Léon X (1515)." *Orientalia Christiana Periodica* 76 (2010): 389–432.

de Ghantuz Cubbe, Mariam. "Le temps de Jérémie de Dmalsa, patriarche des Maronites (1283 environ): Problèmes ouverts et hypotheses." *Parole de l'Orient* 31 (2006): 451–504.

de Ghantuz Cubbe, Mariam. "Les trois expeditions des Mamelouks contre la montagne libanaise en 1292, 1300 et 1305, et les Maronites." *Orientalia Christiana Periodica* 81 (2015): 139–168.

de Ghantuz Cubbe, Mariam. "Maroniti e Crociati dalla prima Crociata al 1215. Le fonti non maronite." *Studi e ricerche sull'Oriente cristiano* 6 (1983): 217–238.

Ghobrial, John-Paul, ed. *Global History and Microhistory*. Oxford: Oxford University Press, 2019.

Ghobrial, John-Paul. "The Archive of Orientalism and Its Keepers: Re-imagining the Histories of Arabic Manuscripts in Early Modern Europe." *Past & Present* 230 (2016): 90–111.

Ghobrial, John-Paul. "Migration from Within and Without: In the Footsteps of Eastern Christians in the Early Modern World." *Transactions of the Royal Historical Society* 27 (2017): 153–173.

Gill, Joseph. *The Council of Florence*. Cambridge: Cambridge University Press, 1959.

Girard, Aurelien. "Comment reconnaître un chrétien oriental vraiment catholique? Élaboration et usages de la profession de foi pour les orientaux à Rome

(XVIe–XVIIIe siècle)." In *L'Union à l'épreuve du formulaire. Professions de foi entre églises d'Orient et d'Occident (XIIIe–XVIIIe siècle)*, edited by Marie-Helene Blanchet and Frederic Gabriel, 235–257. Leuven: Peeters, 2016.

Girard, Aurélien. "Histoire connectée du monachisme oriental. De l'erudition catholique en Europe aux réformes monastiques au Mont Liban (XVIIe–XVIIIe siècles)." In *Scholarship between Europe and the Levant. Essays in Honour of Alastair Hamilton*, edited by Jan Loop and Jill Kraye, 173–194. Leiden: Brill, 2020.

Girard, Aurélien. "Impossible Independence or Necessary Dependency? Missionaries in the Near East, the 'Protection' of the Catholic States, and the Roman Arbiter." In *Papacy, Religious Orders, and International Politics in the Sixteenth and Seventeenth Centuries*, edited by Massimo Carlo Giannini, 67–94. Rome: Viella, 2013.

Girard, Aurélien. "Le Collège maronite de Rome et les langues au tournant des XVIe et XVIIe siècles: éducation des chrétiens orientaux, science orientaliste et apologétique catholique." *Rivista Storica Italiana* 132 (2020): 272–299.

Girard, Aurélien. "*Nihil esse innovandum*? Maintien des rites orientaux et négociation de l'union des églises orientales avec Rome (fin XVIe–mi-XVIIIe s.)." In *Réduire le schisme? Ecclésésiologies et politiques de l'Union entre Orient et Occident (XIIIe–XVIIIe siècle)*, edited by Marie-Hélène Blanchet et Frédéric Gabriel, 337–352. Leuven: Peeters, 2013.

Girard, Aurélien. "Quand les Maronites écrivaient en Latin: Fauste Nairon et la république des lettres (seconde moitié du XVIIe siècle)." In *Le latin des Maronites*, edited by Mireille Issa, 45–76. Paris: Geuthner, 2017.

Girard, Aurélien. "Was an Eastern Scholar Necessarily a Cultural Broker in Early Modern Europe? Faustus Naironus (1628–1711), the Christian East, and Oriental Studies." In *Confessionalisation and Erudition in Early Modern Europe: An Episode in the History of the Humanities*, edited by Nicholas Hardy and Dmitri Levitin, 240–263. Oxford: Oxford University Press, 2019.

Girard, Aurélien, and Giovanni Pizzorusso. "The Maronite College in Early Modern Rome: Between the Ottoman Empire and the Republic of Letters." In *College Communities Abroad: Education, Migration and Catholicism in Early Modern Europe*, edited by Liam Chambers and Thomas O'Connor, 174–197. Manchester: Manchester University Press, 2017.

Górecki, Wojciech. "The Union between *Maronitae* and Rome (1182) as the Context of Relationships between the Franks and the Oriental Churches in the Crusader States in the 12th Century." *Orientalia Christiana Cracoviensa* 2 (2010): 61–66.

Grébaut, Sylvain, and Eugene Tisserant. *Codices aetiopici Vaticani et Borgiani, Barbarinus orientalis 2, Rossianus 865*, vol. 2. Vatican City: Biblioteca Apostolica Vaticana, 1935.

Greene, Molly. "The Early Modern Mediterranean." In *A Companion to Mediterranean History*, edited by Peregrine Horden and Sharon Kinoshita, 91–106. Chichester: John Wiley & Sons, 2014.

Greene, Molly, *Catholic Pirates and Greek Merchants: A Maritime History of the Early Modern Mediterranean*. Princeton: Princeton University Press, 2010.

Grendler, Paul F. *The Universities of the Italian Renaissance*. Baltimore: Johns Hopkins University Press, 2002.

Gribomont, Jean. "Gilles de Viterbe, le moine Élie, et l'influence de la littérature maronite sur la Rome érudite de 1515." *Oriens Christianus* 18 (1970): 125–129.

128 Bibliography

Groebner, Valentin. *Who Are You? Identification, Deception, and Surveillance in Early Modern Europe*. New York: Zone Books, 2007.

van Gulik, W. "Die Konsistorialakten über die Begründung des uniert-chaldäischen Patriarchates von Mosul unter Papst Julius III." *Oriens Christianus* 4 (1904): 261–274.

Gürkan, Emrah Safa. "Espionage in the 16th Century Mediterranean: Secret Diplomacy, Mediterranean Go-Betweens and the Ottoman-Habsburg Rivalry." PhD diss., Georgetown University, 2012.

Hamilton, Alastair. *The Copts and the West, 1439–1822*. Oxford: Oxford University Press, 2006.

Harris, William. *Lebanon: A History, 600–2011*. Oxford: Oxford University Press, 2012.

Hassiotis, J. K. "La comunità greca di Napoli e i moti insurrezionali nella penisola balcanica meridionale durante la seconda metà del XVI secolo." *Balkan Studies* 10 (1969): 279–288.

Hayek, Ignace Antoine II. *Le relazioni della Chiesa Siro-giacobita con la Santa Sede dal 1143 al 1656*. Edited by Pier Giorgio Borbone and Jimmy Daccache. Paris: Geuthner, 2015.

Hershenzon, Daniel. *The Captive Sea: Slavery, Communication and Commerce in Early Modern Spain and the Mediterranean*. Philadelphia: University of Pennsylvania Press, 2018.

Hiestand, Rudolf. "Die Integration der Maroniten in die römische Kirche. Zum ältesten Zeugnis der pästlichen Kanzlei (12. Jahrh.)." *Orientalia Christiana Periodica* 54 (1988): 119–152.

Horden, Peregrine, and Nicholas Purcell. *The Corrupting Sea: A Study of Mediterranean History*. Oxford: Basil Blackwell, 2000.

Housley, Norman. *Crusading and the Ottoman Threat, 1453–1505*. Oxford: Oxford University Press, 2012.

Hofmann, Georg. "L'Oriente nel concilio di Trento." *Studia Missionaria* 2 (1946): 33–53.

Howard, Douglas A. *A History of the Ottoman Empire*. Cambridge: Cambridge University Press, 2017.

Idígoras, Ignacio Tellechea, and Víctor Sánchez Gil. "Testamento del Cardenal Quiñones Protector de la Orden Franciscana (OFM) y Gobernador de Veroli († 1540)." *Archivum Franciscanum Historicum* 96 (2003): 129–159.

Imber, Colin. *The Ottoman Empire, 1300–1650*. 3rd ed. London: Red Globe Press, 2019.

Iordanou, Ioanna. *Venice's Secret Service: Organizing Intelligence in the Renaissance*. Oxford: Oxford University Press, 2019.

Jabre Mouawad, Ray. "The Ethiopian Monks in Mount-Lebanon (XVth Century)." *Liban Souterrain* 5 (1998): 186–207.

Jabre Mouawad, Ray. *Lettres au Mont-Liban d'ibn al-Qilai, XVe siècle*. Paris: Geuthner, 2001.

Jardine, Lisa, and Jerry Brotton. *Global Interests: Renaissance Art between East and West*. London: Reaktion, 2000.

Johnson, Carina L. "Idolatrous Cultures and the Practice of Religion." *Journal of the History of Ideas* 67 (2006): 597–621.

Jones, Robert. *Learning Arabic in Renaissance Europe (1505–1624)*. Leiden: Brill, 2020.

Juel-Jensen, Bent. "Potken's *Psalter* and Tesfa Tsion's *New Testament, Modus baptizandi* and *Missal*." *Bodleian Library Record* 15 (1996): 480–496.

Bibliography   129

Kelly, Samantha. "The Curious Case of Ethiopic Chaldean: Fraud, Philology, and Cultural (Mis)Understanding in European Conceptions of Ethiopia." *Renaissance Quarterly* 68 (2015): 1227–1264.

Kelly, Samantha, and Dennis Nosnitsin. "The Two Yoḥanneses of Santo Stefano degli Abissini, Rome: Reconstructing Biography and Cross-Cultural Encounter through Manuscript Evidence." *Manuscript Studies* 2 (2017): 392–426.

Kennerley, Sam. "Ethiopian Christians in Rome, c.1400–c.1700." In *A Companion to Religious Minorities in Early Modern Rome*, edited by Matthew Coneys Wainwright and Emily Michelson, 142–168. Leiden: Brill, 2020.

Kennerley, Sam. "The Reception of John Chrysostom and the Study of ancient Christianity in Early Modern Europe, c.1440–1600." PhD diss., University of Cambridge, 2017.

Kristeller, Paul Oskar. *Renaissance Thought: The Classic, Scholastic and Humanist Strains*. New York: Harper and Row, 1961.

Kristeller, Paul Oskar. *Supplementum ficinianum*. Florence: Olschki, 1937.

Krstić, Tijana. *Contested Conversions to Islam: Narratives of Religious Change in the Early Modern Ottoman Empire*. Stanford: Stanford University Press, 2011.

Kümin, Beat, and Felicita Tramontana, "Catholicism Decentralized: Local Religion in the Early Modern Periphery." *Church History* 89 (2020): 268–287.

Lammens, H. "Frère Gryphon et le Liban au XVᵉ siècle." *Revue de l'Orient Chrétien* 4 (1899): 68–104.

Lavenia, Vincenzo. "*Quasi hereticus.* Lo scisma nella riflessione degli inquistori dell'età moderna." *Mélanges de l'École française de Rome. Italie et Méditerranée modernes et contemporaines* 126, no. 2 (2014). https://doi.org/10.4000/mefrim.1838

Lefevre, Renato. "Appunti sull'ospizio di S. Stefano degli 'Indiani' nel Cinquecento." *Studi Romani* 15 (1967): 16–33.

Lefevre, Renato. "Giovanni Potken e la sua edizione romana del Salterio in etiopico." *La Bibliofilia* 68 (1966): 389–408.

Leroy, J. "Une copie syriaque du Missale Romanum de Paul III et son arrière-plan historique." *Mélanges de l'Université Saint-Joseph* 46 (1970–1971): 355–382.

Levi della Vida, Giorgio. *Documenti intorno alle relazioni delle chiese orientali con la S. Sede durante il pontificato di Gregorio XIII*. Vatican City: Biblioteca Apostolica Vaticana, 1948.

Levi della Vida, Giorgio. *Ricerche sulla formazione del più antico fondo dei manoscritti orientali della Biblioteca Vaticana*. Vatican City: Biblioteca Apostolica Vaticana, 1939.

Levi della Vida, Giorgio. "degli Albonesi, Teseo Ambrogio." *DBI* 2 (1960). https://www.treccani.it/enciclopedia/teseo-ambrogio-degli-albonesi_(Dizionario-Biografico)

Lucà, Santo. "Guglielmo Sirleto e Francisco Torres." In *Il "sapientissimo calabro". Guglielmo Sirleto nel V centenario della nascita (1514–2014)*, edited by Benedetto Clausi and Santo Lucà, 533–602. Rome: Università degli Studi di Roma 'Tor Vergata', 2018.

Maiarelli, Andrea, ed. *L'Archivio Storico della Custodia di Terra Sancta (1230–1970)*, vol. 1. Bari: Edizioni Terra Santa, 2012.

Malcolm, Noel. *Agents of Empire: Knights, Corsairs, Jesuits and Spies in the sixteenth-century Mediterranean World*. London: Allen Lane, 2015.

Martínez d'Alòs-Moner, Andreu. *Envoys of a Human God: The Jesuit Mission to Christian Ethiopia, 1557–1632*. Leiden: Brill, 2015.

130 Bibliography

Melvin, Karen. "The Globalisation of Reform." In *The Ashgate Research Companion to the Counter-Reformation*, edited by Alexandra Bamji, Geert H. Janssen, and Mary Laven, 391–405. London: Routledge, 2016.

Mércz, András. "The Coat of Arms of Moses of Mardin." *Hugoye* 22 (2019): 345–393.

Meserve, Margaret. *Empires of Islam in Renaissance Historical Thought*. Cambridge, MA: Harvard University Press, 2008.

Messina, Giuseppe. *Diatessaron Persiano*. Rome: Pontifico Istituto Biblico, 1951.

Messina, Giuseppe. *Notizia su un diatessaron persiano*. Rome: Pontificio Istituto Biblico, 1943.

Michelson, Emily, and Matthew Coneys, eds. *A Companion to Religious Minorities in Early Modern Rome*. Leiden: Brill, 2020.

Minnich, Nelson H. "Lateran V and the Call for a Crusade." In *Begegnung der Kirche in Ost und West im Spiegel der synodalen Strukturen*, edited by Johannes Grohe et al, 207–236. Sankt Ottilien: EOS, 2017.

Minnich, Nelson H. "The Participants at the Fifth Lateran Council." *Archivium Historiae Pontificiae* 12 (1974): 157–206.

Mohasseb Saliba, Sabine. *Les monastères maronites doubles du Liban: Entre Rome et l'Empire ottoman (XVIIᵉ–XIXᵉ siècles)*. Paris: Geuthner, 2008.

Moosa, Matti. *The Maronites in History*. Syracuse, NY: Syracuse University Press, 1986.

Moukarzel, Joseph. *Gabriel Ibn al-Qilāʿi († c. 1516). Approche biographique et étude du corpus*. Jounieh: PUSEK, 2007.

Moukarzel, Joseph. "Maronite Garshuni Texts: On their Evolution, Characteristics, and Function." *Hugoye* 17 (2014): 237–262.

Murre-van den Berg, Heleen. "Syriac Christianity." In *The Blackwell Companion to Eastern Christianity*, edited by Ken Parry, 249–268. Oxford: Basil Blackwell, 2007.

Murre-van den Berg, Heleen. "The Transformation of the Syriac Churches: Writing, Reading and Religion in the Ottoman Period." In *Les chrétiens de tradition syriaque à l'époque ottoman*, edited by Bernard Heyberger, 77–92. Paris: Geuthner, 2020.

Naaman, Paul. "La société Maronite a la fin du XVIᶜ siècle." *Parole de l'Orient* 17 (1992): 93–111.

Natta, Gabriele. "L'enigma dell'Etiopia nel Rinascimento Italiano: Ludovico Beccadelli tra inquietudini religiose e orizzonti globali." *Rinascimento* 55 (2015): 275–309.

Neck, Rudolf. "Diplomatische Beziehungen zum Vorderen Orient unter Karl V." *Mitteilungen des österreichischen Staatsarchivs* 5 (1952): 63–86.

Nelles, Paul. "Jesuit Letters." In *The Oxford Handbook of the Jesuits*, edited by Ines G. Županov, 44–72. Oxford: Oxford University Press, 2019.

Noujaim, Halim. *I Francescani e i Maroniti (1233–1516)*. Translated by Bartolomeo Pirone. Milan: Edizioni Terra Santa, 2012.

Noujaim, Halim. *I Francescani e i Maroniti. Volume II: Dall'anno 1516 fino alla fine del diciannovesimo secolo*. Translated by Bartolomeo Pirone. Milan: Edizioni Terra Santa, 2019.

O'Malley, John. *Trent: What Happened at the Council*. Cambridge MA: Harvard University Press, 2013.

Orano, Domenico. *Liberi pensatori bruciati in Roma dal XVI al XVIII secolo*. Livorno: Bastogi, 1904.

Bibliography   131

Panchenko, Constantin A. *Arab Orthodox Christians under the Ottomans, 1516–1831*. Translated by Brittany Pheiffer Noble and Samuel Noble. Jordanville, NY: Holy Trinity Seminary Press, 2016.

Parker, Lucy. "The Ambiguities of Belief and Belonging: Catholicism and the Church of the East in the Sixteenth Century." *English Historical Review* 133 (2018): 1420–1445.

Parker, Charles H. "The Reformation in Global Perspective." *History Compass* 12 (2014): 924–934.

Paulau, Stanislau. *Das andere Christentum. Zur transkonfessionellen Verflechtungsgeschichte von äthiopischer Orthodoxie und europäischem Protestantismus*. Göttingen: Vandenhoeck & Ruprecht, 2020.

Pedani, Maria Pia. *Venezia porta d'Oriente*. Bologna: Il Mulino, 2010.

Peri, Vittorio. "Il Concilio di Trento e la Chiesa greca." In *Il Concilio di Trento nella prospettiva del terzo millennio*, edited by Giuseppe Alberigo and Iginio Rogger, 403–441. Brescia: Morcelliana, 1997.

Petrowicz, Gregorio. "Il Patriarca di Ecimiazin Stefano V Salmastetzì (1541?–1552)." *Orientalia Christiana Periodica* 28 (1962): 362–401.

Piacentini, Paola. *La biblioteca di Marcello II Cervini*. Vatican City: Biblioteca Apostolica Vaticana, 2001.

Piemontese, Angelo Maria. *La Persia istoriata in Roma*. Vatican City: Biblioteca Apostolica Vaticana, 2014.

Pinto Crespo, Virgilio. *Inquisición y control ideológico en la España del siglo XVI*. Madrid: Taurus, 1983.

Pizzorusso, Giovanni. *Governare le missioni, conscere il mondo nel XVII secolo. La Congregazione Pontificia de Propaganda Fide*. Viterbo: Sette città, 2018.

Pizzorusso, Giovanni. "Le lingue a Roma: studio e practica nei collegi missionari nella prima età moderna." *Rivista Storica Italiana* 132 (2020): 248–271.

Po-Chia Hsia, Ronnie, ed. *A Companion to Early Modern Catholic Global Missions*. Leiden: Brill, 2018.

Preto, Paolo. *I servizi segreti di Venezia. Spionaggio e controspionaggio ai tempi della Serenissima*. 2nd ed. Milan: Il Saggiatore, 2016.

Proverbio, Delio Vania. "Santo Stefano degli Abissini: Una breve rivisitazione." *La Parola del Passato* 69 (2011): 50–68.

Quaranta, Chiara. *Marcello II Cervini (1501–1555): Riforma della Chiesa, concilio, Inquisizione*. Bologna: Il Mulino, 2010.

Ritsema van Eck, Marianne P. *The Holy Land in Observant Franciscan Texts (c.1480–1650)*. Leiden: Brill, 2019.

Romani, Valentino. "La stampa del N.T in etiopico (1548–49): figure e temi del Cinquecento romano." In *Studi in biblioteconomia e storia del libro in onore di Francesco Barberi*, 481–498. Rome: Associazione bibliothece italiane, 1976.

Romano, Antonella. "Lingue barbariche. Una sfida per la Roma Cinquecentesca." *Rivista Storica Italiana* 132 (2020): 300–322.

Roncaglia, Martiniano. "Le Relazione della Terra Santa con i Maroniti del Monte Libano e di Cipro dal 1564 al 1569." *Archivum Franciscanum Historicum* 46 (1953): 417–447.

Rota, Giorgio. *Under Two Lions: On the Knowledge of Persia in the Republic of Venice*. Vienna: Verlag der Österreichischen Akademie der Wissenschaften, 2009.

Rouhana, Paul. "Identité ecclésiale maronite des origines à la veille du Synode libanais." *Parole de l'Orient* 15 (1988–1989): 215–259.

132   *Bibliography*

Rouhana, Paul. "La vision des origines religieuses des Maronites entre le XVe et le XVIIIe siècle: de l'évêque Gabriel Ibn-al-Qila'i († 1516) au patriarche Etienne Douaihy (1670–1704)." PhD diss., Institut catholique de Paris, 1998.

Rublack, Ulinka. *Reformation Europe*. 2nd ed. Cambridge: Cambridge University Press, 2017.

Sachet, Paolo. *Publishing for the Popes: The Roman Curia and the Use of Printing (1527–1555)*. Leiden: Brill, 2020.

Salibi, Kamal S. "The Maronite Church in the Middle Ages and Its Union with Rome." *Oriens Christianus* 42 (1958): 92–104.

Salibi, Kamal S. "The Maronite Experiment." In *Conversion and Continuity: Indigenous Christian Communities in Islamic Lands, Eighth to Eighteenth Centuries*, edited by Michael Gervers and Ramzi Jibran Bikhazi, 423–433. Toronto: PIMS, 1990.

Salibi, Kamal S. *Maronite Historians of Medieval Lebanon*. Beirut: Catholic Press, 1959.

Salibi, Kamal S. "The *muqaddams* of Bsarri: Maronite Chieftains of the Northern Lebanon, 1382–1621." *Arabica* 15 (1968): 63–86.

Salibi, Kamal S. "Northern Lebanon under the Dominance of the Gazir (1517–1591)." *Arabica* 14 (1967): 144–166.

Salvadore, Matteo. "African Cosmopolitanism in the Early Modern Mediterranean: The Diasporic life of Yohannes, the Ethiopian Pilgrim Who Became a Counter-Reformation Bishop." *Journal of African History* 58 (2017): 61–83.

Salvadore, Matteo, and James De Lorenzi, "An Ethiopian Scholar in Tridentine Rome: Täsfä Ṣeyon and the Birth of Orientalism." *Itinerario* 45 (2021): 17–46.

Salvadore, Matteo. "'I Was Not Born to Obey, but Rather to Give Orders': The Self-Fashioning of Ṣäga Krestos, an Ethiopian Traveler in 17th Century Europe." *Journal of Early Modern History* 25 (2021): 1–33.

Sanfilippo, Matteo, and Péter Tusor, eds. *Gli "angeli custodi" delle monarchie: I cardinali protettori delle nazioni*. Viterbo: Sette città, 2018.

Sanfilippo, Matteo. "Il controllo politico e religioso sulle comunità straniere a Roma e nella penisola." In *Ad ultimos usque terrarum terminos in fide propaganda: Roma fra promozione e difesa della fede in età moderna*, edited by Massimiliano Ghilardi, Gaetano Sabatini, Matteo Sanfilippo, and Donatella Strangio, 85–110. Viterbo: Sette città, 2014.

Setton, Kenneth M. *The Papacy and the Levant (1204–1571). Volume. 3: The Sixteenth Century to the Reign of Julius III*. Philadelphia: The American Philosophical Society, 1984.

Sirinian, Anna. "La presenza degli Armeni nella Roma medievale: Prime testimonianze manoscritte ed epigrafiche (con un'iscrizione inedita del XVI secolo)." *Atti della Pontificia Accademia Romana di Archeologia. Rendiconti* 86 (2013/2014): 3–42.

Skordi, Maria G. *The Maronites of Cyprus. History and Iconography (16th–19th Centuries)*. Nicosia: UNESCO, 2019.

Subrahmanyam, Sanjay. "Connected Histories: Notes towards a Reconfiguration of Early Modern Eurasia." *Modern Asian Studies* 31 (1997): 735–762.

Subrahmanyam, Sanjay. *Empires between Islam and Christianity, 1500–1800*. Albany: State University of New York Press, 2019.

Subrahmanyam, Sanjay. "Introduction." In *The Cambridge World History. Volume 6: The Construction of a Global World, 1400–1800 CE. Part I: Foundations,*

Bibliography 133

edited by Jerry H. Bentley, Sanjay Subrahmanyam, and Merry E. Wiesner-Hanks, 1–23. Cambridge: Cambridge University Press, 2015.

Surdich, Francesco. "Suriano, Francesco." *DBI* 94 (2019). https://www.treccani.it/enciclopedia/francesco-suriano_%28Dizionario-Biografico%29/

Tedeschi, John, with William Monter. "Toward a Statistical Profile of the Italian Inquisitions, Sixteenth to Eighteenth Centuries." In *The Prosecution of Heresy: Collected Studies on the Early Modern Inquisition*, edited by John Tedeschi, 89–126. Binghamton, NY: MRTS, 1991.

Tedeschi, Salvatore. "Etiopi e Copti al Concilio di Firenze." *Annuarium Historiae Conciliorum* 21 (1989): 380–407.

Teule, Herman. "Les professions de foi de Jean Sullaqa, premier patriarche chaldéen, et de son successeur 'Abdisho d-Gazarta." In *L'Union a l'épreuve du formulaire. Professions de foi entre églises d'Orient et d'Occident (XIIIᵉ–XVIIIᵉ siècle)*, edited by Marie-Helene Blanchet and Frederic Gabriel, 259–269. Leuven: Peeters, 2016.

Tucker, Judith E. "Introduction." In *The Making of the Modern Mediterranean*, edited by Judith E. Tucker, 1–15. Oakland: University of California Press, 2019.

Uluhogian, Gabriella. "Il *Salterio* di Abgar T'oxat'ec'i (a. 1565) e l'avvio degli studi armenistici presso la Biblioteca Ambrosiana di Milano." In *Collectanea Armeniaca*, edited by Rosa Bianca Finazzi and Anna Sirinian, 313–337. Milan: Biblioteca Ambrosiana, 2016.

Vanni, Andrea. "Scotti, Bernardino." *DBI* 91 (2018). https://www.treccani.it/enciclopedia/bernardino-scotti_%28Dizionario-Biografico%29/

Varesco, Riccardo. "I frati minori al Concilio di Trento." *Archivum Franciscanum Historicum* 42 (1960): 95–158.

Varriale, Gennaro. *Arrivano li Turchi. Guerra navale e spionaggio nel Mediterraneo (1532–1582)*. Novi Ligure: Città del Silenzio Edizioni, 2014.

Varriale, Gennaro. "Liricas secretas: los espías y el Gran Turco (siglo XVI)." *Hispania* 76 (2016): 37–66.

Varriale, Gennaro. "Lo spionaggio sulla frontiera mediterranea nel XVI secolo: La Sicilia contro il sultano." *Mediterranea* 13 (2016): 477–516.

Varriale, Gennaro. "Un covo di spie: il quartiere greco di Napoli." In *Identità e frontiere. Politica, economia e società nel Mediterraneo (secc. XIV–XVIII)*, edited by Lluis J. Guia Marín, Maria Grazia Rosaria Mele, and Gianfranco Tore, 47–62. Milan: FrancoAngeli, 2014.

Visceglia, Maria Antonietta. *La Roma dei papi. La corte e la politica internazionale (secoli XV–XVII)*, edited by Elena Valeri and Paola Volpini. Rome: Viella, 2018.

Wallerstein, Immanuel. *The Modern World-System*. 4 vols. New York: Academic Press, 1974–2011.

Wickersham, Jane K. *Rituals of Prosecution. The Roman Inquisition and the Prosecution of Philo-Protestants in Sixteenth-Century Italy*. Toronto: University of Toronto Press, 2012.

Wilkinson, Robert J. *Orientalism, Aramaic and Kabbalah in the Catholic Reformation: The First Printing of the Syriac New Testament*. Leiden: Brill, 2007.

Winter, Stefan. *The Shiites of Lebanon under Ottoman Rule, 1516–1788*. Cambridge: Cambridge University Press, 2010.

Wodka, Josef. *Zur Geschichte der nationalen Protektorate der Kardinäle an der römischen Kurie*. Innsbruck: Felizian Rauch, 1938.

Zagorin, Perez. *Ways of Lying. Dissimulation, Persecution, and Conformity in Early Modern Europe*. Cambridge, MA: Harvard University Press, 1990).

134 Bibliography

Zarzeczny, Rafał. "Su due manoscritti etiopici della Biblioteca Casanatense a Roma." In *Aethiopia fortitude eius. Studi in onore di monsignor Osvaldo Raineri*, edited by Rafał Zarzeczny, 501–537. Rome: Pontificio Istituto Orientale, 2015.

Zekiyan, L. B. "Le colonie armene del medioevo in Italia e le relzioni culturali italo-armene (materiali per la storia degli Armeni in Italia)." In *Atti del primo Simposio internazionale di arte armene*, edited by Giulio Ieni and Levon B. Zekiyan, 803–946. Venice: Toplitografia armena, 1975.

Žontar, Josef. "Michael Černović, Geheimagent Ferdinands I. und Maximilians II., und seine Berichterstattung." *Mitteilungen des österreichischen Staatsarchiv* 24 (1971): 169–222.

Index

Page numbers followed by 'n' refer to notes numbers

'Abd-Isho 74–75
'Abdullah I (Jacobite patriarch) 68–70
'Abgar of Tokat 73
'Adal 61
Adrian VI 31, 113, 117
Africanus, Leo 31
al-Akkari, Musa 31, 36–52, 70, 78–79, 86–94, 95n29, 107–109, 112–118
Albania and Albanians 92
al-Bnahrani, Lūqa 9, 18–19
al-Duwayhi, Stefanos 18–19, 51, 55n57, 99, 102
Aleppo 75–76, 89–91
Alexander VI (Pope) 17
Alexandria 58, 60
al-Ghagi, Johannes 10–11, 99
al-Hadathi, Simon 14–16, 19, 24–27, 29–31, 39, 45, 99, 106
'Ali, Zayn al-Din ibn 42
al-Mun'im, 'Abd 14
al-Mun'im III, 'Abd 38, 110, 112
al-Qilā'i, Gabriel 3, 14–19, 32, 45, 85n124, 99, 101–102
Ambrogio, Teseo 24, 26, 30–31
Amida (Diyarbakir) 75
Antioch 12, 27, 43, 47, 104, 110, 112
Antonio da Troia 11
Antonius (Maronite Archbishop) 38, 96n38, 109
Apamea 8
Arabic 5, 11–12, 15–17, 25–26, 28, 30–32, 44, 48, 64, 66–68, 70, 75, 88, 99
Ara Coeli 14–15
Aranda, Antonio de 91
Armenia and Armenians 10, 38, 48, 57, 65, 68, 72–74, 76, 99, 108–109

ar-Rami, George 16
ar-Russi, Michael 37, 94
Assaf, Mansur 43, 90, 93
Athanasius 12
Augsburg 71
'Ayn Kfa 14

Balbi, Pietro 91
baptism 13, 16, 28, 80n18, 103–105
Bar-Mama, Simon VII 74
Beccadelli, Ludovico 71
Beirut 9–10, 15, 24–26, 29, 44, 60, 67, 70, 75, 90, 100, 103, 114, 116
Bellay, Jean du 68
Bernardino of Siena 17, 88
Beth Maron 8
Bible 31, 47, 59, 65–66, 70–72
Bologna 41, 52n16, 64, 116
book of Clement 13
books and manuscripts 13, 16, 30–31, 41, 47, 51, 62–64, 67, 69–73, 75, 82n77, 88, 91–92, 99
Bourges, Pragmatic Sanction of 29
Bsharri 14, 110
bulls, papal 29, 43, 46–49, 51, 70
Buttigeg, Ambrogio 70, 75–76

Cairo 36, 90
Caldiron 90
Calis, Richard 1, 5, 36
Campanella, Tommaso 92
Capistrano, Giovanni 88
Capuano, Peter 9
Capuchins 51
Carafa, Antonio 55n59, 94
Cardinali, Giacomo 40, 47, 68, 87

136 *Index*

cardinal protectors 39–40, 42, 45, 48–49, 51, 70, 93–94, 99
Carvajal, Bernardino 30–31, 39, 113
Cauco, Giacomo 41
Cervini, Marcello 37–49, 57–79, 86–89, 93, 99–102, 113–116
Cesarini, Giulio 10
Chaldean Church 72, 74–76; *see also* Church of the East
Chaldean language 47, 65
Charles V 37
Cherubino (Franciscan) 89
Chinese rites controversy 28
chrism 26, 28, 30
Chrysostom, John 8
church councils: Council of Basel (1431-1449) 10; Council of Chalcedon (451) 17, 46, 58, 66, 70; Council of Constantinople (536) 8; Council of Ephesus (431) 74; Council of Ferrara-Florence (1438-1445) 10–12, 32, 57–58, 66, 72, 76–78, 85n124, 99–100; Council of Trent (1545-1563) 36–37, 40–41, 47, 51, 58, 61, 78, 94, 100; Fifth Lateran Council (1512-1517) 29–32; Fourth Lateran Council (1215) 9, 12; Sixth Ecumenical Council (680-681) 8, 12
Church of the East 13, 57, 74–76, 99, 101
Cicero 17
Circassians 88
Clement VII 31, 37–40, 42, 49–51
Clissa 92
Cochin 76
Cochlaeus, Johannes 41
College of the Neophytes 72
confession 16, 28
confessionalisation 37, 41–43, 49–51, 60–61, 64–66, 77–79, 99
confessions of faith 26, 28, 69–71, 74–75, 78
Constantinople/Istanbul 8–10, 76, 87–89, 100
conversion 2, 11, 31, 50–51, 64, 88, 93, 100
Copts 10, 17–18, 60, 99
Corfu 41, 88
Corone 92
Cortone da Udine, Bartolomeo 38–39, 107–109
Counter-Reformation 3–4, 18–19, 49–51, 61, 76–79, 99; *see also* church councils; confessionalisation

crusades 8–10, 29, 92
custom 16, 26–30, 44, 46–47, 50–51, 60, 67, 75, 87, 103–105, 117–118
Cyprus 2, 11–12, 15, 19, 26, 29, 41, 68, 71
Cyril of Alexandria 12, 17

d'Aguilers, Raymond 8
Damascus 89–90
David of Lehfed 15–16
Davis, Natalie Zemon 31
Dib, Pierre 37, 39–40
Divo, Cornelio 87–89
Dominicans 17, 70, 73, 75, 92
Dorotheus III (Melkite patriarch of Antioch) 43
Dray, Ibrahim ibn 16
Druze 11, 42–43, 90
Dürr, Renate 36

Ecchellensis, Abraham 19
Efendi, Ebu's-Suud 42
Egypt 32, 36, 41, 60, 72, 90
El-Amsciti, Jeremias 9–11, 13
election and confirmation of Maronite patriarchs 10–12, 15–16, 19, 25–27, 29–30, 38–40, 43, 49–50, 79, 107–109
Eliano, Giovanni Battista 101
Elias (Maronite emissary) 38–39, 109
Elias (*muqaddam*) 29–30
Eliav-Feldon, Miriam 50
Elizabeth I 50
Ephrem the Syrian, Saint 75
Ethiopia and Ethiopians 10, 17, 30–31, 36, 41, 48, 50, 57–66, 69–70, 72, 74–78, 93, 100
Eugenius IV 10–11, 118
excommunication 15–17, 42–43, 46, 68, 70, 111
extreme unction 16
Eymerich, Nicholas 17

Farnese, Alessandro 40–41
Felice da Venezia 42–49, 51, 75, 112–114
Ferdinand I (archduke of Austria) 71, 92
Ferrara, Pietro da 11
filioque 28, 46, 70, 74
Firenze, Marco da 25–27, 103
Florence 10, 41, 57, 88, 101; *see also* church councils
France 17, 36, 40, 68, 92
Francesco (a Maronite) 14

Index   137

Franciscans 9–13, 15, 17, 24–30, 32, 38–39, 42–49, 66, 87–89, 93–94, 99–100, 103, 107–108, 112–114, 117–118
Fugger family 71

Ge'ez 48, 59–66, 68, 70, 78; *see also* Ethiopia and Ethiopians
George (Franciscan Guardian of the Holy Places) 49, 119n28
George (Maronite deacon) 48–49, 75, 84n111, 115
Georgia 73
Ghobrial, John-Paul 45, 77
gifts 39, 41, 48–50, 73, 117–118
Ginepro of Catania 44
Giovanni (Franciscan superior in Beirut) 10–11
Girard, Aurélien 47
Giustinian, Paolo 25, 88
Glassberger, Nicolas 12
Greek and Greeks 10, 13, 15, 17–18, 27, 36, 43, 47, 60, 62–63, 68, 71, 77, 85n124, 92, 99
Gregory XIII 100
Grimani, Marino 40
Gryphon 12–14, 16–17, 19, 28, 32, 38, 45, 99, 101
Gualtieri, Pier Paolo 60–65, 68, 73, 102
Gubbio 41–42

Habsburgs 29, 38, 73, 75, 79, 89–90, 92, 97n50
Hassan, Petrus bar 12
Hayek, Ignace Antoine II 69
Haymanot, Tekla 65
Heraclius (Emperor) 8
Holy Alliance 92
Hormisdas (Pope) 8
Hugo of Aquitaine 87–88
Hungary 88, 90

Ibrahim, Elias ibn 30–32, 67, 99
indulgences 29, 69, 106–107
Innocent III 9–13
inquisition 36, 40–41, 50–51, 71, 74–75
Interiano, Giorgio 88
Islam 9, 27, 41, 43, 48, 50–51, 92
Ismail I 88, 90–91
Italian 44–45, 63, 87

Jacobites (Syrian Orthodox) 4, 10, 12–15, 17, 19, 32, 41, 43, 57–58, 60, 66–72, 76, 85n124, 92, 99, 101

Jerusalem 2, 11–12, 14–15, 27, 38, 42–44, 49, 58, 88, 94, 108–109, 117–118
Jesuits 28, 43, 61, 76, 93–94
Jews and Judaism 30–31, 41, 50–51, 91
Johannes (Maronite bishop of Aqura) 14–15
John VIII Palaeologos 10
Joseph (Jewish translator) 30
Jubileo, Celso 38
Julius III 40–41, 59, 68–71, 73–75, 93

Krebs, Verena 77
Krestos, Şagā 50
Kristeller, P.O. 88

Lammens, Henri 12
Landshut 66–68
Lehfed 14–16
Leo I (Pope) 17
Leo X 19, 24–32, 37–39, 42, 44, 46–47, 49–51, 67, 77–78, 88, 91, 99, 101, 103–106, 112, 118
Lepanto (battle of) 37, 92, 96n36
Levi della Vida, Giorgio 31, 57
Lorenzini, Antonio 41
Louis II (King of Hungary) 90
Loyola, Ignatius 61
Lucius, Saint 14
Ludwig X of Bavaria (duke) 66
Lull, Ramon 17
Luther, Martin 32, 36–37

Macarius (Greek metropolitan) 71
Maffei, Bernardino 41, 59–61, 75
Magnus, Olaus 42
Mamluks 9, 11, 27, 29, 36, 88, 90
Manuzio, Aldo 88
Manuzio, Paolo 88
Manzikert 9
maps 40–41
Marignano 29
Maronite College of Rome 3, 46, 78, 94, 101
Maron, John 8, 12, 18
Maron, Saint 8
marriage 16, 28–29
Masius, Andreas 70–71, 74
Mass 13, 16, 28, 30, 46, 59–62, 64, 70
Maxton, Rosemary 113
Medici Oriental Press 78
Mediterranean 2–3, 36, 38, 40–41, 50, 90–92
Melkites 43; *see also* Greek and Greeks
Monothelitism 8, 12–14, 16

138 *Index*

Montefano 40
Moosa, Matti 7n13, 12–14, 21n34, 37
Moresini, Andrea 91
Morone, Giovanni 71
Moses of Mardin 66–72, 77–78, 92
Mosul 75–76
Muscovy 73
Muzzarelli, Girolamo 74

Naironi, Fausto 19
Nakhchivan 73
Nausea, Friedrich 41
Nicosia, church of St John at 29
Niger, Heliodorus 87–88, 93
Ni'matallah, Ignatius 76

Ochino, Bernardino 51
Orientalist scholarship 3, 15–17,
    24–26, 29–32, 38, 41, 48, 55n57,
    57–79, 100
Orsini, Paolo (Turkish convert) 64
Otto Heinrich (Count Palatine) 72
Ottoman Empire 10, 15, 24, 29, 36–37,
    41–43, 49–51, 65, 75–76, 79, 86,
    88–94, 100

Padua 15, 88
pallium 30, 75; *see also* election and
    confirmation of Maronite patriarchs;
    vestments
papal supremacy 10, 36, 43, 60, 64–65,
    69
Paris 12, 68
Parker, Lucy 60, 74–75, 77, 113
Paul II 12–13
Paul III 40–51, 59–60, 68, 73, 78, 89,
    93, 110–116
Paul IV 41, 70–71, 75, 93, 116–118
Persia and Persians 73, 86, 88–93
Peter of Damascus 66–68
Petrus (Maronite emissary) 24–26,
    90–91
pilgrimage 38, 41, 58–59, 72–73, 76,
    78, 86, 91
Pio da Carpi, Alberto 31
Pio da Carpi, Rodolfo 40–41, 74, 93
Pius V 39
Plato 17
Poland 73
Pole, Reginald 41, 68, 71
Postel, Guillaume 71–72
Potenza, Giovanni Francesco da 29–30,
    34n41, 34n34
Potken, Johannes 24, 30–31, 59

printing *see* books and manuscripts *see*
    Orientalist scholarship
Propaganda Fide 3, 78, 94
Protestantism *see* confessionalisation
    see reformation
Ptolemy 88

Qannubin 11, 15–16, 25, 29, 48, 113,
    116–117
Qansuh (Mamluk sultan) 90
Querini, Vincenzo 25, 88, 97n48
Quiñones, Francisco 39–40, 45

Reatino, Francesco 34n41
Red Sea 41
Reformation 2, 18, 24, 29, 36–37, 41,
    48, 51, 56n91, 58–61, 64–66, 75–79,
    93, 99–101
re-ordination 60, 70–71, 78
Reuveni, David 50
Rhodes 11
Rota, Giovanni 88

Sachet, Paolo 40, 69
sacred history 16–19, 59–66, 75,
    99–101
Saifā, Rizqāllah ibn 14
Salmeron, Alfonso 61
Sander, Bernardino 80n18
Santa Maria della Pace 31
Santiago de Compostela 7, 107
Santo Stefano dei Mori 31, 41, 57–59,
    64, 66, 70, 77
Saorgano, Dionisio 46
Sarkis (Maronite deacon) 44, 113–114
Scotti, Gianbernardino 40, 93
Scotus, Duns 17
Scripture *see* Bible
Selim I 32, 36, 90
Seneca 17
Severian of Gabala 17
Shiites 42
shipwrecks 14, 38, 109
Shāmāt, Daniel of 9
Siena 40
Sigismund II (King of Poland) 73
Simeon (Maronite bishop of Beirut)
    44–45, 55n57, 60, 67, 70, 72, 75,
    100, 114, 116
Sirinian, Ana 72
Sirleto, Guglielmo 62–66
Spain 29, 38, 89–90, 92
Stefanos (archbishop of
    Nakhchivan) 73

Index   139

Stefanos V (Armenian catholicos) 65, 73–74
Suleiman I 76, 89–91
Sulläqä, Yohannan 74–78
Suriano, Francesco 3, 12, 14–16, 24, 27–30, 32, 34n41, 46–47, 103–106, 117
Susenyos (emperor of Ethiopia) 93
Syria 2, 8, 32, 36, 57, 69, 72, 75, 86, 89–91, 93, 104, 109
Syriac 26, 30–32, 44, 47, 55n57, 67–75, 78, 99

Tahmasp I 86, 88–89, 91
Talo 15
Tartars 73
Tasfä Şeyon 59–69, 72–73, 75, 77–78, 80n18
Teule, Hermann 74
Theodoret of Cyrus 8
Timothy (metropolitan of Tarsus) 12, 74
Tümä (Maronite bishop of Kafartäb) 8
Torres, Francisco 62, 64
Tramontana, Felicita 49
translation 14–17, 24–26, 30, 44–45, 60–64, 70, 74, 90, 100
Trent see church councils see confessionalisation see Counter-Reformation
Tripoli 9, 11, 27, 39, 55n57, 86–87, 89–90, 104, 110–111, 113–114, 116–117

Troppau, Martin of 17
Tumanbay 36, 90
Turcoman 12, 43, 90
Tyre, William of 9

Uppsala 41

Vatican Library 31, 41, 67–68, 70
Vecchietti, Giovanni Battista 38
Venice and Venetians 15, 41, 44, 51, 71, 86–93, 96n36
vestments 13, 26–30, 38, 48–50, 73, 103–105, 115–117
Vienna 71, 73
Viterbo, Giles of 31
Vitry, Jacques de 8
Vittorio, Mariano 65, 68

Wallerstein, Immanuel 3
Wickersham, Jane 51
Widmanstetter, Johann Albrecht von 55n57, 66–67, 70–72, 102
Wilkinson, Robert J. 57
Wittenberg 32, 36

Yohannes (Giovanni Battista Etiope) 41, 70, 75, 78, 80n22, 80n35
Yusuf (*muqaddam*) 16

Zagorin, Perez 50
Zahara, Antonino 75
Zapolya, John 88
Zimmermann, Michael 71

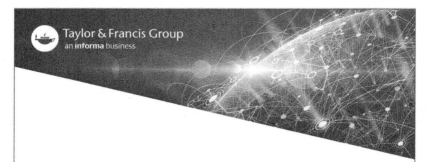